Birgit Gebauer-Sesterhenn

Dr. Manfred Praun

Consulting editor: Michael Msall, M.D.

The Baby Bible

The Complete Guide to Your Baby's First Year

BARRON'S

Foreword

The birth of a child is always a unique occurrence and experience that brings hope, love, happiness, and joy. Now life together begins outside the womb. The child leaves the protective shell and is confident of finding safety and security in loving arms. During the first year of life, a baby is focused primarily on protection, security, and support. In the first twelve months, a child takes big steps in progressing from a newborn infant that must be fed and carried to a little child who can already do a lot independently. That's why the first year of life is so significant.

As a midwife, I am often asked if I can recommend a book about the first year of life, for there is a great need for information. Dealing with an infant seems more difficult nowadays than ever before. In our highly civilized society, solid traditions and the exchanges between generations, which once were common in large families, are now scarce. What do we need for the baby? How much attention does a child need? Will I spoil the baby if I let her into my bed? Why does he yell so much, and why does she sleep so little? Has he eaten enough, and how do I protect my child from allergies? These are only a few of many questions that trouble parents before and after the birth of their child. Certainly nobody wants to do anything wrong.

This how-to book holds the answers to many of your questions. As you make your own way, you will gain understanding and find support in the well-documented information contained in this guide. Beginning with the many changes that occur en route to starting a family, this book will be an invaluable resource as you make all the necessary preparations before the birth, and as you get to know your child after that.

I especially hope that you will take the chapter on breastfeeding to heart. No matter where you are, you can easily supply your child with the best possible nutrition. In this vein, I wish you a wonderful first year with your child, who will have many more wonderful years to look forward to.

Constanze Koschorz, Midwife

Preliminary **Words** *from the Authors*

After the birth of my first daughter Paulina *in November of 1999, someone made a video. Exhausted from a long labor, I was heard to say, "I'll never put myself through that again!" The birth wasn't the only thing that didn't go as I had imagined. Nursing problems? Screaming baby? Baby blues? Sleepless nights? I had never imagined that being a mother would be like that. I would have been grateful if somebody had put some useful advice and a "road map" into my hands during this difficult time. I now understand that most of those problems were of my own making, and with some useful background knowledge things wouldn't have been so difficult.*

That's why this book had to be written. Here you will find valuable support and tips to ease your way into family bliss right from the start. And don't be concerned if your baby's development occasionally deviates from the norm. Don't put yourself under pressure. Trust your parental instincts and your gut feelings, and combine the two with a little composure—your baby will thank you for it. In addition to sections on nutrition for babies, how to encourage babies to sleep through the night, and first aid, there is also one chapter dedicated to a subject that is especially dear to my heart: baby's development. You will find a comprehensive overview of the first to the twelfth month of your baby's development—from the first smile to the first step.

My "never again" attitude following Paulina's birth lasted only a short time. Twenty-one months later our son Samuel was born, and Sophie was born two years after that. Each time everything was totally different, and even more beautiful. Why? Because I had learned to understand the children's signals and to address their needs.

Children are a gift, and all parents should be thankful that this tiny soul has been entrusted to grow in their care. I wish you much harmony and happiness in the first year with your baby.

Birgit Gebauer-Sesterhenn

As a young boy *I often accompanied my father, who was an internist, on house visits. I knew, therefore, at an early age that I wanted to choose this profession. By the end of my studies, it was clear that my future patients would be children. I was impressed not only by their happiness, which they maintained in spite of every illness, but especially by their tenacity of life and their strength. Furthermore, it was an incredible joy to work with children.*

After a good ten years of working in a hospital, I wanted to experience the other side of treating children: How does a young person experience childhood from infancy onward, with all its joys, illnesses, and developmental steps? Naturally, a child's environment is crucial—the questions, concerns, and needs of the parents deserve support. I hope that in the following pages you will find a great many tips and answers to your questions.

Dr. Manfred Praun

DISCLAIMER: All medical advice contained herein should not be taken as a substitute for medical care, and all practices or suggestions should be reviewed with an actual healthcare practitioner before initiating care of a child.

Contents

From Infant to Toddler 94

Contents

Baby's Nutrition in the First Year 176

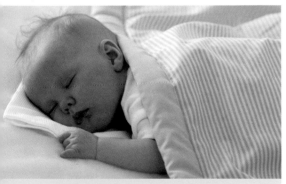

Sleep, Baby, Sleep . . .   232

SOS—My Baby Is Sick   254

We're Going to Have a Baby!

You're expecting a baby, and soon you will be a small family! You and your partner have an exciting time ahead of you—in the truest sense of the word— for there is scarcely anything that will turn your life upside down like the birth of your first child. But just what does it really mean to start a family?

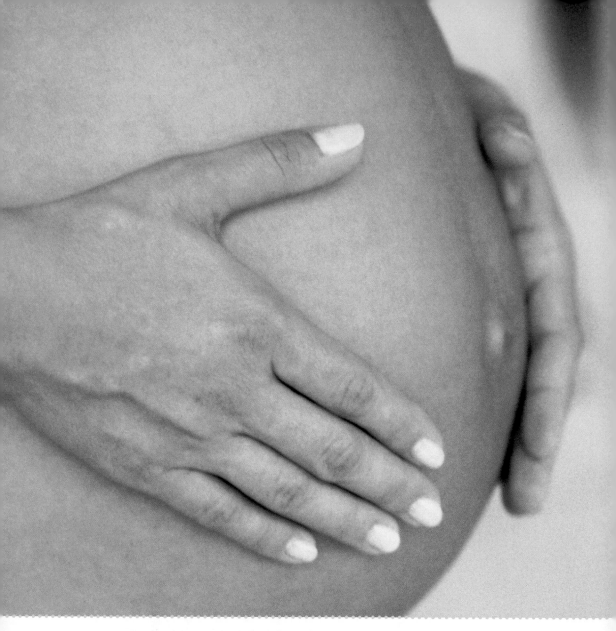

Suddenly Life Is Upside Down . . .

*Everything really could be so easy. In
the ideal situation, a nice couple live
together happily and peacefully and at
some time decide that a baby would
complete the family's happiness.
When a baby first announces its
presence, there is a lot of celebration.*

*The pregnancy goes along without
complication. Then the birth is
imminent—as is the hope that life
with the long-desired child will go as
smoothly as had life up to that point,
just with a little baby. But is that really
how it works?*

The Couple's Relationship

In the beginning, there are two. Generally they are a well-matched team with similar life values. Then there comes the time when the contented duo turns into a trio. Suddenly everything looks different: The previously harmonious twosome becomes a threesome that may not work together perfectly smoothly at the outset. The little one sounds off loudly and makes it painfully clear that she wants what she wants, and at first she doesn't appear ready to compromise. The new baby is small, but she creates a big fuss: Whenever she is hungry, she wants to eat, and right away. When the diaper is full, she needs a new one, and on the double. When a baby wants attention and devotion, she will indicate it loudly. It's important to remember that the third person in the trio is here to stay—and determines how the lives of the other two progress. Even though the new arrival is tiny, she takes over as boss, and she makes it clear whom her favorite "colleague" is. Most of the time it's the mother, who smells good, delivers meals on time, provides loving care, and above all, is always there when needed.

The Price You Pay

Being on call all the time comes with a price—as the two adults will quickly discover. In addition, it's possible for someone to end up feeling like the odd person out. That someone is often the child's father, and it's no wonder—suddenly he has to share his partner with their child.

The Situation

Even though both adults wanted the child, the daily reality is harsh, for it's generally a far cry from what they had imagined. The mother takes care of the baby all day long, she carries the child around with her the whole time, she talks about nothing but nursing problems, the best bottle formula, or the color of what's in the diaper. Sometimes Mom is sky-high with exultation; at other times she is depressed. She can spend the whole day at home, she gets attention from everybody, and people ask her how she and the baby are doing. She is the only one who can calm the baby down; she seems to be one with her baby. There's hardly any room left for the partner.

The Male Reaction

What does the father do? He may feel like an outsider. Typically, he has to get out early every day and make sure there's money coming into the house. When he comes home at night after a strenuous day, the baby is plopped into his arms—and he may long for a relaxing chat and a laugh with his wife, as before, or to go out with her. In short, he may want to have his partner all to himself. Instead, he has to get used to having a little rival around.

Jealousy Doesn't Make Sense

Some partners may experience a bit of jealousy. This feeling can be compared to that of children who experience the arrival of a first sibling. It usually goes

| **HELP! IT'S THE GREEN-EYED MONSTER!**

Many new fathers will feel guilty for feeling jealous of their new babies. After all, this is a time to be happy and appreciative, right? It doesn't make sense to be childish by being jealous of the new bundle of joy you've both been anticipating for months. But bringing home a baby is more than just adding a new member to your family. Many complex emotional issues are involved, and communication can become a problem. Many new fathers tend to ignore or are reluctant to discuss these matters openly with their partners. Perhaps you don't want to bother your partner about your feelings; perhaps you're ashamed of yourself for being jealous of your baby; perhaps you're afraid that your partner will get angry at you or fail to understand where you're coming from; or perhaps you're thinking this is just a temporary thing that will go away in a few months. If you are feeling jealous, accept that this is a natural process of transitioning from a "duet" to a "trio." If you're not comfortable discussing your feelings with your partner, do not force yourself to do so. Instead, set up various tasks you can do to around the house for your new family. Utilize your skills and interests to contribute to the growing household.

like this: Mom and Dad come home with the new baby and say, "Hello, dear, look, this is your little sister. The baby will live with us from now on." Psychologists tell us that the older child perceives the situation on a par with this one: Your husband comes home with a sweetheart (or your wife comes home with a boyfriend) and simply explains it in one sentence: "Hello, darling—I have brought someone else for us to play with you so that you don't get bored." How would you like that? Well, that's what essentially happens to the first-born child—and to many fathers as well. When their partners come home with the baby, some men feel they have been written off. They are no longer number one, but merely a sidekick to the new "boss."

Becoming a Father

When the first baby is born, the father often slips into a new, previously unaccustomed role. He is now the family provider, at least in the traditional scenario in which the mother stays home for a certain length of time to take care of the baby and household. Whereas both partners may have worked previously because they enjoyed it and needed the money, the father must now often take on this task alone. If the couple decides to stick with these roles, the pressure may increase tremendously; the responsibility for maintaining their standard of living now falls solely on the father's shoulders.

In addition, his partner may have changed because she has her hands full with the baby. Housework may fall by the wayside: Growing mountains of laundry, un-ironed shirts, an empty refrigerator, a cluttered living room, and unmade beds are common for young mothers, who have not yet learned how to reschedule their time and reallocate household duties with the father.

The Partnership Changes

One thing is certain: Being parents doesn't always mean peace, happiness, and freshly made omelets. Conflicts suddenly arise over issues that wouldn't have been imagined before the child came. There are differences of opinion on how to deal with and raise a baby. The mother carries the baby differently than the father, and the baby cries more with one than the other, so one may remark "You have to do it my way." That creates tension. In addition, a great deal of uncertainty accompanies caring for a baby. Who knows precisely the right way to do it? We get trained and tested for many of life's experiences (just think about final exams and driver's licenses), but there are few, if any, seminars on dealing with children properly.

A New "Boss" in the House

In addition, with the first baby, both parents feel they are subject to someone else's command: Their baby sets the rhythm in the first days and weeks after his arrival. It's the baby who decides when breastfeeding takes place, how long it lasts, when

A lot changes when a baby is born, including your relationship with your partner. By adapting to the changes, you can calmly look forward to life as a threesome.

15

people can take showers, when it's time to go shopping, and when it's time to do the housework. The baby even controls when you can make a phone call in peace or when you can have a decent conversation with your partner.

It's especially up to the baby when the parents get to sleep. First-time mothers and fathers are totally taken by surprise by this form of subordination: A little person scarcely over a foot long manages to completely dominate two adults.

The Effects of Sleep Deprivation

There's another thing that shouldn't be underestimated: Chronic sleep deficit wears down even easy-going people. Many mothers are so afflicted by this that they can barely open their eyes in the morning. They get up totally worn out, with scarcely any idea how they are going to get through the day, let alone structure it in any sensible manner. There is nothing worse than starting the day in a bad mood. The baby also perceives this—and reacts to it with a similarly bad mood. This is the beginning of a vicious circle, and sooner or later almost every mother will ask herself, "Why am I doing everything? Is this the way I thought it would be? I should have stayed at my old job."

Good Times, Bad Times

Admittedly, all this doesn't sound very encouraging, but it's no reason to enjoy the baby any less. On the contrary, starting a family is a wonderful thing. Just keep in mind that things will not always be good. There will also be highs and lows in family life, and this applies to practically every

family (regardless of what people may tell you). It is also completely "normal" to argue with your partner about trivial or daily occurrences. These bumps are to be expected; there are many new things to adapt to, and it will take some time for your little team to mesh properly. Ignore the expectations of the people around you (especially relatives), who want to see you as a "healthy family" right from the start. In addition, use every crisis as an opportunity, and don't set your own expectations too high.

TIP | WHAT IS HE THINKING?

In the evening after a strenuous day at work, it often happens that a father is handed the baby as he comes through the door. "Good," says Mom, "You're home, I've had it!" And what, you may wonder, is the father thinking? Perhaps he had to get up early, has had a tough day at work, and was looking forward to his night off. He comes home tired and drained and now simply wants to shut down. He hasn't even had time to take off his shoes and jacket, and the baby is already in his arms. And he especially fails to understand why his wife is complaining—she has been home all day and had nothing more to do than take care of the child!

Communication Works Wonders

But communication works only if you and your partner are open with each other. You must describe what you find difficult; talk about what you thought would be different, and clarify the things that disappoint you. Only people who communicate clearly are in a position to do away with conflicts.

Conversations with like-minded people can also be beneficial: Mothers may meet others in their shoes through prenatal classes, at the gym, or in baby playgroups. Always remember that there are no heaven-sent experts, no more than there are perfect parents and babies that never cry.

The Home Front

Do you have an apartment or a house with an extra room for a child? Great. Then what could go wrong? Many parents initially believe that the child will have a private room, and the rest of the house will stay just the way it is. But that's not the way it works.

Pregnancy increases not only your waistline, but also the contents of your home. You buy a changing table, set up a sleeping area, and clean out a closet for the child's clothing. If you were previously a neat freak, you should now accept the fact that chaos may sometimes prevail with a baby around. It's likely that there will be a baby bib and nursing aid lying around, a kiddy car parked in a corner, and the car seat left in the middle of the room. Add pacifiers, baby bottles, training manuals, little coats, and stuffed animals to the list of accessories. This tiny new

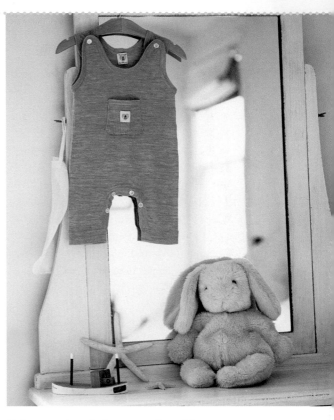

Baby moves into the house—and puts his stamp everywhere!

addition to the human race sure comes with a lot of baggage! It's a fun idea to take a "before" photo of what your house looks like before the arrival of baby and get excited about what it will look like after the baby comes. It's guaranteed that for the next fifteen to twenty years there will be a lot more color and life within those four walls.

17

Definition of "Work"

"And what do you do for a living?" "Nothing right now; I'm just a housewife and a mother." Unfortunately, in our society, it doesn't sound too impressive when a woman is "just" a housewife and a mother, as if this were not a respectable use of time. One should be impressed though! A mother performs several jobs simultaneously every day. She is a cook, a shopper, a nurse, a chauffeur, a psychologist, a companion—and incidentally runs the whole household. Who in their right minds could suggest that mothers don't "work"?

A Trace of Wistfulness

No matter how much a mother manages to accomplish, usually there is a part of her that misses her former profession. Often it's not the actual job that she misses, but rather the fact that she was able to leave the house to go to work. She may miss her colleagues, especially if they were friends she rarely sees anymore. But what she probably misses most is the feeling of having accomplished something. This accomplishment was always visible, at least in the form of a paycheck. Even if you are performing your job at home just as well and there is nothing in the world you would rather do than be a mother, be prepared for the fact that at some point you may be overrun by a longing for your old profession. There you had coworkers who talked to you about more interesting things than baby food or the contents of a diaper. You had a supervisor who might praise you for your work and knew how to appreciate your performance. You had a clearly defined workday, and when it was over, you had some time just for yourself. But now something lies dormant inside you: a longing for recognition. It seems that every mother is familiar with this jumble of feelings. Does anyone truly acknowledge your success when the baby is growing well and thriving, when she has clean clothing to put on every day, when the refrigerator is full, when the baby gets playful encouragement, and when the beds are nicely made? It may seem to you that everything you do is taken for granted and that nobody appreciates your accomplishments. But you should know that this is not the case. Surveys have shown that fathers are happiest when they come home from work and see that the mother and children have had a good day and are in a good mood. As long as his family is happy, he is, too. Just wait—at some point you will get the best recognition there is—from your little "boss." This doesn't come in the form of a salary, but

TIP | MODERN MOTHERS

Fortunately, the image of the modern stay-at-home mom is changing. She has taken on the promotional title of "manager of a small family enterprise." Take inspiration from this thought and develop new self-confidence. All of a sudden you have a demanding full-time job!

as undisguised, true love. Your daughter may whisper words like these into your ear: "You are the best mommy in the world!" or your son may exclaim, "Mom, I want to marry somebody just like you!"

Money Matters

Money becomes an important subject now because, with children, a dollar is worth only half as much. Perhaps this sounds a little dramatic, but that's the way it is. Couples with no children usually have no idea how much children really cost. The reality is that children do cost money. On average, the start-up (stroller, crib, changing table, wardrobe, equipment, diapers, daycare, and so on) cost parents about three thousand dollars during the baby's first year—although it can certainly cost more. Also remember that one of the parents—usually the mother—will stop working for some time after the birth of the child. This means that you are feeding an additional little person, but on a single salary. There is one small consolation: New parents may find that they fall into a lower tax bracket because their income has decreased.

Friendships

Socially speaking, children open doors. This is especially confirmed by mothers who walk a lot with their babies or visit playgrounds. They have practically no difficulty in meeting peers. Mothers who participate in baby yoga, baby swimming, story times, playgroups, or other parent–child programs (see page 173),

will surely make new friendships with parents of children of similar ages.

The Good Old Friends . . .

Things can get difficult with old friends if they don't have children, or if their children are significantly older than yours. They have no restrictions on how to structure their free time and can use their available time however they wish. And this may not always fit in with your schedule. As parents, you are just now learning how to turn your trio into a good team at home. Before you had a child, you may have gone out for leisurely Sunday brunches, enjoyed the theater or sporting events, or relaxed on weekend getaways with friends. But now, with a baby, you may have to modify a lot of all that.

Your spontaneity is restricted, especially in the first few weeks after the baby's birth, and you'll have to consider the practicalities of this new situation. What's the best way to get to where I want to go? How long will it take? Where can my baby sleep? Will I be able to nurse or change diapers without interruption? Where will I put the stroller? Will it be too noisy or smoky for the baby?

Somewhat Different from Before

So, unlike in your "before baby" life, you may decide to spend most weekends peacefully in the circle of your little family. Fine! With a little luck your friends will understand. But don't be surprised if after a couple of weeks someone remarks that you apparently don't have any more time for your friends. Don't pay too much attention to that. You know that's not the **19**

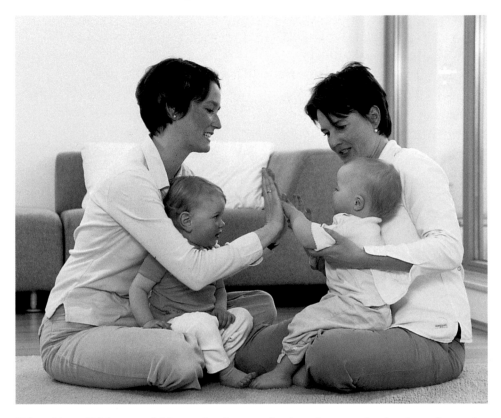

When things click between children at the playground or in a playgroup, the chemistry often works well between the parents, too. This is an easy way to develop new friendships for life.

case. The truth is simply that, for the time being, you simply have different priorities. Your family is now at the top of the list. Soon you will surely meet new friends—probably with children of the same age—for children really do open doors.

Your Love Life

For most new parents there is a major transformation in their sex lives. There are many reasons for this: in the first few weeks after the birth, the mother is processing the birth with all its side effects.

She may have a painful perineum, stitches from a Caesarean section or episiotomy, and other minor aches and pains related to delivery. Since they have just given birth to a large bundle of humanity, most mothers long for peace and relaxation afterward. But, of course, with a newborn, that's not so easy to do—after all, the baby needs care and feeding, in most cases every two to three hours, and throughout the day and night.

Even if a mother really has a relatively pain-free recovery, she still longs for sleep. In addition to her fatigue, there are other dampers on the love life. Engorged breasts, lochia, lower pelvic strain, exhaustion, and hormonal changes don't exactly whet the libido. And there's another unfamiliar twist: in many cases, the new baby sleeps in the parents' bedroom. Walking on tiptoes and whispering to each other, they try to be as quiet as possible—once the baby is finally asleep, she mustn't be woken up!

All these factors can leave romance, libido, and passion in the dust. But don't worry—in the short or the long run, the old passion will return. The important thing here is communication: regular, honest exchanges with your partner. Tell him what exhausts you and how you feel at that moment. Help him understand if you aren't in the mood for a passionate evening, and that you would rather have some rest and a comforting shoulder to lean on.

TIP | **A LIBIDO KILLER**

"So how long do we have to keep our love life on hold after the baby's birth?" This is one of the most common questions new parents ask following the birth of their child. The answer is not simple; it depends on many variables. Surveys have shown that in the first three to six months after the birth, most parents have practically no sex. And yet as soon as the female hormones have switched back to the "non-pregnant" status, the new family trio is living happily together, and the baby is finally sleeping through the night, the desire for sexual intimacy returns. Generally this all takes about six months, but every case is different. Some parents are enjoying sex only two weeks after the birth, whereas others take a year's break after the birth before they feel ready again.

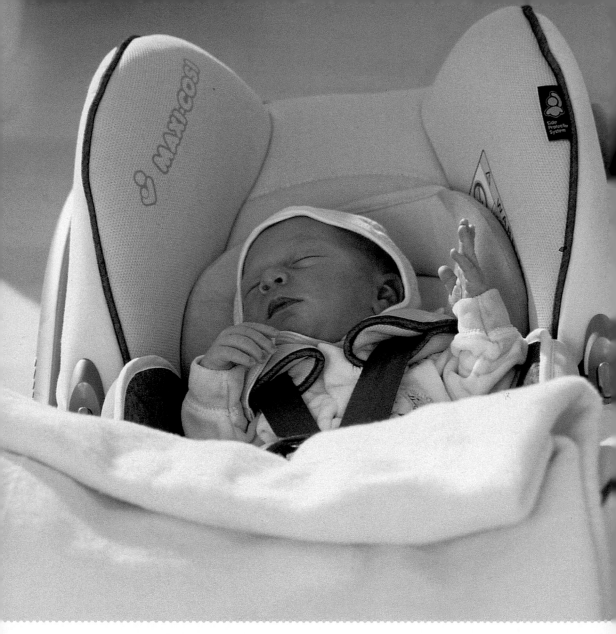

Getting Ready for Baby

As long as baby lives inside the womb, it's still totally undemanding—no feedings, no diapers, no bed, and no stroller. But once the baby is born, everything must be ready so that you can freely take care of your newborn and yourself after the delivery. You may as well put the waiting period to good use and prepare for baby's arrival! There is nothing more stressful than trying to prepare the basics while holding a baby in your arms.

Baby's Layette

Clothing sizes for infants are easy to determine because they are labeled according to age in three-month increments: 0–3 months, 3–6 months, 6–9 months, 9–12 months, and preemie sizes, which are smaller than 0. In general, you should purchase clothing one size larger because babies grow so fast.

Of course, you don't know how big your baby is going to be before she's born. However, your obstetrician may be able to estimate the baby's size. Then you can tell the direction in which your baby is headed (small, average, large) and shop for what you need. Even though it's tempting and pleasant to browse through baby shops, don't buy too many clothes in the smaller sizes! While you can usually count on getting one or more pieces of clothing as gifts after the birth, your baby will very quickly outgrow these tiny sizes. Many mothers are disappointed when a baby has worn a beautiful article of clothing only a couple of times because the baby quickly outgrew it.

Comfort Is Key

It's really nice when baby clothes are pretty. But it's far more important that they be comfortable for your baby and as easy as possible to put on and take off. If you buy one-piece outfits, choose those that fasten along the side or front. That way you don't need to pull them over your baby's head. Also make sure that pullovers and T-shirts have snaps on the side of the neck opening or very large expandable neck holes.

These features allow the head to get through comfortably. Unfortunately there are some clothes out there that are cute but totally impractical because they don't fit over the baby's head—the opening is simply too small. Also, never purchase baby clothes with buttons; they can be a choking hazard.

TIP | STARTER WARDROBE

Here's what you'll need to dress your baby during the first eight to ten weeks:

➤ Three to five one-piece outfits, which ideally fasten at the front or the side
➤ Four to six one-piece sleepers or stretchies
➤ Six or seven light onesies or T-shirts (depending on the season) for wearing as undergarments
➤ One jacket for outdoors (heavy or light depending on the season)
➤ One or two baby hats that also cover the ears
➤ Two or three pairs of socks or booties
➤ Three or four bibs, if you are bottle-feeding
➤ For winter babies, one or two pairs of tights, one snowsuit, and mittens

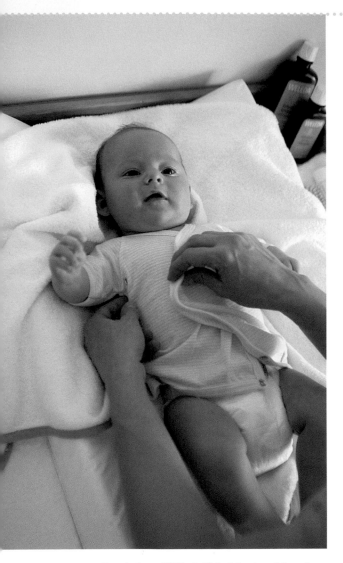

Your baby will like it if clothing is quick and easy to put on and take off.

Hand-Me-Downs

If you are fortunate enough to have a friend loan or pass on baby clothing to you, accept the offer. Even if there are certain items that you don't especially like, they might come in handy. Keep them in a closet and use them if you need extra clothing and have no time to do the wash. If your baby drools a lot, several changes of clothes will be part of the daily program no matter what precautions you take with bibs and so forth. In addition, used clothing has an added advantage that all dyes and other chemicals that could cause allergies in a baby have already been washed out. Used clothing always contains fewer harmful substances than new clothing.

TIP | WHEN TO CHANGE?

As long as the outfit is still clean, newborns don't need to have fresh clothing every day. In addition, they don't need pajamas at night; they sleep just as well in a playsuit. Pajamas make sense later on when babies settle into their day–night rhythms and putting the child to bed turns into a ritual.

Baby Equipment

Whether you get new baby equipment from a specialty shop or opt for used items, you will probably have lots of fun creating a "nest" for your baby. In the beginning, of course, you can do without certain things. But there are other items that you really should have on hand before the due date. Do take into consideration that your baby could very well arrive a few days earlier than planned.

What You Need Before Baby's Arrival

➤ A baby blanket (approx. 28 × 56 inches / 70 × 140 cm), made from a soft, durable, and washable fabric. It's also a fine gift idea.
➤ An infant car seat. Unless you deliver the baby at home, you will need this right away.
➤ A few newborn-sized disposable or cloth diapers.
➤ A diaper pail. A good choice is a small container with a tight-fitting lid. Once it's been used as a diaper pail, it's found its destiny. (Or make arrangements with a diaper service.)
➤ A container of diaper wipes.
➤ A bath thermometer. This will help you make sure the water temperature is always safe.
➤ A digital thermometer in case your baby is ill.
➤ A pacifier in the smallest size available—if you intend to let your baby use a pacifier.
➤ A cradle or a bassinet for the first bed. The latter has the advantage of being equipped with wheels and can be moved into another room.

➤ A baby carrier. This can be either the sling type carrier or the over-the-shoulders harness, some of which can be modified into a backpack. These make perfect baby shower gifts.
➤ A stroller so that you and your baby can soak up as much fresh air and sunshine as possible whenever you want.

Other Practical Items

➤ **A changing table.** You can always change the baby on top of the kitchen table, on the bed, or even on the floor, but it makes sense to set up a designated changing station. This place should be comfortable not only for the baby, but also for you, since in the future you will be spending quite a lot of time here. That's why changing tables are the ideal choice. They should have drawers or shelves so that necessities—such as diapers, lotion, and clothing will be close at hand. As for location, you should also consider that a nearby source of water might be useful. If your budget allows, you might also set up a second changing area in the bathroom, which would be handy after bath-time. All changing tables should come equipped with a safety belt. You should never, ever leave your baby unattended on the table.
➤ **A nursing cushion.** In breastfeeding, your positioning is key in avoiding bad posture and back problems. Nursing cushions come in a wide variety of sizes and fillings; choose one that feels comfortable to you. Make sure that it's not too heavy. **25**

Always use a safety belt on the changing table to avoid the baby falling off!

➤ **A music box.** During pregnancy, many expectant mothers place a music box on their tummy and let their baby experience a beautiful melody. When you choose a music box, look for a slow, calming melody. Babies generally won't doze off to music boxes making a lot of loud, frantic noise. Alternatively, purchase a portable CD player and some lullaby CDs for baby.

➤ **Infant clippers or scissors.** Infant scissors have rounded tips to protect the baby's fingers and toes from injury.

➤ **Washcloths and a large hooded towel.** Choose a large towel, of at least a square yard (meter) for wrapping up baby after a bath.

➤ **Baby hairbrush.** Choose a soft one for gentle head massages.

➤ **A baby monitor.** This device allows parents to monitor a sleeping infant without physically being in the room and standing over the crib. It's a must if the baby's room is out of earshot of the parent's bedroom or other rooms in the house where you usually are. During the day, having a monitor gives the parent the freedom to do other things while the baby is napping; at night, it allows parents to sleep in another room, yet still be able to hear when the baby awakens. Two types of baby monitors are available: audio only and audio-video. Audio monitors pick up sound only. Audio-video monitors allow the parent to hear and see the baby on a screen; a camera is placed at the end of the baby's crib to catch the action. Some high-tech models have infrared technology that makes the baby visible even if it is dark in the nursery.

➤ **A mobile.** Hang a colorful mobile over the crib to keep baby stimulated. Note that once a baby can sit up, a mobile can become a safety hazard.

Things You Don't Need Right Away

➤ **Sleep sack.** Nightgowns with sealed bottoms can be used when babies begin to kick the covers off, which usually happens at around three to four months.

➤ **Pillows.** Babies also don't need pillows. In fact, they pose a safety threat since a baby might pull one over his head and suffocate.

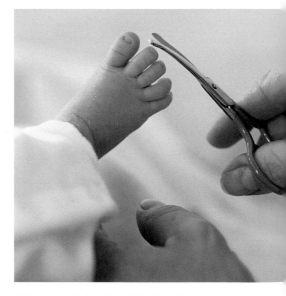

Clip your baby's nails while she is sleeping. Her hands and feet will finally be still, and that will make your task much easier!

A Safe Place to Sleep

Oftentimes a complete furnished nursery awaits the baby before birth, but it usually remains unused at first. Newborns feel most comfortable close to their parents; likewise, many parents feel more secure when their baby initially sleeps with them in the same bedroom. Luckily, in the first four to six months, your baby will have enough room in a bassinet or a cradle. Afterward, the baby's growth will necessitate a move into a crib. Here are some things you should consider when buying a crib and nursery accessories:

➤ Cribs that later can be converted to junior beds are very practical.

➤ The mattress should be adjustable for height. Why? As long as your baby is not yet turning over, sitting up, or pulling himself up, it's much more comfortable to keep the mattress in the topmost position. That way you can reach the baby without bending over too far. Later, when your baby is more mobile, the mattress should be lowered so that the baby won't fall out or climb out of the bed.

➤ The space between slats must be less than $2\frac{3}{8}$ inches (6 cm); otherwise, your baby may get his head stuck between them.

➤ Screws should be countersunk in the wood and inaccessible to the child to avoid risk of injury.

➤ If the crib has rollers or casters, they should be lockable.

➤ Ecologically and healthwise, beds made from untreated wood make sense. Otherwise, ask if the paints and lacquers used are non-toxic and lead-free.

➤ The mattress must be firm and fitted tightly against the crib. Today, many organic options are available that meet safety standards without using the chemicals prevalent in standard mattresses.

➤ Also purchase a washable tight-fitting mattress pad. Children sweat quite a bit, and it's not unusual for vomit or urine to occasionally leak out onto a crib. For this reason, a water-resistant pad also makes sense.

➤ Remember, babies should *not* use a pillow.

TIP | SAFE BEDDING FOR INFANTS

Place your baby on her back on a firm, tight-fitting mattress in a crib that meets current safety standards. Do not use pillows, quilts, comforters, sheepskins, pillow-like stuffed toys, or other soft products in the crib. A sleeper or other sleep clothing is a good alternative to blankets, as babies have been known to get tangled in a blanket and suffocate. If you do use a blanket, place your baby with her feet at the foot of the crib. Tuck a thin blanket around the crib mattress, reaching only as far as the baby's chest. Make sure your baby's head remains uncovered during sleep. Never place your baby on a waterbed, sofa, soft mattress, pillow, or other soft surface to sleep.

A Few More Things

➤ At first a light, airy blanket is adequate; and it should be easily washable. Another good choice: a baby blanket made of virgin wool.

➤ Do not use heavy quilts or comforters, or blankets with fringes or laces—these things can be fatal if babies get tangled up or find their heads under the covers and suffocate.

➤ Don't put the bed right under a window; drafts and direct sun are not good for baby.

➤ At night the optimum temperature for the baby's bedroom is around 65°F (18°C), and the best humidity is about 60 percent. If the air is too dry, a humidifier will help.

➤ One important consideration for a good sleep is the location of the child's bed in the room. Small children sometimes react very sensitively to disturbances. Parents who are open to Feng Shui should consider the basic rules of this Asian art of furniture placement and apply it to the nursery, too. Do an Internet search, using the terms "Feng Shui" and "Nursery," for more advice.

TIP | **WHY IS BABY DISTURBED?**

There has been controversy about the harmful effects of electromagnetic fields (EMFs) on children. If you notice that your baby keeps turning over in bed and adopts bizarre sleeping positions, and you are concerned that this could be connected to electromagnetic radiation (for example, if the crib is upstairs directly above the television or radio), try moving it to a different corner of the room. Also try placing the baby monitor as far away from the baby as possible. The result may surprise you.

Family Case Study

Christine (27), Andy (36), and
Nicky (5 weeks)

Not what we expected . . .

*Andy: Nicky is absolutely the child of our
dreams. We are delighted with him.*
*Christine: We took two pregnancy tests,
because we couldn't believe it.*
*Andy: For the first test we even drove to the
drugstore and asked if we were reading
the results properly.*
*Christine: That was a Friday. Then we
worried the whole weekend that the test was
wrong. So we bought another one. That
was positive, too. It was a dream come true.
The whole pregnancy was a dream. No
problems, no stress, everything was easy.
That's how we thought it was going to be
with the baby, too.*
*Andy: But things turned out differently.
Nicky arrived two weeks early. In the first
couple of days, he slept quite a bit . . .*
*Christine: But then we had nursing prob-
lems. He was too weak to suck, and he kept
falling asleep. So he wasn't really getting
full—and he cried a lot. He still cries a lot.
Nicky nurses, stays awake a little, and then
becomes fussy, so we are always holding
him. It does no good to put him into bed
when he's awake.*
*Andy: While one of us holds Nicky, the other
takes care of breakfast and the housework.
We used to have breakfast on weekends at
eight o'clock after having already gone out
for a jog. Now we're happy if we take our
first bite by ten-thirty.*
*Christine: And we're grateful if we get even
one hour a day when Nicky is sleeping so
that we have time for ourselves.*

*Andy: We thought things would be different.
But, of course, there are also lots of wonderful moments too—like when he's been
nursing and he still has droplets of milk in
the corners of his mouth. Then he looks so
cute and mischievous I could just gobble
him up and forget about all the stress . . .*
*Christine: Andy has even said that he now
has great respect for mothers.*

*Andy: That's right— kudos to all moms!
After the baby's birth I took two weeks of
vacation, but we got almost nothing done!
We were busy with Nicky around the clock.
That's all you can do!*
*Christine: But we understand that Nicky is
still very small and needs lots of closeness.*
*Andy: A baby is like a huge puzzle. Every
day, if you're lucky, you find one more piece
that fits.*

Questions and Answers

1 *I have heard that co-sleeping can be dangerous, is that ever true?*

It's true that some studies have shown that among certain infant populations, co-sleeping can increase the risk of certain specific problems such as suffocation and strangulation. However, it has also been reported (both by doctors and some parents) that the practice of co-sleeping has multiple benefits for infants. This is a topic soon-to-be parents should discuss with their pediatrician.

2 *My husband and I are thrilled with our baby. However, we never imagined that this tiny being would place so much strain on our relationship. What can we do to keep things running smoothly in the future?*

You will realize in the coming months that not only does your baby need endless help and attention from you, but she also determines your daily routine. Most parents find this difficult at the beginning. It doesn't work to continue your "old life" full speed ahead; therefore, there is bound to be some friction and daily frustration. Further complications may come from role sharing and mutually high expectations. Each parent thinks that the other could do a little more, or at least an equal share. This often sets up a vicious circle. What can you do about it? You could lower the demands and the activities a notch for as long as it takes you to establish a family life. It's also important that the partners allow each other some freedom. So if your husband wants to go to

a game or have a beer with friends in the evening, tell him to have a good time instead of asking when you can expect him to be back. Free time is just as important for you; you should also pass responsibility for the baby to your partner from time to time. The feeling is priceless. Ask him to take over the evening duty once a week. Then treat yourself to dinner with a girlfriend, a relaxing massage, or a sauna. Also, speak openly with your partner about which duties at home and in caring for the baby he can (and will) take over. Clearly defined relationships are better than unfulfilled expectations.

By the way, you are not alone. Research shows that 92 percent of parents experience heightened conflict after the birth of a baby. The division of roles and duties is the main cause of arguments.

3 *My partner and I are both ready for sex again. When can we start?*

Naturally, a prerequisite to renewed sexual activity is that the woman feels physically fit and that she has recovered fully from the delivery. Even if the new mother feels physically and mentally ready, she should be aware that the vagina may be uncharacteristically dry due to hormonal changes and that her first attempts at intercourse may be uncomfortable. This problem will regulate itself over the next few weeks. A lubricating cream or gel can help with this. If you had an episiotomy or a cesarean section, you should check with your doctor before resuming intercourse, to make sure that your incisions remain intact until healed.

4 How I can I tell if my child is breathing at night?

During sleep, babies are so still that it is sometimes quite difficult to see if they are still breathing. But there are a few tricks you can use to make sure that everything is in order:

➤ Moisten your index finger and hold it right in front of the sleeping baby's nose. You will feel the soft breath.

➤ When you place your hand on the baby's chest you will feel the slight rising and falling.

➤ When you lightly and carefully press your finger on the baby's forehead, the spot first turns white, and then immediately returns to its natural color—a clear sign of good circulation.

5 Should I go outdoors with my baby even when the temperature is below freezing?

Yes, as long as you've bundled the baby up well against the cold, you can take your baby outside in cold weather. A hat, mittens, layered clothing, a scarf, and warm outer-wear will protect the child from the winter cold. Very cold air is also often dry, and this can cause the baby's facial skin to dry out and tighten. Put a good oily moisturizing cream on her face before venturing out. It's also a good idea to feed your baby before going out into the cold. And finally, if temperatures are very low, you can warm up the stroller with a large heating pack or a microwavable heat pillow (available for purchase at sports stores) wrapped in a towel. Be sure to remove the heat pack before placing baby in the stroller!

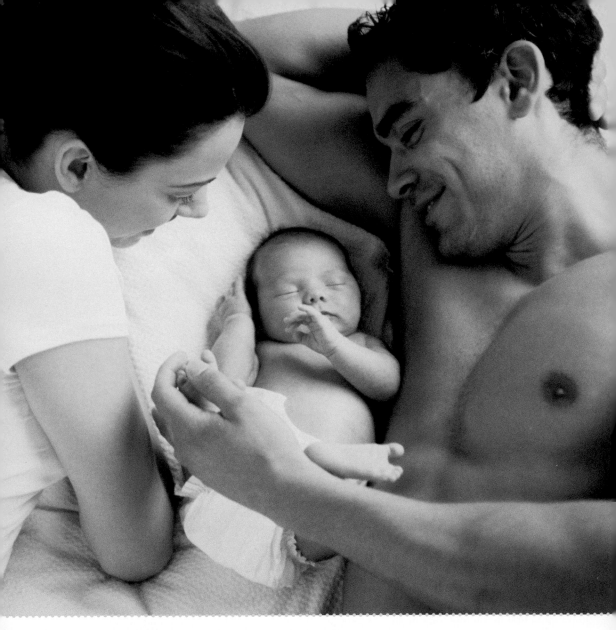

And Baby Makes Three

Welcome, little baby! Finally you're here! The waiting is over, the long-awaited due date has arrived—your baby is born. Congratulations! You have really accomplished something! Be happy that everything has gone well so far, and enjoy these precious first minutes together to the fullest. The strenuous birth is behind you, and you can now relax. Take a deep breath and enjoy the fact that you can finally hold your baby in your arms. For there is scarcely anything more beautiful in this world . . .

Early Days

Enjoy the certainty that your baby is healthy and has everything that belongs on a little person. Take joy in looking at your new baby, picking her up, and holding her in your arms. All these are wonderful moments that often are counted among the most beautiful ones in the life of a mother—and, of course, of a father too.

A Start in Life

Ideally the baby spends the forty weeks of pregnancy as a "tenant" inside the mother's belly. There it was not too bright, not too dark, cozy warm, not too loud, and not too quiet. The baby was able to suck his thumb, never felt hunger, and through the close confinement of his cocoon, always experienced the mother's presence. The baby lacked for nothing. But then contractions suddenly began, and for some reason that the baby could not understand, he was forced downward. What was happening? Why did these waves suddenly palpate his whole body? Why was the mother so agitated? Why did he have to summon up this power and follow the undertow toward the outside? And, most importantly, what's going to happen out there?

Baby's First Demanding Performance

Your baby, during the birthing process, has also completed a magnificent feat. Whether the baby was tentative or was more like a sprinter, the fact remains that she is finally present and wide-eyed. Your baby is happy to see her mother for the first time and seeks direct eye contact with you. In order to be happy now, the baby needs the same conditions outside that she had inside: It should not be too bright, not too dark, cozy and warm, not too loud, and not too quiet. Most of all, baby wants to feel her mother. That's why it's so important to hold your baby in your arms right after birth and to lay her onto your bare upper body. This skin-on-skin contact allows baby to feel, smell, hear, and see the way she did inside your stomach—with every one of her nerve fibers.

TIP | BONDING

Bonding refers to the imprinting of a relationship. Researchers all over the world agree that the first minutes after birth are extremely important for bonding. The sooner the newborn feels the same conditions as inside the womb, the smoother the "change of address" will be, and the more smoothly and harmoniously the baby will grow up in the new environment.

Cesarean Section

With a spontaneous birth, the baby feels that something is changing and that he will soon be born. The baby feels the contractions, the mother's heightened heartbeat, and her reactions to the labor. In short, the baby instinctively knows that it will be time to move out. This is often not the case with a planned cesarean section. In this instance, the baby lies unsuspecting inside the womb, and then suddenly the roof opens up. Two large gloved hands reach for the baby and remove him from the familiar womb. Instantly, it's uncommonly bright and loud, it's colder, and it's not as cozy as before. "What happened?" the baby must wonder.

Babies delivered by cesarean section have a different birthing experience. Some scientific studies show that many babies delivered by cesarean section experience a sudden transition from intrauterine (meaning inside the uterus) to extrauterine (meaning outside the uterus) life. There are those who believe that C-section is disruptive for the baby. Closeness to the parents shortly after birth can be a great help with this. Also, cesarean babies adapt quickly to their environment. An important factor is that they experience warmth, touch, and their mothers soon after birth.

Dad's First Major Deployment

If a father actively participates in the pregnancy of his partner, his baby will immediately recognize his voice. This is an important consideration for the baby's well-being, for if the mother is unable to take and greet the newborn in her arms because of a cesarean, or other complication, the father will have to take over this important early role. In this case, the male is responsible for the initial bonding and must provide the baby with the necessary tender loving care.

Forceps and Vacuum Extractors

During the expulsion phase, progress frequently stalls, and delivery cannot advance because of labor pains or the mother's exhaustion. The baby is often deep inside the pelvis and is practically "knocking at the door," as birthing assistants say. In these cases, a birthing implement is generally used to help bring the child into the world.

Forceps

Forceps are a pair of large metal "spoons" that are introduced into the vagina and placed around the baby's head. Then the doctor or midwife gently pulls in synch with the contractions and brings the baby into the world. A prerequisite for the use of forceps is that the cervix is completely opened and the baby's head is almost crowning.

TIP | NOT FOREVER

It was once believed that "once a cesarean, always a cesarean." This may not always be the case, though. Some women have had vaginal births with their subsequent children in spite of having previously had a cesarean. However, the risk of uterine rupture is not minuscule.

The Vacuum Extractor

This birthing instrument can be used in when the child is farther up inside the pelvis. The vacuum extractor involves a type of metal bowl that is placed on the back of the baby's head. A vacuum is created between the bowl and the baby's head by means of a pump, and the baby is then pulled along with each successive contraction.

Baby's Recovery

Some children who are delivered with a vacuum extractor or forceps, or by cesarean section experience an extended period of restless sleep phases and cry a lot. They may experience painful hematomas or bumps of varying sizes that may produce headaches. (So stroke the hair gently.) It often helps these babies to feel the closeness and the care that they have been accustomed to up to now. So hug your baby and press her tenderly to your body so she knows she's being loved and feels protected.

Not All Peaches and Cream

Few children come into the world with bright pink facial complexions. On the contrary, most babies are initially rather pale or bluish right after birth. This changes as baby cries and takes initial breaths. And, oxygen levels in the bloodstream rise dramatically with baby's first breaths—giving color to the face.

Ready for Life

As long as the baby is still attached by the umbilical cord, his lungs are not yet solely responsible for supplying oxygen. As the pulsation in the umbilical cord decreases,

Whether delivered through vaginal birth with forceps or a vacuum extractor or by cesarean section, newborn babies need as much closeness and tenderness as possible.

babies take on a rosier hue—this usually begins on the buttocks, then on the head, and then on the arms and legs. By the time the umbilical cord ceases to pulsate, most babies begin to cry, and their own

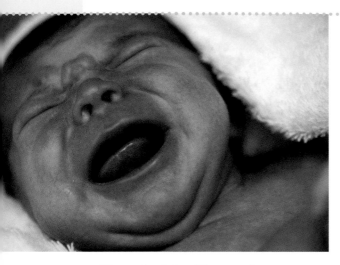

The cry that brings life—new air streams into the lungs, and the baby is now breathing independently.

breathing begins. With babies whose cord is cut immediately after birth, the doctor or midwife will use every means to coax a cry out of the baby. Usually they rub the baby gently to stimulate the breathing. In some cases there is also the traditional slap on the bottom. The sooner a baby cries, the better, for that is a sign that the breathing is functioning on its own. The lungs along with all other baby organs must function immediately.

The Apgar Test— Baby's First Checkup

Now, for the first time it is determined how well the baby is dealing with life outside the protective shell. The condition of the newborn is observed three times in brief intervals: the first time one minute after birth, and then five and ten minutes after the birth. Depending on the criteria, points from 0 to 2 are awarded for each result. In all, five criteria are considered so the maximum score relative to a baby's health condition is 10. Still, there's no need for concern if your baby falls short; very few babies get an Apgar value of 10. With a healthy child and a "normal" birth, most infants will score 8 or 9 points by the five minute mark.

After a pH test . . .

Cord blood is routinely collected right after delivery, and if the baby experiences difficulty in breathing, a blood pH test is conducted. This gives the doctor an idea of how the baby's circulation adapted to the stress of labor and delivery. In addition, many clinics measure the partial pressure of carbon dioxide and oxygen in the blood, which provides more precise information. For this purpose a couple of drops are painlessly removed from the umbilical cord.

. . . and the First Checkup . . .

Normally during the first few hours after birth a pediatrician conducts the

TIP | FIVE CRITERIA

This scale was developed in 1950 by Virginia Apgar, an American pediatrician. The five criteria are

➤ Breathing
➤ Heart rate
➤ Muscle tone
➤ Color (skin tone)
➤ Reflexes

TIP | INTERPRETING THE APGAR TEST

	0 Points	1 Point	2 Points
➤ **Breathing**	none	weak	regular
➤ **Pulse**	imperceptible	below 100	over 100
➤ **Basic Tone**	limp; no movement	little movement	active movement
➤ **Appearance**	pale or blue	pink body, blue arms/legs	pink all over
➤ **Reflexes**	none	grimaces	cries

first checkup (see page 100 for more information.)

... comes the First Bath!

In most clinics, newborns are bathed, providing them with a feeling of home: romping in the warm water is nearly as nice as being inside Mom's tummy. If the baby still has any vernix caseosa, or the white cream-like substance that coat's baby's skin at birth, on its body, it is carefully washed off. This layer, which protected the baby's skin from the amniotic fluid in the mother's womb, is no longer necessary after birth. After the relaxation bath, the baby is fitted for her first diaper and wardrobe. Finally—nicely dressed and swaddled—she is calm and nicely recovered, and ready to land in the arms of the waiting parents. After so much hard work, a well-earned, lengthy sleep is usually appropriate for the mother and child.

Other Delivery Room Procedures

There are a few other things that will be done either in the delivery room or the nursery depending on the facility's protocols. The baby will be weighed and measured. He will receive an injection (in the thigh) of vitamin K to help with blood clotting. Babies will also get eye drops to guard against any infections they might have been exposed to in the birth canal.

Before You Go Home

A blood test is done to check for serious medical problems (including thyroid, metabolic problems, PKV, and sickle cell anemia). Several drops of blood are taken (usually from the baby's heel) and placed onto a special filter paper. The hospital and the baby's pediatrician will be notified in a few days if there are any problems. The baby is also given the first in a series of immunizations to protect against hepatitis B (an inflammation of the liver). Hospitals do a newborn screening including a hearing test on the baby before she goes home. Two different techniques can be used. Both are quick and painless, don't require any active participation on the baby's part, and can be done while she is sleeping.

Mastering Life With Baby

A newborn feels most comfortable when life outside the womb is not too different from life inside Mom's tummy. For example, the baby has a great need for warmth and longs for familiar boundaries. Meet your baby's desires as closely as possible by always keeping him warm—but not so warm, of course, that the baby starts to sweat. Provide security by putting him in an infant wrap or swaddling him up snugly in a baby blanket. That way the whole body and the arms are tucked in so that only the little head peeps out.

Babies like things snug but not too tight— that's what this environment felt like for the past forty weeks.

38

Nursing and Resting on Demand

In the womb, your baby was accustomed to sucking his thumb and drinking amniotic fluid any time he wanted. So why try to forcefully impose a rhythm onto your newborn? Nursing on demand means that you give your baby the breast whenever she wishes, at least in the first days of life—provided that this doesn't harm the breast. Additionally, the mother's womb wasn't too bright, too dark, too loud, nor too quiet. Try to provide your baby with similar conditions by keeping your baby far away from noise and loud conversations, repeated visitors, hassles, and everything that would annoy you after a long trip. With regard to sleep, you should follow your baby's wishes. Peace ruled inside the womb, so the baby could sleep whenever she was tired. Make it possible for your baby to meet her need for sleep whenever she's ready for it.

Fostering Baby's Health

In addition to providing the best possible conditions for your baby's arrival, you must also remember to take care of other essentials: namely, *preventative health care*. Pediatricians recommend the following program to prevent certain illnesses or disturbances right from the outset.

Vitamin K
This fat-soluble vitamin is commonly referred to as the blood-clotting vitamin.

A vitamin K deficiency can lead to dangerous hemorrhaging, including bleeding in the brain in extreme cases. Adults are able to produce this vitamin independently so that it is always available in case of clotting factors, but the digestive tract of a newborn can't do this to the extent that an adult's can. As soon as the infant nurses or consumes vitamin-enriched formula, he gets this important vitamin (provided that the child's digestive tract can handle fat digestion and fat intake). There is no confirmed research on how much vitamin K there is in mother's milk, and the content can vary significantly on a daily basis (the mother's nutrition is an important factor in this). For this reason, the baby is given an injection (in the thigh) of vitamin K while in the delivery room to ensure adequate clotting ability.

Vitamin D

Vitamin D is important in helping the body absorb the minerals calcium and phosphate in the intestines and deposit them in the bones. If this vitamin is deficient, the result may be a softening of the bones and even bone deformation called rickets. Some vitamin D can be supplied in food; in combination with sunlight, the human body can produce another portion independently in the skin and transform it into the active form in the liver and kidneys. The current American Academy of Pediatrics' recommendation is for breast-fed babies to have an additional 200 I.U. of vitamin D daily beginning at two months of age. Vitamin D comes in a liquid preparation. Formula-fed infants do not need this as the

> **TIP | WRAPPING THE BABY UP**
>
> Babies like to be wrapped up snugly. Here's how to do it: place your baby onto a baby blanket (measuring about 32 square inches/approximately 30 sq. cm.) with her head in one corner. Now fold the point opposite the head over the feet. Then fold the left corner of the blanket over the baby's tummy with the arms held tight to the sides, and then tuck the right side over that.

formula is already supplemented with vitamin D.

Fluoride

Fluoride is a chemical that occurs naturally in minerals among other places. It is also present in small amounts in water and in the air, which explains why fluoride is found in nearly all plant and animal tissues.

What Does Fluoride Do?

Studies have shown that fluoride can protect the teeth from decay. Decay occurs when bacteria on the surface of the teeth transform sugar into organic acids. These acids destroy the enamel—and in the worst case produce a cavity in the tooth. Fluoride can offer protection by hardening the dental enamel so that the acids have less chance to destroy it. Because of their size, infants need much less fluoride than older children and adults.

What's the Recommendation?

The current recommendation from the ADA (American Dental Association) is that babies from zero to six months should not receive any fluoride drops or pills and babies up to twelve months should not consume fluoridated water. Although fluoride is important in preventing dental cavities, too much at this age can lead to a permanent discoloration of the tooth enamel.

Supplemental fluoride is not recommended within the first six months of life.

TIP | DENTAL CARE FOR BABY

➤ Most pediatric dentists recommend using toothpaste when the first tooth pokes through. An unfluoridated baby toothpaste is recommended. Teach your child to spit out the toothpaste, instead of swallowing it after brushing.

➤ During your baby's first year, if you mix infant formula with bottled water, use water that is fluoride-free or contains very low levels of fluoride. This includes water that is labeled purified, demineralized, deionized, distilled, or reverse-osmosis filtered water.

➤ Avoid putting a baby to bed with a bottle. Allowing a baby to go to sleep with milk or juice in her mouth is bad for her teeth.

➤ Establish good dental habits early on by using special baby and toddler toothbrushes as soon as the first tooth appears.

Caring for Baby's Bottom

For the next several months, you will be spending a lot of time with your baby—especially at the changing table. That's why it makes sense to provide a pleasant atmosphere and set up a changing station that is comfortable and practical for both you and your baby. The changing table doesn't have to be an expensive piece of designer furniture. In fact, an inexpensive plastic one, a changing table add-on for an existing dresser, or an insert for the bathtub are equally good options. A fabric surface, preferably washable, will make the baby comfortable—choose something soft that baby will like. A storage area for your diapers, washcloths, baby wipes, and so forth should be within reach. All your equipment needs to be close at hand. Whether you use a changing table, the bed, or the floor, it's important that the place be comfortable and pleasant for you and your baby so that the trip to the changing station is fun—or at least as fun as possible! And don't forget that safety requirements in the United States require safety belts on all changing tables!

Time for Tenderness

Changing time is the right time for playing with baby, for cuddling, or for singing a song. Your baby likes being able to wiggle and stretch a few minutes and loves your undivided attention. Getting out of the restricting diaper and playing with Mom or Dad is not only good for the baby's bottom but is also a great opportunity to bond.

Diapers—Disposable or Cloth?

More and more parents are considering the type of diapers they want to use for their babies before they are even born. They have three choices: cloth diapers that you can wash yourself and reuse many times, cloth diapers that are available through a diaper service, or the common disposable diapers. There are convincing arguments for all three.

Cloth Diapers

The basic equipment for a reusable diaper system consists of cotton diapers, either foldable or fitted, with a stretchable waistband that's adjustable for size with snaps or Velcro. They fit babies from about 7 to 38 pounds (3–17 kg). A three- or four-day supply of diapers is recommended. At about ten to twelve diapers per day for a newborn, you would need thirty to forty-eight diapers. In addition, diaper covers protect against moisture; they may be made from virgin wool, fleece, soft polyester, or nylon. Since they don't have to be washed with every change, a supply of three or four of them in the present size is adequate (about three different sizes are needed until the baby becomes potty trained). You will also need one insert for every diaper and a few extras for doubling up at night.

Diaper Services

A diaper service is very handy. The service drops off fresh diapers and picks up the used ones every few days. If you opt to use such a service, you should still purchase a few cloth diapers for other uses or in case you need extras.

INFO | A COMPARISON OF DIAPER SYSTEMS

Which type of diaper is right for you and your baby? For a fairly complete overview we have compared the two options.

	Cloth Diapers	Disposable Diapers
➤ Practicality/ application	Costly; diaper, insert, and diaper cover must all be ready to go.	Fast; quick to put on and a snap to dispose of.
➤ Cleaning requirements	Diapers must be sorted, washed, dried, and folded.	None; toss dirty diapers away and you're done.
➤ Purchasing	Once you own them, there are no further purchases.	You have to buy and lug heavy packages of diapers over and over.
➤ Cost	High (one-time) purchase price.	Cost spread over entire time.
➤ Cumulative costs until child is potty trained (about three years)	Relatively economical; may be around $500 for basic equipment plus $250 for ongoing costs.	Expensive; may be more than $800 by the time the child is potty trained.
➤ Environmental impact	Cloth diapers do not contribute to daily waste.	Less demands on water and using of washing chemicals.
➤ Gentleness to the skin	Very gentle on the skin; the fabric allows air to circulate more freely.	Basically plastic underpants; newer diapers do wick moisture away from the skin.
➤ Comfort	There is a bulky lump of diaper between the legs.	Innovative models are contoured so they can scarcely be felt or seen.
➤ Potty training	Children feel the unpleasant dampness and generally become potty-trained earlier.	Since modern diapers are fairly comfortable, there is less pressure to become potty-trained.

TIP | DIAPER SUBSIDY

Here is an example of the impact of diapers on solid waste. Around 1,200 children are born every year in Starnberg, Germany, resulting in about 10 percent (or an estimated 1,600 tons) of household trash from disposable diapers. This equals over 1,300 pounds (600 kg, or about 4,000 diapers) per baby until the child becomes potty-trained. The waste authorities intervened and since 1997, parents who use cloth diapers or a diaper service get a subsidy of about 20 percent of the resulting expenses. Other locations with scarce space for solid waste disposal could emulate this example. In the United States and United Kingdom, several organizations have studied the environmental costs of cloth diapers versus disposable ones. So far, it appears that neither method is environmentally superior. Once used, disposable diapers cannot be recycled and are sent straight to landfills as waste products. Cloth diapers on the other hand, can be used over and over again. However, washing cloth diapers involves using clean water, releasing chemicals into the environment (i.e., laundry detergents and bleach), and using energy to heat the water for washing diapers, and using the dryer if one does not air dry.

Disposable Diapers

Using disposable diapers doesn't require much advance planning, and is easy on the child. Disposable diapers are quick to buy, unwrap, use, and discard. The range of sizes runs from "newborn" to "toddler" diapers for babies who weigh as much as 55 pounds (25 kg).

A Happy Medium

But not everything is black and white with respect to diapers—why shouldn't parents benefit from the advantages of both diaper systems? At least it's worth considering if both systems can be used according to need. For example, more and more parents are choosing cloth diapers to avoid irritating tender baby skin. But when they are on the go, they also reach for the more practical and convenient disposable diapers.

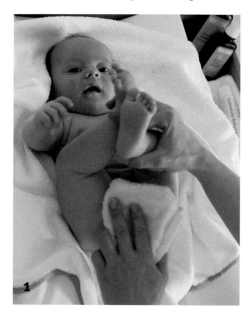

Carefully wipe the baby's bottom from front to back with a baby wipe or a clean washcloth.

Diaper How-to

Before changing a diaper, you should have all the necessary components handy: a clean diaper, diaper wipes (or fresh warm water and a washcloth), and if needed, diaper cream. Remember that you should never leave your baby unsupervised on the changing table! A single moment of inattentiveness is all it takes for your baby to fall off the changing table! Always use the safety strap, even if your baby has not yet begun to roll over.

➤ Step 1: Lay your baby on her back on the changing table, fasten the safety strap, and take off the diaper when you have the new one ready. Be aware that when you open up the diaper, fresh air will hit your baby's bottom, often causing her to pee again. For this reason, it makes sense to leave the baby lying on the old diaper for a

minute or two after opening it up—of course, as long as it only contains urine.

➤ Step 2: Wash the baby's bottom with a moist cloth. This can be a washcloth with lukewarm water, a baby wipe, or a paper towel moistened with oil or lotion (photo 1, page 44). When changing girls it's important to always wipe residue of stool and cream from front to rear—that is, away from the vagina and toward the anus—and never in the opposite direction. Otherwise, germs from the stool could get into the vagina and cause an infection. Also be sure to wash all traces of stool from the outer genitalia. With boys, carefully lift up the scrotum and thoroughly clean the area beneath it. The foreskin on uncircumcised boys must not be pulled back, however.

➤ Step 3: Now place a clean diaper under the bottom. Practice putting your entire

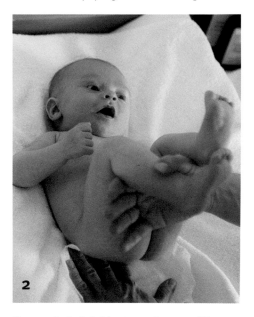

Protect the baby's hips as much as possible as you lift her up. Slide a fresh diaper underneath.

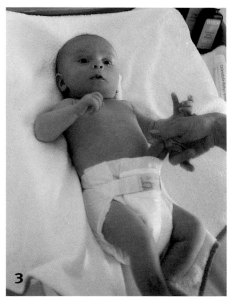

Check around the waist and the legs to make sure that the diaper is not too tight.

45

hand and forearm under one of the baby's thighs and using this hand to grasp the other thigh from above (see photo 2 on page 45). This hold is much safer for your baby's hips than grabbing the baby by the ankles and lifting him up.

➤ Step 4: Fasten the diaper—not too tight, not too loose. It should fit snugly, but without constricting. Check the fit by sliding two fingers along the inside of the diaper at the leg and tummy (photo 3 on page 45).

Caring for Baby's Tender Skin—Less Is Often More

Tender baby skin is five times thinner than that of an adult, and it is not completely developed in its function as a protective barrier against external influences. Creams, oils, and other products used on your baby should therefore be made only from natural ingredients.

Creams and Lotions

Times are changing so don't get irritated if your mother, mother-in-law, or grandmother remarks that the baby's bottom needs lotion. Babies used to be smeared with lots of lotion after every diaper change—with the result that these children were often sore. Today the trend is toward naturalness, and healthy skin needs no cream. The greasier the lotion, the more it clogs the pores of the skin. And the more artificial ingredients it contains, the more irritations you can expect on sensitive baby skin. However, if baby's bottom is really sore or raw, it should be treated with plenty of diaper cream so that stool and urine can't get onto the open

areas on the skin. Special salves for this purpose contain the trace element zinc, which helps control inflammation (see page 257). Your pediatrician can give you advice on this. Additionally, when you do purchase products for baby, keep your selections small—in every sense of the word. Many lotion bottles are so large that their contents could last for several years.

Into the Tub!

Normally the baby doesn't need a bath in the first few days after birth. (It's better to wait until the umbilical cord has dropped off.) But as soon as the navel has healed properly, the time for the first bath has arrived. This bath can take place in a large bathtub, a baby basin, a baby bathtub, or even in a dishpan. Regardless of where your baby gets his bath, you have to be able to stand comfortably during the process. The bathwater needs to be body temperature with a water temperature between 95 and 100°F (between 35 and 38°C). To check the temperature you can hold your dry wrist or elbow in the water; if the temperature feels pleasant, it will be fine for the baby. To be absolutely certain you can use a bath thermometer. If you want to raise the water temperature a little, don't add hot water while the baby is in the tub! If you hold your baby on your forearm and lower it into the water, you can use your free hand to go over the baby's body with a washcloth. The little body should be cleaned thoroughly but gently behind the ears, under the chin, on the neck, in the armpits, and in the genital area. If necessary, you can also wash the baby's head. It doesn't even matter if a

Interview

Baby Care—Tips from a Pro

The selection of baby products out there is huge, and the price range is immense. What should parents need to look for when they buy lotions and baby care products?

What do I need to be aware of when caring for my baby's skin?
Since baby skin is about five times thinner than the skin of an adult, it is particularly susceptible to all outside influences. It's also not fully developed in its function as a protective barrier. So, it's important that care products be designed specially for baby's skin. They should contain only a few, high-quality, natural ingredients.

What should we avoid putting on baby's skin?
Things such as mineral oils. These include by-products from the breakdown of fossils. Just like synthetic silicon oils and paraffins, they are foreign to human skin and stick to the surface of the skin as an insulating layer. In many cases, they can even interfere with healthy skin functions. On the other hand, baby skin "recognizes" the fatty acid structures of natural plant oils such as almond and sesame oils. They are easily absorbed and incorporated into the body's lipid mantle.

What about preservatives?
These are used to protect the product from spoiling. But if a manufacturer is careful in developing the formula (appropriate pH, low water content, etc.), preservatives can be left out entirely. Parents who prefer preservative-free products must read the labels closely.

What's the story on artificial aromas?
Synthetic aromas are supposed to improve the scent of the products. Their health effects on humans are largely unknown, however. Recently, some harmful effects have been noted in certain products. Good alternatives are ethereal oils, which are simply valuable plant essences. In nature, plants represent growth and metabolism—the same things that make it possible for people to live. Artificial ingredients don't have this quality.

Is it harmful to the baby's skin if we keep changing care products?
Continuity is recommended. Skin irritations or even allergies may result more frequently with frequent product changes.

For babies, bathing is about much more than just getting clean. In the bathwater, they can splash around in near weightlessness and discover their own body.

little water gets into the ears. You should just avoid submerging the baby from neck down in the first couple of weeks.

Bathtub, Sink, or Basin?

Once the umbilical cord falls off and the circumcision (if your baby had one) is healed, it's time to decide how you will bathe your baby. There are plastic tubs specifically designed for newborns. Or you can use plain plastic basins or inflatable tubs that fit inside the bathtub. Lined with a towel or rubber mat, the kitchen or bathroom sink may be another option. Baby bathtubs give parents a controlled environment for cleaning a wet, slippery baby. And the angle of the seat helps free a parent's hands for washing. No matter which method you choose, safety is the most important consideration. If you purchase a baby bathtub, be sure it has slip-resistant backing to keep it from moving. Look for a tub made of thick plastic that will stay firm in the center, even under the weight of the water. Avoid bath rings, baby flotation devices, and suction seats without restraining belts. These can flip over and lead to drowning. Most important of all, never leave your baby alone in the water, not even for a few seconds.

Bath Products: with or without?

A bathwater additive is not really necessary. You can bathe a newborn simply with warm water. If you would like to use something more, select a mild, moisturizing soap without scents or lotions, which can irritate baby's sensitive skin and clog the pores.

Navel Care

The navel generally doesn't require special care. The important thing is to keep the area around the navel continually clean. This is especially crucial in the first days after delivery, when the stub of the umbilical cord dries up and falls off. If this area isn't kept clean in the early days, it could become infected with germs, which, in the worst case, could contaminate the internal organs. Watch for redness at the base of the umbilical cord, which is a sign of infection. If you think your baby's navel might be infected, call your pediatrician for advice.

The Best Scenario: Dry and Exposed to the Air

The goal of the care is to keep the navel dry. This is why keeping it open makes sense. In other words, the navel should not be enclosed in dressings but rather left to heal in the air. If the remainder of the umbilical cord becomes soiled with urine or stool, you can carefully clean it with water and/or tincture of arnica (from the drugstore). Arnica prevents infections and checks bacterial growth. If there is already a small, local red area at the base of the navel, you can treat it with a non-burning first-aid spray from the drugstore. Report any redness to your pediatrician or midwife. If the remainder of the umbilical cord has already dropped off, once a day for the first three to four days you should dab some arnica onto the base of the navel. This can protect against possible infection. Many midwives and mothers can confirm

INFO | NO BATHING

Until the remainder of the umbilical cord falls off, you should not submerge the umbilical stump when bathing the baby. The moisture might cause an infection. However, the umbilical stump can be cleaned with a washcloth.

that the remainder of the umbilical cord spontaneously falls off between the seventh and fourteenth day. Of course, as always, there are some babies for whom it falls off a couple days earlier or later. That has no effect on the care you provide.

The Umbilical Granuloma

Once the remainder of the umbilical cord falls off, yellow granulation tissue (a type of connective tissue) can form in the navel itself. It may weep and lead to inflammation and infection. Your pediatrician can use a silver nitrate swab to cauterize this granulation tissue. This sounds more drastic than it really is: The treatment takes less than a minute and is totally painless for the baby.

Nail Care

Your baby has it all—including fingernails. They grow quickly and can become surprising long. Quite frequently, a mother will take her baby out of the bassinet and find that the baby has another scratch on the face. That is to be expected because the nails have very sharp edges. It is often said that in the first days and weeks following birth a baby's nails should not be clipped, but only picked at. That is supposed to keep the nails from becoming ingrown. But this method leads to more frequent inflammations in the quick of the nail. We recommend trimming with special baby nail clippers with rounded tips (you will find a good selection in drugstores). When you cut the nails, make sure that they are cut straight. If your baby still manages to scratch itself in spite of it all, you can slip some thin wool or cotton gloves or socks over his hands.

The First Days in the Life of a Baby

The first minutes after the birth are incredibly suspenseful. Often newborns look at the world with their big eyes, as if they wanted to say, "Hi, here I am. And so that's you—I have been listening to you for many weeks. I know you. Nice to meet you."

The First Half Hour: First Wide Awake . . .

Newborns can not only gaze alertly but also suck surprisingly well. In the first half hour after birth your baby will be wide-awake and equipped with a huge sucking reflex. This is the ideal time for the baby to be placed at the breast. That allows the baby to satisfy the need to suck, and simultaneously be as close as possible to the mother.

. . . and then so-o-o-o Tired!

Tired out from the strain of the birth and the first sucking at the breast, your baby will probably fall asleep. And things won't be much different for the parents. After the stimulation of the last few hours or days, the joy of holding the baby in your arms will make you too long for rest. Most parents enjoy with happiness and fatigue the view of their newborn—the baby is finally there, looks so sweet, and sleeps. At this moment, it seems improbable that things could ever be anything other than perfect.

Balance of Warmth

In this time after the birth, it is important for your baby to be surrounded by constant warmth so that all bodily functions can work smoothly outside the mother's womb. Newborns are able to regulate their temperature only to a limited degree. If it's too hot for them, they begin to sweat, and their heads turn bright red. When it's too cold for them, their body temperature can drop significantly. The problem is that babies don't always tell us that they are too warm or too cold. Many simply keep sleeping and put up with the temperature.

INFO | TEMPERATURE CHECK

From time to time check to see that your baby is at the right temperature: when the head and the fingers are supplied with blood so that they are rosy and warm, everything is fine. A good place for checking the body temperature of a newborn is the neck. If the temperature here is about the same as your warm hand, your baby is dressed properly. You should also regularly check the temperature in the baby's bed and adjust it accordingly by adding or removing covers.

The baby was able to sleep in Mom's tummy whenever she was tired. Let your baby enjoy that luxury in this world, too.

The Need for Sleep

In the first twelve to twenty-four hours most babies are so tired from the strain of birth that they sleep right through the rest of their birthday and want just one thing: rest! But then there are babies who lie peacefully in their cradle, the bassinet, or the parents' bed while they gaze in wonder at every little detail.

But things can be different! For there are babies who are ready to go after one or two hours of sleep and want to be in mom's arms—or better yet, at her breast. For it is nice and warm, smells and tastes like mom, and awakens familiar feelings in the baby.

But that's not all—these babies are simply hungry. They already need milk at regular intervals—sometimes every two hours—to supply their body with the nutrients they urgently need to maintain their metabolism. In the first days, the nutritional intake is needed for life support; what's taken in is used right away. This explains why many babies want to be nursed so frequently in the early days. And what about the babies who sleep through the day of their birth? After a prolonged sleep, they wake up with just one thought in mind: satisfying their hunger as soon as possible.

Meconium

When newborns empty their intestine for the first time there is green and black stool in the diaper with a sticky, tough consistency that suggests tar. This is the meconium, which reflects everything that the baby swallowed inside the womb: amniotic fluid, dead skin cells, mucous membrane, vernix caseosa, lanugo, and a few others. As soon as newborns drink their first gulp of milk, the contents of the stomach and the intestines move down a step and are excreted. It's no simple matter to clean a baby's bottom smeared with meconium. But abundant warm water and a little oil help in washing off the sticky mass.

In the following days, the meconium becomes lighter with every stool, until at three to four days (but sometimes as soon as one to three days) the first ochre-colored "milk stool" appears. Naturally, a prerequisite is that the baby is consuming adequate mother's milk or baby formula. The transition from meconium to (mother's) milk stool is an important step in the baby's life: It's a sign that the infant is getting adequate milk.

Red Urine

But the intestine is not the only thing that evacuates and releases the meconium in the first days after the birth. The bladder also releases what it has collected. Don't be alarmed if you see a light red urine spot in the diaper—sometimes referred to as "brick dust" urine. This urine is excreted by many newborns, particularly before the mother's milk has come in. The red particles are urate crystals, which form when the urine is very concentrated. It is a sign that the baby will very soon need a supply of fluid (from milk).

Swollen Breast Glands (Witch's Milk)

It often happens with breastfed babies that their breast glands swell up in the first days of life. The cause is the hormones that are transferred to the baby in the mother's milk. In the last weeks of pregnancy, expectant mothers form hormones that are intended to prepare their breasts for milk production and simultaneously enlarge the breast. These hormones can also enlarge the breasts of newborns (both girls and boys). Every once in a while, light pressure can even cause milk to flow (witch's milk). This is a source of amazement to both mothers and fathers. But this is no cause for concern. Never press or squeeze the breast, for it may be very sensitive to pressure. To keep the body and body suits from exerting pressure on the baby's breast and causing discomfort, you should put small gauze pads onto the nipples. The gauze provides a little relief from the discomfort, which is roughly comparable to that of a breast full of milk. Ask your pediatrician for advice. Generally this unplanned milk production lasts no more than a week or two. Children who are not breastfed rarely produce witch's milk.

Crusty Eyes

A few days after birth, many newborns have crusty eyes, a yellow secretion that sticks the eyelashes shut and collects in the corners of the eyes. In extreme cases, the newborn can't even open the eyes. The cause for this is usually excessively

TIP | THE NEED FOR WARMTH

Most newborns are quite content in a cozy, warm environment. Warmth is necessary for effectively sustaining all bodily functions. In contrast to adults, babies can't regulate their body temperature by themselves, so in extreme cases they become too cool or too warm. That's why it's important for the parents to check the temperature regularly in the first weeks of life. Rosy cheeks and hands are a good sign. In case of doubt, lay your hand under the baby's blanket and feel the temperature there.

narrow and consequently clogged tear ducts. The reasons may include a shifting of the facial bones during birth or a swelling of the mucous membranes. Generally all you have to do is carefully wash the secretions out of the eyes. You should use a gauze pad moistened with a saline solution (available in drugstores) and wipe the eyelid from the outside toward the inside—not the other way around—so that the germs are not rubbed into the eye. Get advice from your pediatrician if one eye is very red, because there may also be a bacterial superinfection that requires antibiotic eyedrops.

Nasal Congestion

Many newborns sneeze with surprising frequency in the first few days. Usually this is not a cold caused by a virus. Generally this involves amniotic fluid that is still lodged in the upper respiratory region. If small dust particles collect in the nose, crusty formations clog the nose. Treatment involves freeing up the nose with a few drops of mother's milk or a solution of saline (see above).

Newborn Jaundice

In the first few days, the skin of all newborns takes on a yellow hue to a greater or lesser extent that is caused by an increased concentration of bilirubin in the skin. Usually the amount of bilirubin in the blood increases between the third and sixth days of life to a maximum of 15 mg/dL and then falls back to a normal level (below 1 mg/dL) by the tenth day of life.

A different case is non-physiological newborn jaundice, which can become significantly more severe through other influences. The most common cause is incompatibility between the mother's and the child's blood (rhesus negative mother and rhesus positive child; rhesus positive child, blood-type O mother; blood-type A or B child) as well as diseases of an acute or chronic type. Even birth-related injuries (see page 35) can cause an increase in bilirubin. As long as the newborn jaundice remains in a normal range, it requires no treatment. However, high levels of bilirubin can be toxic to the baby's developing brain. You can help to bring down the bilirubin level by making sure that your baby is taking in adequate fluids to help excrete the bilirubin in the urine and stool. At home, you can place the newborn in a sunny area (but not in direct sunlight due to the danger of sunburn) because natural sunlight encourages the breakdown of bilirubin. In the hospital, the pediatrician may recommend using an artificial light called phototherapy to help break down the bilirubin in the skin.

Phototherapy

This involves laying the blindfolded child (because of the danger of damage to the retina) in a warm bed and shining a light of a specific wavelength onto him. The blue light portion of the phototherapy has the capacity to transform the bilirubin built up in the skin into water-soluble substances that can be excreted through the urine and stool.

Skin Problems with Babies

In the first few months after birth, the transition from intrauterine life to extrauterine life includes changes in the skin of the newborn. To help you understand your baby's skin, here is an overview of newborn skin problems and information on what you can do to treat them.

Strawberry Hemangioma

These common newborn skin conditions can appear on any part of the body and affect about 2 percent of all newborns, girls more frequently than boys. They are raised swellings of capillaries under the surface of the skin that feel bumpy to the touch and can occur in any size. Generally hemangiomas grow very quickly in the first year but begin to recede afterwards. By the age of two to three years, 90 percent of all capillary hemangiomas have disappeared. Treatment: Most hemangiomas do not require treatment, but those that occur on the head, are excessively large, or continue to grow may need laser treatment or surgery.

Cradle Cap

Cradle cap refers to small, bark-like, yellowish, greasy, shiny scales that form tightly on the scalp (also called seborrheic dermatitis). The dried crust looks like overcooked, dried milk and is similar to adult dandruff. Cradle cap forms during the first days and weeks after birth and may last until school age, although only in exceptional cases. In 50 percent of affected children, cradle cap spontaneously disappears by the end of the first year of life.

Remedy: Gently massage baby oil (or olive oil) into the scalp and let it work overnight. The next morning you can try to carefully comb out the softened scales with a soft brush. Finish up by washing the head with a mild shampoo.

Milia

Milia are small (pinhead-size) and yellow and look like a grain of sand; they occur mainly on the face (tip of the nose and cheeks). In 60 to 70 percent of newborns, milia (or whiteheads) occur also on the hard palate as well as on the dental ridge. Milia are small skin cysts that are filled with hardened keratin (pimples, in contrast, also contain sebum). Milia appear approximately at the same time as newborn acne and disappear within a few weeks. Treatment: None required.

Mongolian Spots

Mongolian spots are dark, blue-black spots occurring especially on the lower back or buttocks. They are congenital, but there is no reason to worry. The pigmentation is totally harmless and tends to fade during childhood.

Newborn Acne

Newborn acne involves small pustules and pimples with a reddish color. It generally occurs two to three weeks after birth and spontaneously disappears after a few days. With breastfed infants, newborn acne is more prevalent because of the hormones ingested with the mother's milk. Treatment: None. Do not squeeze. With severe pustule formation anti-inflammation therapy should be considered.

Erythema Toxicum

Erythema toxicum is a skin eruption that occurs usually on the second and third day after birth in approximately 60 percent of full-term babies. Small pustules, pimples, and red spots appear primarily on the upper body, while the surfaces of hands and feet are spared. Individual spots can appear and disappear within hours, but the overall eruption should resolve within two weeks. Treatment: None. Do not attempt to pop or squeeze.

Infant Acne

Infant acne usually begins in the second to third month of life. The condition springs from a heightened secretion of the sebaceous glands due to hormones; it recedes in the following six to nine months. Rarely is real acne therapy (as in adolescence) or an antibiotic skin therapy necessary.

Eczema

Eczema, or atopic dermatitis, can begin in infants between the third and sixth weeks of life, although it may be present at birth. It starts as a bright red crusty rash on the cheeks, which spreads to the neck and area behind the ears, arms, and legs. These areas itch and can be uncomfortable. Often the skin will heal spontaneously during the first year of life, but you should talk to your pediatrician about treatment to prevent complications. Non-prescription creams containing evening primrose oil and zinc may help.

Stork Bite

Stork bite is a clearly delineated red coloration of the skin caused by a prolifera-tion of tiny surface blood vessels. It is also called an angel's kiss or a salmon patch, but in medical terms it is a nevus. It is particularly common on the neck and the back of the head, but it also appears in the midline of the face—thus on the forehead between the eyes and to the root of the nose. When you press on it, the skin will blanch, but when your baby cries, it may appear darker. Generally stork bites fade within the first two years of life.

Dry Skin

Many newborns are born covered with the protective vernix caseosa ("cheesy wax"), a type of greasy film that coats the skin. Once this is washed off, your baby's skin will be sensitive and wrinkled. It is also usually quite red—appearing almost like a sunburn—and very dry and rough. On the stomach, the legs, or the feet, it can form scales, and sometimes, small shreds of skin can be pulled off. But this should

TIP | WELL PREPARED

Before a baby massage, you should make sure that your baby will feel comfortable. In addition to a room temperature of about 70°F (24°C), you need a place that you and your baby are familiar with. It's also a good idea to assemble your supplies before you start so you don't have to interrupt the massage. Lay the baby down inside a protective covering. Then away you go . . .

TIP | TIMING FOR PHOTOS

If you plan to put photographs of your cute little rascal into thank-you notes, you may have concerns about what people will say if your newborn suffers from acne. The solution is black-and-white film, which reduces the appearance of acne and shows off your baby's beautiful face.

be no cause for concern: A massage with a pure, natural oil such as almond, olive, or avocado can help. Mix a small amount of this vehicle with a drop of real rose oil (this works well in an eggcup). Before applying the mixture to the baby's skin, you should moisten your hands with warm water. Then rub a few drops of the oil into your hands and carefully massage the baby's body. An alternative is to use a store-bought baby oil—just take care that it doesn't contain any artificial colors or fragrances. Using oil or cream is good for your baby in several ways: You take care of the skin, protect it from further cracks, and give your baby a beneficial massage.

INFO | COLICKY BABIES

There are always some babies who, after a few days or weeks, begin to cry incessantly. It doesn't matter if Mom or Dad carries them around, bounces them up and down, swings them, or feeds them—nothing helps.

➤ **What is a colicky baby?** Experts have a definition for this: A colicky baby is an infant who cries continually for at least three hours a day on at least three evenings in the week, for at least three weeks. Colic usually occurs in the late afternoon and evening, and it begins in the first month and can continue until the sixth month. But listen to your gut feeling. Even if your baby cries "only" two hours a day and you are at your wit's end, you have a colicky baby in your arms.

➤ **What causes colic?** Scientists have several theories about the cause of colic. Infants may cry because of sensory overstimulation, which reaches a "breaking point" sometime late in the day. They may also cry due to digestive problems, such as gas and reflux.

➤ **How can you calm the baby down?** There are ways to calm a crying baby. Here, the magic wand involves reducing stimuli rather than increasing them. Therefore, it's not necessary to wind up the music box for a tenth time or whirl the baby through the air. A crying baby doesn't need distraction, but rather calming. Feeding the baby at the first signs of hunger, or putting him to bed at the first yawn seems to help. In addition, it helps to introduce a calm, regular daily rhythm. In short: you have to satisfy the baby's needs without hustle and bustle.

➤ **How can we turn things around?** The baby may have difficulty adjusting to life outside the womb. You can help your baby feel more comfortable by swaddling him up tight (see page 39), keeping him moving in a repetitive, rocking motion, and providing soothing sounds like a heart beat, ocean, or even the washing machine! By re-creating some aspects of life in the womb, you can help give baby some peace.

➤ **Other things that may help:** Be sure to take a break from your crying baby. If there are two parents at home, take turns trying to calm the baby. Occasionally try to take a break together, leaving the baby with a babysitter or other family member. And if you are at home alone and are at your wit's end, remember that you can put the baby in a safe place like a crib and step away for a few minutes to regain your sanity and composure.

➤ **When do we need help?** When you no longer know what to do, it's time to consult your pediatrician to rule out organic causes. Your healthcare provider may also suggest simethicone drops or fennel tea, or various resources on the Internet. In the United States, the Fussy Baby Network can help support parents during this stressful time (http://www.fussybabynetwork.org/). Luckily, colic will eventually run its course, and peace will return to your home.

Questions and Answers

1 *Is there some indication of when my baby needs to be changed?*

A fresh diaper is always appropriate whenever you can smell that the baby has had a bowel movement. Otherwise, you should change the diaper at least every three to four hours so that the baby's bottom doesn't stay in a wet diaper for too long. A full, heavy diaper is unpleasant not only for the baby, for it becomes hard, leads to a sore bottom, and cools the baby's body. It is also worthwhile to change babies after every feeding, for there is a direct correlation between sucking and evacuation.

2 *When changing a baby boy, is it necessary to push back the foreskin of the penis?*

No. At first the foreskin is so tight that there is just a tiny opening. Manipulating or forcing it back can result in painful injuries or even the formation of scar tissue or an infection.

3 *As my baby grows older and stronger, he is becoming more resistant to diaper changing. Is there any way for us to make him stop thrashing around and screaming?*

Yes there are. First, you can keep a supply of small toys by the changing table. Use them as distractions while you change your baby. When the novelty of the "changing toys" runs out, try playing peek-a-boo with your baby while changing or sing his favorite song. Using a variety of diversions is the key. Also, make changing time into fun time.

4 *How, where, and especially how often should I bathe my baby?*

You don't need a separate baby bathtub. Of course, it's a help, but a small wash tub will work, too. Many mothers simply put their baby in a wash basin. For the past several years, there have also been small plastic baby baths available. They should make your baby feel particularly comfortable (see page 48). Forty years ago babies were bathed daily. But today's recommendation is to bathe the baby once or twice a week. You don't need to use a bathwater additive; a soothing baby wash is perfectly adequate. Avoid products that contain preservatives and artificial scents.

5 *Why is it that baby care products from different sources bear the same seal of approval ("natural," for example) but vary so widely in price?*

Costs are based on various considerations such as quality control, research and development, and pharmaceutical production process. Expensive organic products contain only natural ingredients that usually come from carefully controlled biological cultivation. The cultivation and the care of the plants are consequently much more demanding and costly than with conventional cultivation.

6 *I keep finding a crust (nasal discharge) in my baby's nose. Should I get it out of there? If so, what's the best way to do it?*

You should remove the crusts only if they interfere with the baby's breathing; you can tell that by listening. Here's an easy tip for removing the crusts: Take a gauze pad for removing makeup and separate it so you have two thinner pads. Moisten your fingers and roll one of the halves of the pad into a thin cylinder. Carefully introduce one end into the nostril and move it back and forth. With luck you will fish out the crusts. This also works with a soft facial tissue. Don't put your finger into the tender nostril, for you might damage the mucous membranes in the nose. You could also use the baby's sneezing reflex to catapult the crust out by tickling the baby's nose.

7 *Is it alright for the father to bathe with the baby?*

Of course, there is no objection. It is often a neat experience for fathers to splash around in the tub with their offspring. That way the baby experiences direct skin contact and security. However, the baby should not bathe with the mother as long as she continues to experience lochia (for more information on lochia, go to page 70).

8 *I have heard that a delivery using forceps or a vacuum extractor is a stressful experience for the baby. It that true?*

Even natural birth can be a very stressful experience for the baby: A birth using forceps or a vacuum extractor is not imperceptible to your baby. The goal is to help quickly deliver your baby. After the birth, the fact that both devices were used is clearly and immediately visible on the head. When forceps are used, many babies have reddish-blue marks in the area between the ears and the temples. Vacuum extractor babies, on the other hand, usually have a circular reddish-blue spot the size of a tennis ball. In addition the whole head may become stretched by the strong suction. Many parents are alarmed when they see this, but they needn't worry: the molding of the head is usually gone a day or two after the birth. In as many as 3 percent of newborns, the scalp may fill with blood and produce a large bruise (cephalhematoma). This will gradually go away with time (see page 55).

Lying-In

With the birth of the first child a new stage of life begins for the parents. From now on there are new duties: finding a transition as smooth as possible from duo to trio, figuring out the baby's needs, and understanding her signals. In addition, a mother also has to come to grips with a major physical change:

She not only has to process the birthing experience but also let her injuries heal, produce milk, and get back into shape. From this point until eight weeks after the birth used to be referred to as lying-in, or confinement—to indicate that this should be a special kind of time off.

The Early Stages After Delivery

The first ten days after giving birth are very important for both the baby's early growth and the mother's recovery from delivery. Everyone can now recover from the stress of the birth; injuries can heal, and milk production should start up. You and your baby experience ways to foster your heartfelt relationship in daily life.

Help, My Stomach!

Initially it feels strange to be as soft and voluminous as a ball of dough. When you press your finger onto your stomach, it nearly disappears in the soft layer. Many women automatically hold their stomach below the navel when they stand up for the first time. They have a feeling that it will drop down if they don't. You feel a pressure in the pelvic region—almost as if you had a worn-out trampoline in your stomach. There are a tremendous number of things going on inside you in the hours and days after the birth: All the organs are happy to have their space back. Stomach, intestines, bladder, and other organs get sorted out. Your stomach has changed even on the outside: There may still be a dark line (the linea fusca) visible between the navel and the pubic bone. If stretch marks appeared due to the large girth of the stomach during pregnancy, the skin now appears wavy. But don't worry; that will change. The brown line will fade in the next few days and won't return until the next pregnancy. Any stretch marks from pregnancy don't disappear, but they do fade significantly.

What You Can Do

A gentle stomach massage (e.g., with lotion) will help you to bring your stomach muscles back to life. Stroke them with circular motions as you lie down or take a shower, or use two fingers to pinch the skin along the stomach fold. This will stimulate circulation. In the first days after birth, lie frequently on your stomach to take strain off your perineum and pelvis. Place a cushion under your hips so that your bottom is raised. If you also put your head onto a cushion, your body can relax thoroughly. This position relaxes the stomach, simultaneously encourages recovery of the womb's muscles, and encourages the flow of the lochia.

Improvement in Sight?

Patience, patience! Nobody is expecting you to leave the hospital with a flat stomach or fit into your favorite blue jeans right away. Up to the end of your pregnancy, your stomach gradually stretched to the maximum, and now it needs time to become smaller. There's a reason people say, "nine months coming, nine months going."

The Perineum

Nearly every woman who has given birth to a child—especially if it's her first child—feels discomfort in the area of the perineum. Because of the stretching of the tissue there are nearly always small tears or abrasions on and around the labia—and very probably the area is swollen. You may even have a more serious birthing injury such as a torn perineum or have experienced an episiotomy. But whether or not you have an injury—your lower abdomen now needs lots of attention and especially good care.

Caring for Stitches in the Perineum

The opening of the vagina had to stretch to the maximum to create easier passage for the baby's head. Whether this resulted in a tear or an episiotomy, stitches in the perineum are painful. How much they hurt and how long the pains last depend on several factors: the length and depth of the wound, the stitching technique, and the way the individual wound heals. Take the time to look at your perineum. This is best done lying down in the bath or in bed. Make yourself comfortable and hold a small mirror between your legs. When you look at the genital area, the injuries that you have felt so far take on a new meaning: are the labia still very swollen? Are they red? Are hemorrhoids causing a problem? How big is the stitch, where does the thread go, and do the edges of the wound mate properly? Many women are pleasantly surprised. For their perineum feels more uncomfortable and irritated than it really is. But is even more astonishing how quickly the injuries heal.

What Encourages the Healing Process?

The highest priority now is to take the strain off your perineum. Every injury heals better if it is not pressed or torn. So in the first days after giving birth, avoid sitting directly on the perineum. For now you absolutely must avoid sitting cross-legged. If you want to get out of bed and it is very high, you can either put a step stool at the foot end or simply crawl out of bed on all fours.

A Flotation Ring for Sitting

To keep the pressure off the perineum while sitting, many women commonly use a donut-shaped cushion (sometimes simply called a "donut") or a towel rolled up and shaped into a circle. The hollow in this type of ring really helps protect the perineum from any uncomfortable pressure. Still, new recommendations from birthing assistants are increasingly insistent that in the first days after giving birth a woman should avoid sitting whenever possible. The less you sit—with or without the mitigating sitting ring—the quicker healing proceeds.

Cold

All swelling goes down quicker if it is kept cool. So try to cool your perineum. You can use a cold pack (a cushion filled with gel that you can buy at a drugstore); however, don't put it directly on the wound, or there will be a danger of excessive cooling.

Wrap the cold pack in a thin cloth diaper or other cloth. In the clinic, you should have a new cooling pouch brought every couple of hours. Here is a good tip for at home: moisten a clean washcloth in clean water and put it into a freezer bag in the freezer for a little while. Take it out when it is still squishy. You could also use a real ice pack. But this poses a particularly high risk of excessive cooling, so put the ice pack into a cloth before placing it onto the perineum.

Air

Wounds often heal quickly when they are kept dry. The perineum is often difficult to keep free of moisture because the area is thickly packed in soft bandages. This continually damp, warm environment interferes with healing. You should thus occasionally treat your genital area to an air bath. Lie in bed with no panties, preferably on a towel folded in two (because of the lochia), and place your feet onto the mattress. If you need to you can put a blanket tent-like over your legs to keep you warm. This way the perineum receives a healing air bath.

Arnica

Arnica reduces swelling. Moisten a compress with essence of arnica (from the drugstore) and place it on the perineum. It is also effective to soak gauze pads (from a drugstore) in arnica and place them directly on the affected parts of the genital area, where they help reduce swelling.

TIP | ARNICA PELLETS

The use of arnica in pellet form is known for healing injuries. Midwives, gynecologists, and alternative medicine specialists know that arnica pellets reduce pains from stitches, help reduce swelling in injuries, and support the healing process from within.

Sitz Bath

A sitz bath may provide relief starting with the fourth or fifth day after giving birth. You must avoid bathing the genital region sooner because the stitches could soften and come apart. Even without stitches in the perineum, a sitz bath can be refreshing. Run warm water in the shower or into the bathtub and sit in it for ten to fifteen minutes. Or get a sitz bath/bidet insert for the toilet.

You can get these either from large mail-order companies or in medical supply stores. Good bath water additives include oak bark, chamomile, and sea salt; a teaspoon per liter of water is adequate. It's a good idea to ask your aftercare midwife or the doctor if you can use sitz baths or which bath mixture she would recommend in your case. One example of a frequently recommended mixture consists of yarrow, geranium, lavender extract, Turkish rose, and blue chamomile. A pharmacist can also help you with questions of this nature.

Rinsing and Washing

It's highly likely that the stitches in the perineum burn when you urinate. Before going to the bathroom, mix some fresh, lukewarm water in a fairly large container (a measuring cup, for example). As you urinate, pour this water onto your labia. That will keep the urine from stinging and leave you with a pleasant, fresh feeling. Then carefully pat your private parts dry. Doctors often times recommend that you use TUCKS® pads after you urinate.

When Will Things Get Better?

Depending on the extent of your injury, you will feel significantly better after a few days. Most women have no further problems after the first week.

Cesarean Stitches

There are several versions for the origin of the term *cesarean*. The most plausible one is that in July of 100 or 102 B.C. the future emperor Julius Caesar was the first person reported to be delivered by this method. Some evidence for this could be that there was a Roman law that required cutting the unborn child from the belly of a woman who died just before delivery so that the mother and child could be buried individually. The Latin name *Sectio caesarea* can be translated literally as "cesarean section."

Modern Adaptation

Nowadays a cesarean section means an operation. The suture is about 6 inches (15 cm) long and runs along the top of the pubic hair region. Obstetricians say "in the bikini zone," by which they mean that later on the scar will hardly be visible even if the mother wears a bikini. Formerly the incision was wrapped with thick compresses and held together with a large adhesive patch; but today it is usual to protect the wound with an adhesive bandage for just a day. Thereafter, the wound is allowed to heal in the open without the bandage.

A Respectful Glance

For most mothers, the first glance at the suture involves a mixture of uncertainty and respect. Women continually report that at first they didn't dare to look at the incision. And yet other women are very interested in the sutures and immediately take a look, which is not so easy because the stomach of women lying-in usually obscures the incision. If you use a mirror you can see the sutures—as close as possible above the shaved pubic region. The thread used to stitch together the outer layer of skin generally is transparent and

---

TIP | TAKING IT EASY

If you have such severe birthing injuries that you can scarcely sit because of the pain, your body is trying to tell you that you need three things above all else: rest, rest, and more rest. Give your body a chance to recover and, especially, time to heal. Take care of yourself and stay in bed, whenever possible, during the first few weeks.

made of synthetic materials. It doesn't need to be removed, for it dissolves by itself after eight or ten days. Depending on the surgeon, there may be a drain left in the incision. That is, a thin tube sticks out of the incision, with a plastic bottle on the end. This collects the secretions that seep out of the sutures from the incision. This drain is removed after about a day if there is no more seeping.

Dealing with the Sutures

At first the sutures must be checked daily. The attending physician regularly checks the incision and oversees the healing process.

Rest Helps with Healing

In the ideal situation, the following days consist of a mixture of rest and activity— the latter in moderation, however. Even if you feel tired and run-down, you should go to the bathroom regularly. On the one hand, this empties the bladder and lets the lochia flow at the same time, helps the uterus recover, and prevents a buildup of urine. On the other hand, it prevents thrombosis and keeps the circulation stable. But don't rush into things: For the first trip, the nurse will literally hold you under the arms.

Coping with the Strain

At first it is difficult to hold the baby, for the pressure on the scar hurts. Don't forget that you had to have an operation! In the first two days, the pain is usually so severe that mothers are glad to have help getting out of bed, lifting the baby out of his crib, laying him down, and changing

TIP | AFTER-PAINS

Naturally, mothers who have experienced a cesarean delivery also have lochia and more or less pronounced after-pains. To make sure that the injured uterus recovers properly, most clinics provide pain medication after the operation.

the diapers. But as early as the third day, most mothers are able to care for the infant completely on their own.

Getting Digestion Started

Regular digestion is important after every birth. As the baby grew inside the mother's tummy, the mother's intestine was pushed upward. As soon as the baby is born and the amniotic fluid and the placenta have been expelled, the uterus shrinks, and the intestines once again have room to spread out and resume their original position.

When Will Things Get Better?

Women who have had a cesarean delivery generally spend three nights in the hospital. The cesarean incision usually heals so quickly that after a week there is nothing visible but a fine line with a small scab. The stomach generally still hurts when pressed at this point. The skin above and below may still feel numb—permanently, in rare cases. Around the fourth day after the birth, most women can carefully bend over, and things are significantly better three to four days after that.

Post-Delivery Uterine Contractions

The delivery is over once the baby is there. But for the birthing assistants, it's not done until the whole placenta has emerged. Then you will be congratulated as parents. The mother is still not quite done with the birth, however—for there are after-pains.

Dealing with Contraction Pain

To understand which measures are well suited to reducing after-pains, you have to understand where the pains come from. At the beginning of the pregnancy, the uterus was the size of a fist; and at the end, it was the size of a large basketball. When the baby is born, the uterus must return to its original size, and the after-pains help with this process. In the process, the muscles of the uterus contract. The mother feels this acutely, sometimes as acutely as birthing pains.

As Needed: Pain Medication

There are just two possibilities for dealing with the pain: Either you put up with it or you get pain medication. First-time mothers normally get by fine without pain medication. But if you have had your second or third child, you may be offered pain medication by your doctor. Suppositories have also been proven effective. There are also some alternative medicines (or herbal remedies) that may reduce pain; they will not eliminate the pain completely, but they will take the edge off. In addition to arnica, these include chamomile, caulophyllum, and cuprum.

You should, however, take these medications only under the advice of your physician and a pediatrician.

Warmth and More Warmth

It is important to keep your lower abdomen warm! While you are lying-in, you should always have a hot-water bottle ready. It's generally acknowledged that warmth helps with abdominal cramps.

Herbal Teas: Gentle Help from Nature

Non-caffeinated herbal teas, such as chamomile, may help you relax and assist in milk production.

When Will Things Be Better?

Admittedly, you need to be patient. In the first day or two, the after-pains may be very severe; after three or four days, they recede significantly. It takes about a week for them to become imperceptible to most women lying-in. There is one small but important comfort: The sharper the pain, the quicker the recovery of the uterus, and the less lochia there is.

Retraction

Right before the birth, the uterus extended as far up as the rib cage. But just a few hours after birth, it is so small, because of the after-pains, that it can be felt as a firm ball in the vicinity of the navel. From this point on, it recedes about the width of a finger every day.

What Helps the Uterus Retract?

During postpartum care in the hospital, the midwife or doctor checks the size of the uterus daily. This is always a good opportunity to find out which of the following measures make sense for you.

Frequent Nursing

The perfect coordination of hormones demonstrates how well nature is prepared for birth and the time that follows: as soon as a woman on the childbed places her baby on the breast, her body releases the hormones prolactin and oxytocin, which cause the milk to flow. The latter hormone is also responsible for the retraction of the uterus and the after-pains. The more frequently you place your baby at the breast, the quicker the uterus retracts and the quicker the after-pains disappear. Many mothers immediately feel how well the hormones work together: When the baby begins sucking at their breast, they experience less severe after-pains a few minutes later.

Relaxing on Your Stomach

Use the time between the birth and the start of the milk flow to lie on your stomach as frequently as possible. This position reduces pressure on the uterus, which helps the retraction process. The blood has a chance to flow out, and you also take pressure off the perineum (see page 63).

Emptying the Bladder

Go to the bathroom frequently to empty your bladder. A full bladder interferes with the shrinkage of the uterus. Don't wait until you feel the need to urinate; it's best to go at least every two hours. One problem is that after giving birth it is often difficult to urinate, and the bladder is

> **TIP | SEVERE PAIN**
>
> The more children a woman has borne, the more usual it is to find pain medication on the bedside table for the treatment of after-pains and other severe pains—at least in hospitals. Many women are glad to accept the offer. But what about breastfeeding? Are the effective ingredients transferred through the mother's milk? Yes, but if the medications are taken in moderate doses, there is no negative effect on the baby. Talk to your physician and pediatrician about safe pain relief while breastfeeding.

emptied only halfway; this encourages urine retention and raises the risk of a bladder infection. So try to empty your bladder as completely as possible by using the proper sitting posture and one little trick: sit erect on the toilet and with your back straight. Spread your legs as far as possible and rock the pelvis back and forth a little. You will be amazed at how much urine is left in the supposedly empty bladder.

When Will Things Get Better?

After about ten days, the uterus can no longer be felt from the outside, for it has retracted to its original position in the pelvis.

Lochia

To put it simply, lochia is postpartum vaginal discharge, which can last for four to six weeks. It is not menstrual discharge, since lochia contains blood, mucus, and placental tissues. Basically, your body is flushing out whatever substances it has left in the uterus, since they are not needed anymore. Whether you had vaginal birth or cesarean section, you will have vaginal discharge following delivery. During pregnancy, the placenta was responsible for carrying nutrients from the mother's circulatory system to that of the child. It is the size of about two hands, and it was attached from the inside to the uterine

A cup of tea in a calm moment is a help— and it helps mothers relax.

wall. At the location where it was formerly "hooked up" there is now an open wound that bleeds as long as it takes for it to heal. Along with remains of mucous membranes this blood leaves the body and is visible as what's known as the lochia. Generally, this lasts for several weeks; the heaviest bleeding occurs in the first three to four days after giving birth, and it gradually subsides.

Color Change

In the first few days after the birth, the blood is light red, an indication that the wound is still very fresh. When you go to the bathroom, coagulated blood may flow out the vagina. When you lie down it collects in the uterus and flows in small clumps (which look like a piece of liver). Don't be alarmed. This is entirely normal. Tell your obstetrician or midwife about it. He or she may once again check the size of the uterus to see how the shrinkage is progressing—and also make sure that nothing is blocking the flow of the lochia.

When the first major flow of lochia is over, its color changes: From the initially light red, it turns pink after a few days and has some mucus mixed in with it; after about a week, it appears brownish. By the second week after delivery, your discharge will be yellowish or white. Still, it is not uncommon for the lochia to stop flowing for a couple of hours, and then resume after nursing, going to the bathroom, or walking around.

Dealing with the Lochia

Immediately after giving birth, you will bleed so much that you will have to place

TIP | NOT BREASTFEEDING?

In nursing, hormones that foster retraction are continually released. So what about mothers who don't breastfeed? The uterus also retracts with these mothers, but the process takes from one to three days longer in comparison to nursing mothers.

thick, absorbent cloths between your legs—preferably two of them that overlap a little lengthwise. That way you can be sure that you are largely "leakproof." This cloth packing is so thick that normal underclothes are too tight. So most clinics provide disposable underwear. It is important to change the cloth pads every two to three hours at first. On the one hand, the moist, warm environment interferes with the healing in the uterus; on the other, the discharge quickly begins to smell unpleasant when it comes into contact with the air. You will also want to freshen up a little down below.

When Will Things Get Better?

After three to four weeks, the discharge takes on a yellowish color. By then the quantity has reduced to the point that conventional panty liners are sufficient.

The "Baby Blues"

Usually the "valley of tears" hits the recovering mother around the third day after the birth. Then the mood seems to change on short notice from sky-high jubilant (finally the delivery is over, the pains are gone, the baby is healthy and in my arms, my partner is providing devoted service, and the congratulations of friends and family are a source of joy) to deathly sad. All it takes is one tiny trigger—maybe the tea was too hot, the baby's playsuit was too big in the feet, or the partner had to go to the office for a while—and the tears start rolling and won't stop.

So What's Wrong?

The hormone levels are changing quickly: The hormone that was responsible for maintaining the pregnancy rapidly subsides, while other hormones that take care of the milk supply shoot up in the twinkling of an eye. These tremendous swings in hormone balance also cause mood swings. Sometimes there is also a feeling of total exhaustion because the last few days have been very strenuous. Then if there are after-pains or injuries to the uterus, the smallest trifle is all it takes . . .

One other thing can influence the baby blues: the anxiety of responsibility, of being forever after responsible for this tiny being. But other thoughts are also high on the list, such as "Will I be a good mother?" "How will this affect our relationship?" "What will happen with my former job?"

Dealing with the Bawling

First of all, you must realize that it is entirely normal if you hit bottom emotionally a few days after giving birth. The important thing is to accept the fact and let the tears simply roll if you feel like it! Your feelings and hormones are taking you on a roller-coaster ride—and who can just sit there radiating joy? Your partner can be a huge help. Also talk with your healthcare provider. He or she is thoroughly familiar with the situation and can help you with some hints to cheer you up.

When Will Things Get Better?

Normally the baby blues are over in a day or two; in individual cases, they may last a few days longer. If the mood lasts for several weeks and physical problems such as headaches or circulatory problems arise, this may be a case of postpartum depression. Significant depression in the tenth through the thirtieth days should be taken seriously. In this case, you must get advice from your doctor.

Other Effects of Hormone Changes

Given the powerful hormonal changes that are going on inside your body, it would be remarkable if there weren't some additional physical side effects.

Hair Loss

"If this keeps up, pretty soon I won't have any hair left on my head!" Gynecologists are familiar enough with this concern. Fortunately they can give the all-clear signal: Hair loss after giving birth is a function of hormonal changes. The causes are the tremendous decline in estrogen after the birth and the separation of the placenta. Sometimes an iron deficiency is suspected of contributing to hair loss. This is not permanent. You may lose a lot of hair now, but it will all grow back.

A scalp massage in the morning and evening will boost new hair growth.

When Will Things Get Better?

Generally the hair loss is worst four to six months after the birth. Around the same time your hormonal balance reestablishes itself, the hair loss will slowly subside. Maybe this is the right time for a new hairdo . . .

Sweats

Some new mothers feel as though they are going through menopause: they sweat so profusely all over their body that they have to get completely undressed, especially at night. The reason is totally understandable. During pregnancy, a lot of water was stored up, and now it's leaving through all the pores of the body.

When Will Things Get Better?

The problem goes away rather quickly: The sweats generally become history two to three weeks after giving birth.

TIP | **LUSH, NEW HAIR**

Hormonal changes can also have a positive effect on hair growth. Many new mothers are happy because their hair is noticeably thicker and fuller after giving birth. Additionally, previously straight hair may become curly, and vice-versa.

Intestines and Digestion

After the delivery, the intestines finally have room to stretch out; they return to their original position. During this time, they sometimes work a bit sluggishly. Precisely when you have your first bowel movement after giving birth depends on whether or not you had an enema beforehand. If so, you may have a bowel movement on the third day; if not, it will probably be a little sooner.

Dealing with Digestion

You can play an active role in this. When you have achieved a bowel movement, sufficient liquids and proper nutrition will help get the intestines working properly again.

Fluids

Now it's more important than ever to drink enough, for you need lots of fluids to stimulate milk production. You also need to compensate for the water loss caused by repeated sweats. Both breastfeeding and sweating increase loss of water to the body, and the result is a thickening of the intestinal contents. So you should be sure to increase your daily fluid intake.

Anxiety About Going to the Toilet

Many new mothers with a perineal injury are concerned that by squeezing when they go to the toilet they may open up fresh tears. But this approach is incorrect. If the intestine is not emptied regularly, it keeps filling up. Then the contents of the lower intestine harden further, and evacu-

ating the bowels will become more painful. Speak with your or obstetrician or midwife to allay your concern.

Proper Nutrition

It is not necessarily good advice to increase at this time the intake of foods high in fiber, such as whole grain products, raw fruits and vegetables, and cabbage. On the one hand, the roughage swells up quite a bit inside the intestine and thus increases the stool quantity. On

> **TIP** | **HELP FROM THE PARTNER**
>
> It would be ideal for the partner to know what can now happen: his partner can instantly dissolve in tears in front of him without any real cause. It's important that the partner not get cornered into a position of explaining (why he had to phone the office, or why it took too long to go shopping) because that has nothing to do with it. It's the hormones that are turning everything upside down in the new mother. What can the partner do? Lovingly hug the mother and offer understanding. Admiring the wonderful baby also is effective. Conflict resolution techniques would be out of place here; attention and understanding alone are called for. This is also a good time to present a birth gift.

TIP | **GENTLE HELP**

If you are apprehensive about going to the toilet, an enema may help. That way you can empty your lower intestine gently and without side effects.

the other hand, foods that are extremely high in fiber can cause gas in you and your breastfeeding child. It's much more important to provide the body with plenty of fluids to keep the stool soft. The best choices are non-carbonated mineral water and unsweetened herbal teas, ideally in the quantity of around three quarts (liters) per day. Along with the blood you lost in giving birth, your body has also lost the important electrolytes magnesium and potassium. Both minerals help keep the intestine active and the intestinal contents moving along. So it is important for you to eat foods that are rich in potassium and magnesium. Potassium is found in such foods as potatoes, meat, legumes, tomatoes, and bananas; there is lots of magnesium in berries, nuts, whole-grain products, and meat, as well as in bananas.

Hemorrhoids

The knotty structures on the anal opening, which are referred to as "external hemorrhoids," are a type of varicose vein on the anal opening. Depending on their severity, they can itch, make sitting or walking unpleasant, and cause real pain during bowel movements. The thickened

INFO | **GRADE III TEAR**

The situation is different if you have a grade-three perineal tear—that is, if the perineum is torn as far as the sphincter. This situation requires medical care, which you must discuss with your gynecologist.

veins may rupture so that bright red blood is visible in the stool. Unfortunately, no one is immune to them. Women who never had problems with them before pregnancy are bothered with them after giving birth because they arise from impeded circulation during pregnancy and the strong pressure during birthing.

What You Can Do

It is very important that you thoroughly clean your genital area after every bowel movement. Then you should apply TUCKS® pads, which reduce swelling in the veins. Ask your midwife about this. Here too it is important to drink enough to keep the stool soft. That's the only way to avoid exerting too much pressure when you go to the bathroom. If the hemorrhoids are severely swollen after giving birth, a sitz bath will soothe the swelling. In addition, you can train your pelvis with exercises, thus killing two birds with one stone. The exercises are not only good for the pelvic floor but also strengthen the tissues and shrink the hemorrhoids. See instructions later in this chapter for more on exercise.

Wrist Trouble

It's quite possible that you will experience wrist problems sometime after giving birth. Depending on your movement

TIP | ALTERNATIVE MEDICINE

Herbal remedies such as arnica and witch hazel can also help with hemorrhoids. You should get expert advice on the precise choice and dosage; ask your after-care midwife or your gynecologist.

and posture, there may be a strong pulling or even a stinging in the wrist. It can be so severe that you don't want to grasp anything with the affected hand. Presumably the cause is strain in the tendons and ligaments. It is also conceivable that the hormonal changes contribute to a loosening of the ligaments and tendons.

Dealing with the Pain

Pay attention to how you hold your wrist, because—especially while breastfeeding—you may be using an unaccustomed hand position. In extreme cases, your doctor may prescribe a wrist splint that protects the wrist from strain. Ideally, though, you should see what new, unaccustomed movements you are making with your wrist. Then you can avoid them whenever possible.

Exercises for a New Mother

Please note that there are no specific guidelines for exercises. Any form of gentle movement can help, but women need to consult with their doctors first before beginning any physical exercise.

Here are some suggestions for an exercise program. This involves easy exercises that boost metabolism, quicken the circulation, and help prevent thrombosis or blood clots (especially important for everyone who has delivered by cesarean section). We're not looking for fitness and conditioning here; that won't be appropriate until a few weeks later when the birthing injuries are completely healed, and you have stocked up on new strength and energy. Of course, the following exercises can help your pelvic floor, which recently underwent serious strain and can use all kinds of support. Starting on page 80 you will find precise information on how the pelvic muscles function and why it is so important for them to become fit again after giving birth.

All in Due Time

Just when you feel fit enough to begin your lying-in exercise program depends on the extent of your birthing injuries. If, for example, you have a major perineal tear or an episiotomy, you should allow yourself and your body a few extra days of rest. It is important that you not put yourself under any pressure. On the other

Exercise 1: Ten reps breathing in and out.

hand, if you have weathered the delivery in good shape and feel fit, then make an effort and start the following exercises on the second day after the birth.

1 Lie on your back so that your spine is straight. Stretch your legs out straight and slightly apart and let the toes fall loosely to the sides. Place both hands on your stomach, with your left hand under your left breast.
➤ Close your eyes and breathe consciously: breathe in through the nose and out through the mouth.
➤ As you breathe in, feel the lungs and the diaphragm stretch so that your breast and stomach rise. All organs now have room and enjoy it.

2 Carefully sit on one side. Keep the legs close together and stretched out.
➤ Keep your arms stretched out behind you to provide support and begin to circle alternately left and right with the pelvis. Your legs also make small circling motions.
➤ The goal of the exercise is to make you conscious of your pelvis—and simultane-

ously stimulate circulation to the pelvic floor.

3 Lie flat on your back with your legs outstretched and your arms parallel to your body. Cross your ankles.
➤ Now it's time to build and maintain muscle tone. Relax and breathe in a few times through the nose and out through the mouth.
➤ The next time you breathe out, tense the muscles of your lower body in sequence from bottom to top: first the feet, then the calf, the thigh, and finally the bottom. Hold this tension for about ten seconds—and let your breath out.
➤ Relax and loosen the muscles once again.

4 Remain lying on your back. Bend your right leg and place your right foot on the floor. Stretch the left leg straight up in such a way that the thigh of the straightened left leg is parallel to that of the right leg held in position.
➤ Now tense the foot of the straightened leg for five to ten seconds by curling your toes.
➤ Release the tension and stretch the foot down to the toes.
➤ Repeat the exercise with the other leg.

➤ Variation: Assume the same starting position and stretch the foot of the extended leg down to the tips of the toes. Now make circles by rotating the foot from the ankle. Then relax the leg and repeat the exercise with the other leg. Do twenty repetitions per foot.

Exercise 2: Circle ten times right and ten left.

Exercise 3: Repeat ten to fifteen times.

Exercise 4: Ten repetitions per foot.

79

TIP | THE PELVIC FLOOR

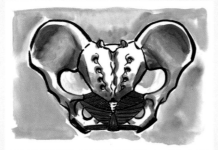

For many years the pelvic floor was scarcely worth a mention. This oversight was incorrect, especially because it has a very important function in the female body. The pelvic floor refers to a layer of muscle that covers the bony pelvis from within. So the musculature of the pelvic floor literally forms the bottom of the abdominal cavity. It also keeps the organs from falling down among the pelvic bones. Like a type of hammock, it carries the weight of the internal organs such as the bladder, the intestines, and the uterus.

The Pelvic Floor—
A Really Versatile Player

On the one hand the musculature of the pelvic floor must be very stabile and firm (with pregnant women it also supports the weight of the baby). On the other, it must also be capable of stretching and flexing. It's not a continuous harness but rather is pierced for urinary ducts, the vagina, and the anus. To empty the bladder and intestines, the musculature of the abdominal floor must be very relaxed. It is particularly elastic during birth—so soft and stretchable, in fact, that it even lets a baby pass through.

The Pelvic Floor After Giving Birth

Because of the baby's weight and various hormone changes, the pelvic floor is stretched out like a rubber band that's lost its tension after birth. If it remained in this condition, it would lead over time to a sagging of the internal organs. This would have the unpleasant consequence of uncontrollable urine loss during coughing, sneezing, or any type of physical exertion.

New Tone Through Training

It doesn't have to come to this. For nature sees to it that the elasticity returns when the muscles are trained early and regularly. That's why you should start exercises while still lying-in (see page 78) and proceed with reconditioning a few weeks later.

More Lying-in Exercises

A week after giving birth, you should perform the following two exercises in your daily program; they provide conditioning for the pelvic floor.

1 Get down on all fours so that your hands are directly on the floor beneath your shoulders.

➤ Now let your head relax and hang down. Breathe in deeply so that the air flows in toward the pelvic floor.

➤ As you breathe out, tense all muscles in the lower abdomen (urethra, anus, vagina) and hold the tension for about five seconds. Release the tension when all the air is exhaled, and relax your pelvic floor as you breathe in again.

➤ Keep up the rhythm: relax and breathe in deeply, tense the pelvic floor, and hold it as you slowly breathe out.

2 Lie flat on your back on the floor for the "elevator" exercise. Bend your legs so that they are as close to your bottom as possible.

➤ Take two or three deep breaths. As you breathe out the last time, tense the muscles of your pelvic floor and tip your pelvis in the direction of your upper body.

➤ Imagine that your pudenda are tipping toward your navel and that the navel is being pulled toward your back. Don't arch your back!

➤ Hold this position for ten seconds as you breathe in and out evenly.

Exercise 1: From the starting position . . .

. . .flex six times and relax again.

Exercise 2: Six ten-second repetitions.   **81**

Reconditioning

Starting around the sixth week after giving birth, mothers should start reconditioning exercises. In contrast to the lying-in exercise program, this involves no training for the pelvic floor. The following exercises will enable you to work on your conditioning, coordination, muscle strengthening, and general fitness.

A Little Program for Home

Try to make time for these important exercises—ideally twice a week for twenty to thirty minutes over the course of several weeks. The more frequently and intensively you do this little program, the stronger your pelvic floor will become, the greater your physical awareness, and the better your overall fitness.

Warming up . . .

It's true that, when even working out at home, nothing works well without warming up. To keep things light and fun, find some lively music, and get started.

➤ Warm-up 1: March in place; swing your arms and lift the knees as high as possible.
➤ Try to keep up the tempo for the length of a song or two. This should cause you to break into a sweat.
➤ Warm-up 2: If you are not warm enough after marching, you can do some stationary cycling on your back. An exercise consists of cycling ten reps forward and ten reps backward.

. . . and then relax!

After the stationary cycling, you should relax for a minute. Put your feet back onto the floor and let them slide out. Extend

Warm-up 1: Forward march!

Warm-up 2: Repeat the exercise ten times.

Exercise 1: Five to ten repetitions per side.

Exercise 2: Twenty repetitions.

your arms and legs and stretch while lying down. Then tense and relax your buttocks several times. This movement relaxes the muscles in your buttocks. Now you are ready to handle the following four exercises, all of which condition the muscles of your pelvic floor.

Here goes

1 Lie on your back and bend your legs. Place your arms next to your body. Breathe in and out regularly.
➤ Now build basic toning step by step: As you breathe out, tip your pelvis forward (vagina and pelvic bone toward the navel) and hold the tension in your stomach and vagina. Don't forget to keep breathing.
➤ Now put pressure onto your heels so that your upper body up to your shoulders slowly lifts off the floor. Keep breathing gently.
➤ Maintain the base tension in your pelvic floor and make the fingers of your left hand crawl parallel to your leg along the floor toward your left foot. When the fingers get as far as they can go, they

slowly wander back. Lay your upper body back down, release the tension in your pelvic floor, put your pelvis back down, and let your legs slide out. Repeat the exercise with your right hand.

2 Lie on your back and place your legs as close to your bottom as possible.
➤ Let your knees fall to the right and left like butterfly wings. In this position, tense your vaginal muscles. This works best if you imagine that you are trying to pick something up with your vagina.
➤ Relax the muscles and then tense them again.
➤ Let your legs slide out, and relax and loosen all muscles.

Exercise 3: Six repetitions per side.

Exercise 4: Two repetitions.

3 Lie on your back and bend your legs. Place your arms next to your body. Breathe in and out regularly.

➤ Now build basic tone step by step: As you breathe out, tip your pelvis forward (vagina and pelvic bone toward the navel) and hold the tension in the stomach and vagina. Keep breathing calmly.

➤ Now lift your bottom and upper body from the floor by pushing against the floor with your heels. The cheeks of your bottom should not be tense; tighten only the vaginal and lower pelvic muscles.

➤ The arms lie next to your body, and the weight is borne on the soles of the feet and shoulder blades. Make sure you have a solid position on the right side, and stretch the left leg toward the ceiling so that the thigh is parallel to the right thigh.

➤ Hold this position for a few seconds and continue breathing.

➤ Let your upper body back down, and then let your pelvis and legs slide. Shake out your legs briefly, relax them, and do the exercise with the other leg.

4 Assume a kneeling position and sit on your lower legs.

➤ Lay your stomach as flat as possible on your thighs and stretch your arms straight to the front. Even the fingers are extended. Stretch in this position.

➤ Place your arms close to your lower legs so that the fingers and arms point forward. The head is positioned as an extension of the spine.

➤ Now move one arm after the other from rear to front, as if you were stalking like a cat.

➤ Slowly press with your arms so that you first kneel and then get up on all fours.

Contraception After Birth

Breastfeeding as a Birth Control Method

There is a persistent dictum that says that women who breastfeed can't become pregnant. The truth of this saying was the subject of a major international study that included, among others, women from Germany and the United States. It investigated the issue of when breastfeeding women experienced their first period after giving birth. In addition, the participating women were advised to use no other means of contraception while they were nursing. The intent was to demonstrate how many women became pregnant during the time of full-time nursing. In Germany, out of 300 women, one became pregnant.

What This Study Tells Us

Under certain conditions, breastfeeding makes women temporarily infertile. How quickly fertility resumes depends mostly on how frequently and how regularly the woman breastfeeds. The cause for this is the milk-producing hormone prolactin. It is produced as soon as the baby sucks at the mother's breast. In other words, when the milk flows, prolactin is active in the mother's body. It suppresses other hormones (the follicle stimulating hormone FSH and the luteinizing hormone LH), which are responsible for ovulation. As long as adequate prolactin is active in the body, no new pregnancy is possible.

The LAM Method

LAM stands for lactational amenorrhoic method; it refers to avoidance of menstruation through breastfeeding. When used correctly, that is, when the LAM basics mentioned below are adhered to, during the first six months after birth it provides a 98 percent reliable protection against conception. After that, the protection decreases. In other words: of 100 mothers who nurse their babies and take the LAM basics to heart, two will become pregnant. After giving birth, if you absolutely want to avoid becoming pregnant, you should also use another means of contraception. You should also be aware that LAM does not protect against STDs. If that's a concern, you must use a condom.

INFO | LAM BASICS

The LAM method offers 98 percent protection as long as all of the following points are observed:

➤ No menstruation has resumed since giving birth.

➤ The baby is younger than six months old.

➤ The baby is nursed exclusively and gets at least six meals daily through breastfeeding.

➤ The interval between breastfeedings does not exceed six hours.

➤ The baby is given pumped breast milk if the mother is not available for every breastfeeding session.

Hormonal Contraception Methods

The pill, mini-pill, hormone spiral, contraceptive implants, and contraceptive patch all contain a synthetic sexual hormone that is similar to the body's own hormones estrogen and gestagen.

The Pill

With the pill, we must make a distinction between combination preparations and the mini-pill.

INFO | PEARL INDEX

In the early 1930s, the American doctor Raymond Pearl developed a statistical measurement that makes it possible to compare various birth control methods with one another: the Pearl Index. It specifies the number of unplanned pregnancies that occur among a hundred women using a particular contraception method. Although it may sound confusing, but it simply involves a hundred women practicing a method for one year or fifty women for two years, and so forth. The Pearl Index of a birth control method thus says something about its dependability. For example, a Pearl Index of 1 means that one of 100 women became pregnant in one year.

Combination Preparations (Estrogen and Progestin)

You take this pill for twenty-one days and then take a week off. During this pause, the hormone level declines, producing menstruation.

➤ How it works: It suppresses ovulation, so combination preparations are also referred to as ovulation inhibitors. It also blocks the formation of uterine mucous membrane and renders the mucous plug in the uterus impermeable to sperm.

➤ Dependability: With proper use, it is very dependable. Pearl Index 0.3.

➤ Advantages and disadvantages: It allows for spontaneous sex, can prevent acne, and offers protection from ovarian cancer. However, side effects from the permanent hormonal strain are possible (such as headaches and weight gain). There is no reliable protection during an upset stomach or indigestion, vomiting, and diarrhea.

➤ Price: Around $10 to $30 dollars a month (prescription required).

➤ Appropriate for: Every healthy woman. It is not appropriate for nursing mothers because the hormones may interfere with milk production. It also carries increased risk of thrombosis in women who smoke or are older than thirty-five years old.

Mini-pill (Progestin only)

The mini-pill involves a pure progestin dosage that interferes with fertilization and implantation of the egg cell.

➤ How it works: The hormone progestin keeps the mucous plug in the isthmus of the uterus tough and impermeable to sperm.

➤ Dependability: Pearl Index 1–3.

➤ Advantages and disadvantages: The mini-pill also allows spontaneous sex, and it can still be taken while breastfeeding, which is important for nursing mothers. This is a pure progestin preparation, and the hormones have no perceptible effect on the baby. It must, however, be taken daily without a break and precisely within a three-hour period. It can lead to irregular or overdue menstruation and is effective only after fourteen days.

➤ Price: Around $10 to $30 dollars per month (prescription required).

➤ Appropriate for: Women who want to use hormonal contraception while breastfeeding and for all who cannot tolerate estrogen preparations.

The Hormone IUD (Mirena)

This interuterine device (IUD) looks like a small anchor; it is placed inside the uterus.

➤ How it works: The spiral emits a certain amount of the progesterone hormone levonorgestrel in the uterus, thereby thickening the mucous plug in the isthmus of the uterus and significantly reducing the monthly buildup of the uterine mucous membrane.

➤ Dependability: Pearl Index 0.2.

➤ Advantages and disadvantages: After implantation in the uterus, the spiral remains effective for five years. In this time, the period slackens significantly. However, in the first months unexpected bleeding may occur, and 10 to 20 percent of all women may miss their periods altogether. Regular ultrasound checks with a gynecologist are necessary.

➤ Price: Around $400.

➤ Appropriate for: Nursing mothers, for the device deposits only progestin into the female body, and this has no negative consequences on the baby. It is also appropriate for women who previously have suffered from severe, painful menstruation. It should not be used by women who have a history of pelvic infections or ectopic pregnancies, or HIV/AIDS.

Three-month Shot (Depo-Provera)

This long-acting shot is a progestin preparation that is injected into the bottom or the thigh. Over the following three months, the hormone is released from the resulting "depot."

➤ How it works: It prevents ovulation in the first four to eight weeks; thereafter, a contraceptive effect is produced by the thickened mucous plug in the isthmus of the uterus and by reduced production of uterine mucous membrane.

➤ Dependability: Pearl Index 1–2.

➤ Advantages and disadvantages: Three months of contraceptive protection, no installation defects, spontaneous sex possible. It does, however, contain a large dose of hormones with possible side effects (weight gain, headaches) and is mpossible to remove. With extended use, it can take up to a year for ovulation to resume after discontinuation.

➤ Price: Around $50 for three months.

➤ Appropriate for: It is theoretically appropriate for nursing mothers, for only progestin is released. In practice, it is rarely used, for there are methods that involve less strain on the body. It is especially practical for women who are finished having a family.

Vaginal Ring (Nuva-Ring)

The vaginal ring is a thin, flexible ring a little over 2 inches (5.4 cm) in diameter.

➤ How it works: The woman inserts the ring into her vagina (like a tampon), where it remains for three weeks. It contains two hormones (estrogen and progestin), which it continually gives off during this time. It is removed after three weeks. Then there is a one-week break for menstruation.

➤ Dependability: Pearl Index 0.65 (according to manufacturer).

➤ Advantages and disadvantages: The vaginal ring doesn't need to be taken regularly; the hormones can be dispensed in lower doses. During sexual intercourse, the device may remain lodged in the vagina, but it can also be removed for up to three hours and then reinserted. There is a possible sensation of pressure inside the vagina.

➤ Price: Around $45 per ring/month.

➤ Appropriate for: Women who tolerate the pill well but who don't want to bother with daily contraception. It is not appropriate for nursing mothers because the hormones (estrogen and progestin) can be transferred to the baby through the mother's milk. It is also not appropriate for smokers.

Contraceptive Patch (Ortho Evra)

Every week a new $1\frac{3}{4} \times 1\frac{3}{4}$ inches (4.5 × 4.5 cm) skin-colored patch must be stuck onto the stomach, bottom, or upper body. Every fourth week no patch is used.

➤ How it works: It continually gives off hormones (progestin and estrogen) to the skin, preventing ovulation and altering the mucus in the isthmus of the uterus.

➤ Dependability: Pearl Index 0.9.

➤ Advantages and disadvantages: Taking hormones every day is not necessary; however, the reliability of this method may suffer in women weighing more than 200 pounds (90 kg). If the patch falls off, it must be replaced in a matter of hours.

➤ Price: around $35 for a one-month supply (prescription required).

➤ Appropriate for: Women who tolerate the pill well but don't care to be bothered with contraception every day. It is not suited to nursing mothers because the hormones (estrogen and progestin) can be transferred to the baby through the mother's milk.

Mechanical Birth Control Methods

Mechanical birth control methods are also known as barrier methods because they use a barrier to keep the sperm away from the fertile egg cell. They are used only when needed; however, they must be put into place immediately before or during foreplay, which may be perceived as an annoyance.

Condoms

A condom is a rubber, latex, or latex-free "cover" for the erect penis.

➤ How it works: The sperm are intercepted by the condom.

➤ Dependability: Pearl Index 4–9.

➤ Advantages and disadvantages: Condoms are the only effective protection against infectious diseases. Not only is there no chemical or hormonal stress, but it is small, handy, and economical. The material can tear and cause allergies. Additionally, putting one on can interrupt foreplay.

➤ Price: Around $0.50 apiece.

➤ Appropriate for: Nursing mothers because no hormones that could be transferred in the mother's milk are discharged. Women who want protection in addition to other methods or who do not see a possible pregnancy as a problem may also want to use condoms.

Diaphragm

A semicircular latex dome of fairly large diameter ($2\frac{1}{2}$ to 4 inches / 6–10 cm). The size must be fitted by a gynecologist.

➤ How it works: The diaphragm is first coated with a spermicidal or sperm-blocking gel; the woman then inserts it into the uterus. The diaphragm blocks the uterine isthmus like an inverted umbrella and keeps sperm from getting in.

➤ Dependability: Pearl Index 4–7.

➤ Advantages and disadvantages: The diaphragm is nearly free of chemical stress and provides no hormonal stress. It can be inserted up to two hours before intercourse (so it doesn't interfere with foreplay). It is effective for only one ejaculation; new gel must be applied before the next time. The diaphragm must remain inside the vagina at least six to eight hours after intercourse to make sure that all sperm have been killed.

➤ Price: Diaphragm costs around $20; the spermicidal gel, around $8 per tube.

➤ Appropriate for: It should be used by nursing mothers (no hormones are given off) and women who are disinclined to use hormonal methods. It is inappropriate in cases of vaginal prolapse.

Cervical Cap

Like the diaphragm, the cervical cap must be fitted by a gynecologist. It is shaped like a thimble and is very similar to the diaphragm in use and function. It is placed tightly over the isthmus of the uterus (the portio), but it stays more tightly in place than a diaphragm. It offers greater security when used with a spermicide.

➤ How it works: It closes off the isthmus of the uterus and keeps sperm from getting into the uterus.

➤ Dependability: Pearl Index 4.

➤ Advantages and disadvantages: Minimal chemical, no hormonal stress. Can be inserted up to two hours before intercourse. Disadvantage: It is not so easy to locate the correct size; it requires experience and skill in use.

➤ Price: Around $25, no prescription required

➤ Appropriate for: Nursing mothers, since no hormones are given off that could be transferred to the baby through the mother's milk; for all women who are disinclined to use hormonal methods.

Lea's Shield®

A silicon cap the size of an egg, it is a one-size-fits-all reusable vaginal barrier contraceptive device; it is pushed into place before the isthmus of the uterus. Air is forced out through a valve so that the device sticks tightly to the isthmus of the uterus. It can also be used with a spermicidal gel.

➤ How it works: The way for the sperm into the uterus is blocked.

➤ Dependability: Pearl Index 2.2–2.9.

➤ Advantages and disadvantages: One size fits all, so no extra fitting is required. The

89

Lea can be inserted hours before intercourse and remain in place up to forty-eight hours. With repeated sex a spermicidal gel must be used again. Disadvantage: because of its size it may be perceived as a nuisance during sex.

➤ Price: Around $70 (prescription required).

➤ Appropriate for: Nursing mothers because no hormones are given off. Women who are disinclined to use hormonal methods may find it practical. It is a good solution for weekend relationships.

The Non-Hormone IUD (Para-Gard)

Modern coils usually consist of a small, T-shaped plastic body with a stem wrapped in copper wire. But there are also purely plastic coils. At the lower end of the spiral, there is a small string for removal. Generally a gynecologist inserts the coil during menstruation, for during this time the mouth of the uterus is slightly open and more penetrable.

➤ How it works: It is presumed that the presence of this foreign body inside the uterus prevents the implantation of a fertilized egg. In addition, copper wire coils give off copper ions, which kill sperm.

➤ Dependability: Pearl Index 0.5–4.6.

➤ Advantages and disadvantages: The coil can remain inside the uterus up to ten years; checkups are required. Periods are frequently more painful and longer lasting. There is also a heightened risk of infection and tubal pregnancies.

➤ Price: Around $300 every ten years.

➤ Appropriate for: Nursing mothers because no hormones are given off. It may also be useful for women who are disinclined to use hormonal methods, who want to put off having children, or who are done with having a family. It should not be used by women who are allergic to copper, have a history of pelvic infections or ectopic pregnancies, or have HIV/AIDS.

Fertility Monitor

The monitor measures hormone levels in a woman's urine each day and calculates when she is fertile. During fertile times, a barrier method of contraception should be used.

➤ How it works: Test strips are dipped into the first morning urine each day and then inserted into the monitor. The monitor measures leutinizing hormone and estrogen levels to determine if ovulation is approaching, occurring, or past.

➤ Dependability: Pearl Index 1–6.

➤ Advantages and disadvantages: The woman becomes familiar with her cycle and learns on which days contraception is required; however, the urine must be tested every day, and it can take two or more menstrual cycles before the monitor "learns" a woman's cycles and can accurately predict ovulation. In addition, there is a high purchase price for the monitor and an ongoing expense of test strips every month.

➤ Price: $300, plus approximately $50 per month for the test strips.

➤ Appropriate for: Women who want to know on which days in the cycle birth control is required so they can use mechanical methods will want to consider this method. It is not appropriate for nursing mothers during the entire breast-feeding time, for the hormones are running wild.

Chemical Birth Control Products

Chemical birth control products include vaginal suppositories, gels, foams, vaginal tablets, sponges, and ovules.

➤ How they work: This varies depending on the preparation. They may kill sperm or render them immobile, and/or form a barrier against sperm. All means must be inserted about ten minutes before intercourse.

➤ Dependability: Pearl Index 9–25! Because chemical birth control products are relatively undependable, they should be used only in combination with a condom or a diaphragm.

➤ Advantages and disadvantages: They are flexible to use and have no long-lasting hormonal strain. They are not, however, a reliable protection against conception by themselves. Additionally, they may cause burning and itching in the vagina or on the penis and may lead to a temperature rise in the lower abdomen and are not always aroma- and taste-free.

➤ Price: $10 to $15 per package.

➤ Appropriate for: Women who occasionally use birth control or who want to boost the dependability of condoms may want to use on of these products. Be aware that many preparations are incompatible with the materials from which condoms are made. Ask your pharmacist. Many preparations are inappropriate for nursing mothers because the effective ingredient may be transferred in the mother's milk. A doctor or druggist can provide more information here.

Fertility Awareness Method

It is possible to use the physical symptoms and basal body temperature method to monitor a woman's natural fertility signs throughout the time she is breastfeeding. You will clearly see when your normal menstrual cycle and ovulation gradually resume. Basal body temperature, checked first thing each morning when you wake up, remains low prior to ovulation and then spikes. In addition, checking cervical mucus and cervical position can indicate when fertility has resumed. There are very specific instructions for using this method, so for more information on this type of birth control you should consult a book dedicated solely to this topic.

Questions and Answers

1 *Will the brownish line that runs from the pubic area to the navel remain visible after giving birth?*

Only for a few weeks. It is a sign of the hormonal changes during pregnancy. This pigmentation is most noticeable with dark-haired and brown-eyed women. The so-called linea fusca will fade no later than the time when the hormones level off, your baby is weaned, and the first menstruation occurs. Normally it is completely gone six months after giving birth.

2 *I have stretch marks around my stomach. Will they disappear?*

Unfortunately not. Stretch marks occur where the connective tissue became stretched so far by the growing stomach that it eventually tore. At first the stripes are dark pink to purple, but later they fade. After bith, they usually become much less apparent.

3 *What heals better—a uterine tear or an episiotomy?*

Most physicians say that a tear heals more quickly and with fewer complications than an episiotomy. In addition, scientific studies show that women with a perineal tear experience less discomfort while lying-in. Depending on the size of the tear, it is more difficult to suture, but it heals better. Still, there are good reasons to opt for an episiotomy in individual cases, for example,

when the baby's head is very large, in the case of a forceps or a vacuum machine birth, or when the birthing must be completed quickly for medical reasons. In any case, the duration of the active pushing phase plays an important role in the healing of the perineum. The longer it lasts, the greater the chance of damage to the perineum.

4 *How long is it before the stitches from perineal sutures can be removed?*

This normally takes between four to six days. In that time, the stitches must not be subjected to any pulling.

5 *What should I do if the lochia stop flowing after a week?*

There may a variety of reasons for this starting with a full bowel (the recovering mother may not have had a bowel movement for quite a while) which prevents the uterus from returning to its original position. The cause may also be a fold in the uterus. The important thing is to quickly determine the cause, for the lochia must in no case dry up too soon. Be sure to consult with your obstetrician.

6 *How much less does the average woman weigh once the birth is over?*

Let's look at it this way: A baby weighs an average of seven and a quarter pounds; the placenta, around twenty-one ounces;

the amniotic fluid, a little over a pound; and the increase in the uterus, around thirty-five ounces. You can subtract this total immediately after the birth. What's left behind is the weight of the water in the tissues, the increased blood volume, the increase in the breasts, plus the fat and protein stores that your body has put aside. This can add up to about an additional fourteen or fifteen pounds.

7 *Is it true that mothers become forgetful after giving birth?*

That statement is too sweeping; however, it is true that in the first few weeks after giving birth, many women complain of an inability to concentrate. That's a small wonder: They really have their hands full. It may be a phone number or part of the shopping list that evades recall, but usually this is just a temporary condition. Forgetfulness can, however, be a symptom of anemia (blood deficiency). So don't hesitate to have your blood checked during your next visit to the doctor.

8 *When I look at my figure, I find it hard to believe that I will ever be as slim as I was before getting pregnant. What are the chances that I will get my old figure back?*

Have a little patience! Think of the proverb, "Nine months coming, nine months going." This refers to the belly. As long as you eat sensibly, you will have your old figure back after a few months. While you are breast-

feeding, however, it is essential that your diet includes good-quality fat in order for your baby to fully develop. Once you have stopped nursing, you will have plenty of time to take care of your figure.

9 *I would really like to lose the weight left over from pregnancy. Which diet is the best one for the purpose?*

There isn't one! Stay away from a strict diet. Shortly after giving birth is not the time for it because you need strength and energy for the baby. If you are breastfeeding, you even need additional calories (see page 195). In addition, a diet that involves avoiding certain foods is usually not much fun. So don't subject yourself to the additional pressure in the stressful time with the new baby. For the time being, your baby and smooth family life should be your first priority. Once everything settles down, the nursing is going well, and you can sleep regularly at night, you will have enough time to get involved in a possible diet or a fitness program. For now, look for healthy, varied nutrition with lots of fruits and vegetables. Use fat sparingly and eat as little sugar (sweets and cakes) as possible. Activity will make you fit again, so take your baby for frequent walks at a brisk pace. Or start a gentle fitness program, including reducing exercises, of course. See the exercises on page 78.

From Infant
to Toddler

During the first year, development proceeds at a fast pace—your baby will never again develop as quickly as during this time. As parents, you can accompany your child and experience with amazement the giant steps by which a helpless infant is transformed into an active toddler . . .

How Your Baby Develops

Even a pregnancy that has lasted for forty weeks ends essentially as a "premature birth," for newborns are essentially "undeveloped" and totally dependent on the care of their parents. In comparison to other mammals, a newborn starts out behind in terms of learning: A creature like a calf can stand and run minutes after being born, but a human usually requires a year or longer for these steps. Still, newborns are equipped with some amazing abilities that ensure their survival. As soon as the umbilical cord is severed, the child can breathe independently, keep his body temperature largely constant, take in nutrients, and excrete undigestible remains. Babies can suck and swallow immediately after being born. If they first had to learn these skills, they surely would starve.

From Reflex to Conscious Action

An infant's reflexes are inborn, and they can recede when they are superceded by conscious actions. In other words, the more the central nervous system develops and the cerebrum takes over management duties, the more the early childhood reflexes recede into the background. The nervous system, especially the brain, is responsible for this control of human behavior. Along with the spinal cord, it constitutes the central nervous system. Its basic building blocks are the nerve cells. Every nerve cell is connected to up to 10,000 others, which leads to an unimaginably high number of connections.

The First Month

Welcome to our world, little person! Even though your baby still looks so tender and vulnerable, he has already brought many skills into this world to guarantee survival. The favorite lying position reminds the baby of the position inside the mother's womb. In this "closed" posture, all joints are bent, arms, legs, and toes drawn in, and the tiny fists are tightly clenched.

TIP | AN OVERVIEW OF THE MOST IMPORTANT REFLEXES

➤ **The Rooting Reflex:** As soon as you stroke a baby's cheeks, she turns her head in that direction and begins to suck.

➤ **The Sucking Reflex:** If you touch your baby at the corner of the mouth, she opens her mouth and begins to suck. Rooting and sucking reflexes are evident up to the third month.

➤ **The Grasping Reflex:** When you place a finger in the palm of your baby's hand, he immediately grasps it. He often bends his arms, as if he were doing a pull-up. Sometimes the grip is so tight that newborns can even hold their own weight for a couple of seconds. The reason for this reflex can be found in the distant past when babies had to cling to their mother's fur. This skill is also referred to as the Darwin Reflex. It disappears by the fifth month.

➤ **The Moro Reflex:** When a baby feels that it he falling, he spreads his arms out and then puts them onto his stomach—as if the intention were to hug himself. Dr. Moro, a pediatrician in Heidelberg, Germany, discovered this reflex in 1918; it remains clear up to the third month, but by the sixth month it is fairly faint.

➤ **The Bauer Reflex:** If the baby is lying on his stomach with bent legs and you touch his feet, he pushes off with the feet, as if he wanted to flee. This reflex can be triggered up to the third month.

➤ **The Striding Reflex:** When a baby in an erect position touches the floor with her feet, she lifts a foot, bends a knee, and takes a step forward. This reflex is detectable around the third month.

Fostering Connections

With the exception of the eye, a child's brain is the organ that is closest in mass to that of an adult. Almost all nerve cells are present upon birth. However, the weight of the brain, around 12 ounces (450 g), is about a quarter of that of an adult. After six months the weight is 50 percent; after two and a half years, 75 percent; and at five years, 90 percent of that of an adult brain. This comparison clearly shows how important it is to encourage babies' senses so they can continue forming new nerve connections. The more the senses that are stimulated, the more nerve connections result and the sooner your baby can perform conscious actions—such as reaching for something with the hands, rolling from the stomach onto the back, or lifting a spoon to the mouth.

At first, make sure that mobiles and similar objects are always about 10 inches (25 cm) from the baby's eyes. That way your baby will be able to recognize the shapes more clearly.

Your Baby's Senses

In the first days following birth your baby must get used to the new surroundings—using all her senses. She lived for weeks doubled up inside her dark cave filled with amniotic fluid, waiting for her big arrival day.

Hearing

In contrast to the sense of sight, a newborn's sense of hearing is very well developed. It's no wonder; long before birth, the baby was able to perceive all kinds of noises while inside the womb—the rushing of the blood, the heartbeat, the rumblings inside the stomach and intestines. But the baby was also able to hear noises from the outside clearly.

In the first days after the birth, the ears may still be clogged with a little amniotic fluid or vernix caseosa. But soon your child can register a broad frequency spectrum: She can hear soft sounds, such as bird songs, steps, and the ticking of a clock, very well. A particularly trusted sound is the mother's voice, which the baby can distinguish from other voices within the first twelve hours after birth.

Basically, babies prefer gentle, fairly high tones; deep and especially loud (male) voices tend to frighten them. It's good that most adults use a higher voice for baby talk, so that grandma's "Well, how's the little muffin doing?" sounds right.

Vision

Among all the senses, vision is the last one to develop. That would be expected because there was scarcely any stimulation for it because the eyes were closed inside the dark environment of the womb. After birth, your baby's eyes first had to get used to the brightness. The vision is now fairly poor for things that are far away, but your baby can see things that are 10 inches (25 cm) away. This is about the same distance between the mother and the baby when she is drinking from the breast. The baby sees everything farther away as a blur.

Visual acuity after birth is only about 4 percent of that of an adult. The newborn is best at recognizing contrasts—such as black outlines against a white background. That's why he prefers looking at lines and clearly delineated shapes rather than a confusion of colors. As for colors, babies can distinguish red from yellow, but not blue from green.

Smell and Taste

From the beginning, newborns have a keen sense of smell. As soon as the baby is placed on the mother's stomach after being born, he stores the specific scent in his memory bank. After a few days the baby also recognizes the mother's milk and can distinguish it from unfamiliar milk. That's why babies can usually find their way to the nipple even in the dark; they simply follow the scent signals from the nipple. At the age of two days, children already react

> ### TIP | MOM'S SCENT
>
> Ideally, in the first days and weeks after giving birth, you should avoid using perfumes so you don't irritate the baby's sense of smell. Nature has set things up so that your baby will learn to recognize your individual body scent. Your scent is good for your baby, and it offers his nose more pleasure than any expensive perfume ever could.

with increased thrashing motions to strong smells; they also breathe more rapidly, and their pulses increase.

The senses of scent and taste are closely connected. From the outset, your baby can distinguish among the four taste categories, sweet, sour, bitter, and salty, and she clearly prefers sweetness. Babies have more taste buds in their mouths than adults do, and they are distributed over a larger surface. The buds are located on the tongue, the palate, the throat, and the jaws, as well as the insides of the cheeks. And every baby takes special pleasure in one food source: mother's milk.

Touch

In every square inch of baby skin there are about six million cells and nerve fibers. It is no wonder that the skin is a very sensitive organ. Touching begins immediately after birth: The baby is picked up, stroked, and wrapped up tightly. Such skin contact is essential because it produces a sense of security. But loving touch such as a massage is also good for a baby because he feels accepted and loved—an important foundation for bonding. Even though babies can't grasp anything with their hands in the first few days, it is important to stroke their hands to stimulate the sense of touch.

Continual Progress

Toward the end of the first month, your baby will get better at controlling the position of her head. While lying on her back, the baby makes an effort to raise her head; while lying on the stomach, she lifts her head for a few seconds. If the baby gets into a sitting position (but this should mostly be avoided at this age), she can hold her head up for a moment. If you hold some object in the baby's field of view, she can focus her eyes on it; when you move it back and forth, the baby can follow it with her gaze. The baby clearly reacts to light and sound: She wrinkles her forehead, blinks, thrashes, and starts to cry loudly when things get to be too much.

Medical Checkups

As early as during the pregnancy everything is documented—you medical records are carefully updated at every visit. After the delivery, the child begins accumulating a medical track record. By the age of five, your child will accumulate a number of regular checkups.

The First Checkup
Almost immediately upon arrival in this world, a newborn undergoes the first in a series of checkups. The Apgar test (see page 36) is used to determine the baby's overall condition. It provides information about the baby's breathing, pulse, and appearance. Recording weight and height plus the results of a physical evaluation are part of the program: The doctor checks the heart, lungs, and pulse and makes sure the hands and fingers have the right number of digits, the genitals are positioned normally, and there are no holes in the palate. In addition, the baby receives a dose of vitamin K and antibiotic eye ointment at this time.

The Second Checkup
Weight and height are again part of the program at this checkup usually around two weeks. Has the baby regained his birth weight or put on weight? Is development proceeding normally? Are all metabolic functions stable? Is the baby breathing regularly? Is the heart capacity normal? How are the reflexes and drinking behavior? Is there any possible jaundice?

There is also a newborn state screen, which is usually performed before the baby leaves the hospital. If it was not done at that time, it will be done at this checkup. For this purpose the doctor takes a couple drops of blood from the baby's heel or a vein and drips them onto a special filter paper. Multiple tests for possible metabolic diseases and some genetic diseases are performed in a lab. Several disorders, such as phenylketonuria (PKU), if caught early can be treated successfully. This is also the time to discuss any questions or concerns you may have about your baby's behavior or development.

Personal Experience Report

Carol (42), mother of John (14) and Millie (6 weeks)

Two children fourteen years apart—were things any different with the second birth?

My first child, John, was born two years after I got married. The pregnancy was carefully planned to accommodate our living and financial situation at the time. I was also in my late twenties when I gave birth to John, so I felt that I adjusted to the labor, my new baby, and the dynamic changes in our life without too much emotional or physical stress. I had several miscarriages in my subsequent pregnancies, so after a few years, my husband and I came to accept the fact that John would be our only child. To our surprise, soon after my forty-first birthday, I learned that I was pregnant. Feelings of shock were soon replaced by excitement and fear. We always wanted a sibling for John, but my history of previous miscarriages as well as my advanced age made me more nervous about this pregnancy than my first one. Every time we went in for a checkup I was paralyzed with fear in case the doctor found something wrong with the baby. It was like I was starting all over again as a new parent. We read

books and medical journals on babies born to middle-aged mothers. We did research on the latest baby products, which had made many strides and advances in the past fourteen years. But there were many unanswered questions: Will my body be able to handle another labor and raising a baby? How smooth would the transition from three persons to four persons be?

Luckily, my family and friends were supportive throughout the whole pregnancy. John was excited about the idea of a younger sister. My doctor and the medical staff were helpful in addressing my questions and concerns.

Playful Encouragement for Baby

Touch Makes Babies Happy

One of the highlights in a baby's life is a gentle massage. This doesn't always have to be the full routine: even if you now and again stroke the palm of your baby's hand, tickle the soles of her feet, or massage her tummy or back, it will have a positive effect on further development. You can also count the toes from time to time: when your baby is undressed on the changing table, stroke or tickle every toe and greet it. Then you needn't be surprised if the little feet are stretched up to you in expectation . . .

It's just as much fun to count the fingers and toes using the old counting rhymes: This little piggy went to market; this little piggy stayed home; this little piggy had roast beef; this little piggy had none; this little piggy went wee-wee-wee all the way home!

A Mobile in View

If you want to stimulate your baby's vision, the best choice at this point is geometric shapes in black, white, or red that stand out clearly on a white background. Babies are also very interested in faces. Babies also like to focus on everything that moves. Once they discover a mobile over the bed or the changing table, they will continue to hold it in their gaze. By occasionally replacing the mobile with a different one, you playfully encourage the development of the child's sense of sight. Move the mobile and similar items back and forth slowly and calmly in front of the child's eyes so that he doesn't become frightened. The optimum distance between the child's eye and the mobile is around 10 inches (25 cm).

"Sleep, Baby, Sleep"

What's more beautiful than lying in Mom's or Dad's arms and being rocked to sleep? Even big children dream of this. Small wonder, then, that this type of gentle rocking back and forth usually provides calm and relaxation. Your child benefits from this even more if you simultaneously sing a song or hum a melody. It's not important to sing a new song every day. On the contrary, if you keep singing the same song to your child, he will soon grow accustomed to the melody and your voice. This situation can turn into a ritual in which your child already know which notes are coming next.

Listen, Something Is Rustling!

You can stimulate your baby's sense of hearing by bringing different sounds to the child. Gently shake a rattle near the

TIP | CUDDLE CLOTH

If your baby wants to be with you all the time and acts uncomfortable when you lay her down, offer her a cuddle cloth or a cloth diaper that you have kept on your skin for a night or two. The cloth will smell like Mom and may calm the baby.

ear or behind her head so that she has to turn around to see the rattle. You can also try gentle rustling with a paper bag or ringing a little bell. There is one sound your baby likes to hear best of all: the voice of her mother, and in all variations. Talk to your baby at various pitches, read the baby a story aloud, or sing a nice song.

Your baby also enjoys a colorful but simple mobile, or a mobile with chimes, hanging over the changing table. Your baby will usually become acquainted with this place very quickly, for this is where she can always get caresses and loving words from her parents; thus, it's a place where all attention is focused on the baby. Soon the ringing of the mobile also becomes familiar and is like music in the baby's ears. The same is true of a music box: When you open up a music box and put it into the baby's crib, she will listen to the melody with interest. And soon the baby will understand that sleep comes next whenever she hears the familiar melody. This playing of the music box can become part of the bedtime ritual and an

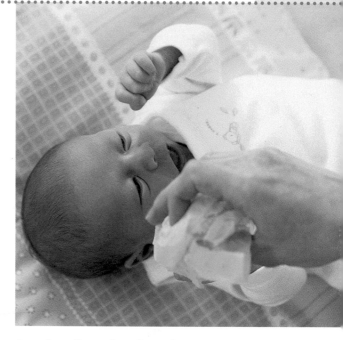

A gentle rattling, a piece of wrapping paper—the choices for stimulating the baby's sense of hearing are fairly simple.

important point in the events of the day. See page 128 for more information on how rituals help your baby to get oriented to the daily routine.

TIP | CONTINUITY

Studies have shown that babies carefully observe faces around them. They register various characteristics, such as the shape of the head, the hairstyle, or the facial contours. So if you get a new hairstyle two to three months after giving birth, your child may not recognize you at first glance.

Questions and Answers

1 *Which sleeping position is right for my baby?*

Today experts are unanimous in saying that lying on the back is the best and safest sleeping position for your baby. When your baby is awake and you are supervising him, you should still change his position from time to time; for example, while lying on his stomach, the baby can practice lifting his head and upper body and develop his back and neck muscles (see also page 110).

2 *Do I need to disinfect my hands when I want to pick up my baby?*

No, even though nurses in the hospital recommend that you disinfect your hands, this applies mainly to the time that you are in the hospital. There can be a lot of bacteria and germs on door handles, shelves, and beds, or in the air. In addition, there are always lots of unfamiliar people in a small space, giving pathogens a good chance to spread. Once you are back home, this strict order to disinfectant no longer applies. Of course, your hands should be clean when you pick up your baby. But all you need to do is wash them with soap, especially after going to the bathroom or touching a pet. Advise visitors to wash their hands before coming into contact with the baby, knowing full well how difficult that may be for a grandma who wants nothing more than to embrace her grandchild after a long trip. But these two minutes of hygiene for the benefit of the child must simply be observed.

3 *I have heard that babies shouldn't be brought outdoors in the first two weeks after being born. Is that correct?*

As long as the outside temperature is comfortable for you, there's no reason to keep the baby indoors. Fresh air and light, especially, are good for the baby. The important thing is for you to dress your baby appropriately for the weather. When summer babies, who have to deal with outside temperatures up to the high eighties, are in the stroller they must be parked only in the shade. Babies easily become overheated, and heat can build up dangerously in a baby stroller or a car. In warm temperatures, babies are adequately dressed if they are wearing a body suit over a diaper, they do not need to wear a cap. If your baby sleeps outdoors in a baby carriage, you can cover the child with a light cloth. If you live in an area with a lot of mosquitoes, don't forget to pack a mosquito net; you can get this in a drugstore, baby shop, or outdoor shop. You can also get light cotton cloths with a built-in UV protection that makes good sense for really hot, sunny summer days. For cold winter days, keep the stroller inside your home—not in your garage—to keep it from getting cold. When you do decide to go for a stroll outdoors, you should put a thicker jacket over the playsuit, and winterproof the baby with mittens, cap, and scarf. Make sure your baby is protected from the wind in the stroller by keeping the hood up and attaching the windscreen.

4 How should I take care of what's left of the umbilical cord if urine or even a little stool sticks to it?

This situation may arrive in the first two weeks of the baby's life. First of all, don't panic. Urine is sterile and will cause no infections; neither will it harm the healing navel. The stool, however, does contain intestinal germs, but generally they don't cause illness. Thus, all you have to do is to carefully but thoroughly clean the navel with a washcloth previously dampened with lukewarm water. Then pat the area dry. Try to avoid wrapping the remains of the umbilical cord in the diaper. Inside the diaper the environment is always warm and damp, and this interferes with the healing of the navel.

The Second Month

Right now your baby is working every day to get more control over his body. When he lies on his stomach, he can lift his head about forty-five degrees for a while—many children manage to hold it for up to ten seconds! This performance is even more remarkable when you consider that with little babies the head amounts to nearly a third of their overall weight.

How Your Baby Develops

When your baby is in a sitting position, his back is no longer so rounded. This shows that the back muscles are getting stronger. In the sitting position the baby can likewise hold his head up for a few seconds before it suddenly falls forward limply and out of control. If the baby is lying on his back, he generally turns his face to one side, especially while sleeping. When the baby is awake, he can thrash strongly with his legs and move his arms. And gradually the fists loosen up and the little hands open. Perhaps you have already noticed that babies cry without tears in the first four to six weeks. This is because the nerve paths that are responsible for the formation of tears are not yet working. But now the time for flowing tears begins. With a little luck you may also get your first gift of a smile.

Skin to Skin

Physical contact is important even for very tiny babies. They love nothing more than lying naked on naked skin. See for yourself: In a room at a comfortable temperature, lay your baby on your naked stomach and watch his excitement when you fondle him on the neck or stroke his back. Of course this will work only when your baby is neither hungry nor tired.

Observant, Alert, and Very Talkative

Now your baby can focus her eyes on an object and follow it when it moves back and forth or up and down in her field of view. The ears are just as alert: the baby hears a sound and looks for the source with her eyes. The baby can do more than listen: She can also produce sounds on her own. In addition to the accustomed crying, she now babbles. Many babies manage to coo the vowels up and down the scale (like, "oooo," "ah," and "ee"). Consonants will come later. The baby babbles on without periods and commas, with particular enjoyment after waking up or before going to sleep. This is not only pleasant to listen to—especially when the baby occasionally shrieks with delight—but it also has an important side benefit: your baby is training her vocal cords and developing the ability to listen and speak.

Singing Makes Babies Happy

In some cultures, music and singing enjoy a higher esteem than in the West, so mothers commonly sing or hum to the babies as they carry them in front of them or on their back. Many young mothers in our latitudes, on the other hand, don't like to sing. They prefer merely to play a music box or rely on recorded music. These melodies are usually pleasant to listen to,

TIP | EARLY PRACTICE

Parents who sing communicate good mood and happiness, which quickly infect their child. It won't take long at all for your baby to "compose" her own songs. Try it with some classic children's songs such as *Row, row, row your boat gently down the stream,/Merrily, merrily, merrily, merrily, life is but a dream.* The sooner you begin singing aloud, the sooner your child will become familiar with the melody and enthusiastically clap and "sing" along. It's twice as much fun when you carry out the appropriate movements, which your child soon will imitate.

but your baby would much rather hear the voice it likes better than all others: yours! So don't hesitate to pull some old children's songs out of the memory bank (or a collection of songs) and sing them aloud! It won't matter a bit to your baby if the pitch is right, or the song sounds a little distorted—the baby is most interested in hearing your voice! And don't worry if you miss notes, it will have no effect on the baby's future appreciation for music. Also, grandmas usually are very happy when people ask them about old songs, traditional lyrics, and singing games!

TIP | IMMUNIZATION

A great place to look up the current immunization schedule online is the American Academy of Pediatrics website (http://www.cispimmunize.org/). The schedule is updated annually because new combinations of vaccines are being developed and released every year. It's important for you to keep a record of your baby's immunization in case your family moves and your baby will have to be seen by a new pediatrician. You are required to show your child's immunization records before enrolling your child into school.

The First Smile

Most parents remember this moment forever. Sometime around the sixth week, they talk to their baby and then they see it: First, the corners of the mouth twitch, and then they move upward until suddenly a big, broad smile radiates toward the parents. What a glorious sight! It's also an important moment, for this first smile shows you that from now on your baby can make conscious contact.

We Know Each Other!

Your baby is able to distinguish people she loves and knows from strangers. For the infant already recognizes recurring patterns: She identifies her parents by their faces, which she sees every day. She feels the hands that stroke her every day, she recognizes the voices that regularly speak to her, and she feels the consistent grip with which she is held. She has also stored up the scent of her parents in her memory. Scientists even maintain that nursing mothers give off a specific scent. During the nursing time, substances are emitted that also were present in the amniotic fluid and that the baby recognizes full well.

The Third Checkup

Recording weight and height are also part of the third checkup, which takes place at two months of age. It also includes a check of mental and motor development: Can the baby follow moving objects attentively with her eyes? Can she focus on a point in front of her eyes? When lying on her stomach, can she turn her head from one side to the other? This is also the first checkup where immunizations will be given.

How large is the baby's field of vision? Does the baby lift her head and hold it up when in a sitting position? Does she drink regularly and enough? Can she thrash strongly with both legs?

And there it is—the first smile. At the beginning of this skill in smiling, the charming gift is reserved for the people the baby knows best and trusts.

The child's heart and circulatory system are given particular attention in this third checkup. Is there any irregular noise detectable in the heart? Does the pulse in the arms and the groin feel the same on both sides? Are there any skin changes (such as baby acne) that have recently cropped up (see page 55)? The pediatrician will pay special attention to the hip exam. The pediatrician checks the baby's motor and neurological development with various reflex tests. Don't be alarmed if the doctor suddenly grasps your child by an arm and a leg and lifts her up. This helps reveal normal movement patterns. This and other simple tests make it possible to evaluate development in a few steps.

Playful Encouragement for Baby

I Can Do Everything You Can Do

Nearly all babies like to imitate facial expressions. Hold your baby in front of you on your lap so that he can look at you. Talk with your child. If you also smile, raise your eyebrows, or stick out your tongue, the baby will try to imitate you. Conversely, your baby will like it when you imitate his sounds, for he sees that he can communicate with you. The echo-game is also great fun; you each repeat the sounds that the other one makes. For the baby, this is like being in front of a mirror, and it helps the baby know himself better.

Heads Up, Little One

During the first weeks of life, your baby's head makes up around a quarter of his total weight. Small wonder that babies at first have to train strenuously to lift their heads. When your baby is awake, put him on his stomach frequently; that way he will practice lifting his head for a few seconds. He is developing his muscles and at the same time he has a chance to discover the world from a different vantage point. In addition, lying on the stomach encourages the child's motor skills: This is the only position in which the baby learns to lift and turn his head, and sometime in the following weeks, he will be motivated to move forward. However, not every baby likes to lie on his stomach. If your baby is one of these children, you should give him a little stimulation: Lie on your stomach facing the child. Encourage the baby with a gentle, friendly voice. Make faces, sing a song, or draw the baby's attention by showing him a toy. You can also lie on your back and place your baby face down on your stomach. That way he can look you right in the face. This type of play makes it possible to for your baby to forget for a moment how difficult it is to hold up his head. This also helps to keep baby's head rounded: Babies who sleep on backs and are in strollers or car seats all of the time will get flattened occipital bones.

A Little Training for the Nose

Of all human senses, the sense of smell is the first to mature. When the sense of smell is appropriately trained, over a thousand receptors in the nose can recognize and distinguish countless substances in the tiniest details. So don't hesitate to introduce fine aromas to your baby by letting him sniff a bundle of lavender or freshly plucked rose petals. At this age, baby will enjoy the smell of freshly mowed grass in the summer and the scent of spices for baking at Christmas time.

Everything in Sight

Babies like to be carried a lot in the first year of life, because when they are being held they feel secure and can scout out their surroundings. In addition, carrying your child also encourages his mental development. This doesn't refer to just a quick pick-me-up for something like opening the door. There are good carrying games that stimulate your baby's senses. For example, you can lay your child on your shoulder so he can support himself with his arms on your shoulders. He has

Show your baby how beautiful the world is by returning all the love and tenderness that she gives you.

a great view from this position and learns to keep his head steady. You can also carry your baby in front of your stomach so that he sits on your forearm and leans against your stomach with his back. Your child feels held securely and learns to keep his head in balance.

Look, There's Something Hopping!

A simple, plain mobile over the crib or the changing table is always good as long as your baby is not overexcited.

Caresses for Intelligence and Happiness

Warm, soft baby skin invites stroking and kissing. Accept the invitation and fondle your baby as frequently as possible. On the changing table, your baby will enjoy not only a big kiss on the tummy, but also a walk with the fingers from head to toe. Every touch is balm for the baby's soul. Massage the soles of the feet, run a dry washcloth over the back, tickle the baby's neck, gently stroke her head, and carefully brush her hair. All of this stimulates circulation and stimulates the baby's metabolism.

Questions and Answers

1 *How much weight does a baby normally gain, and how much does he grow?*

On an average, newborns are about 20½ inches (52 cm) long and weigh about 7½ pounds (3400 g); boys are generally slightly larger and heavier than girls. During the first several days of life, your baby at first loses weight, for he loses extra water that has accumulated in his tissues during gestation. In addition, the baby is learning how to nipple feed and may not be drinking very much. By two weeks of age, the newborn should regain his birth weight and continue to gain weight from that point on. In general, a newborn will gain 7 ounces (or, approximately 200 g) a week up to the end of the third month. Between the first and third months of life, a baby grows an average of about an inch (2.54 cm) per month. Remember, however, that every child grows differently! At the end of the first year, children are an average of about 13 pounds (approximately 6 kg) heavier and 10 inches (25.4 cm) longer than at birth, depending on birth weight.

2 *Is it true that after birth a baby's bones are relatively soft?*

Yes, the long bones (in the thigh and upper arm) have mature bone mid-shaft but only cartilage at the ends. That's good because that way nature keeps young bones from breaking easily (such as during birth). This is also why the plates of the skull are not yet totally fused, so they can slide over one another during the passage through the birth canal. The bones harden during infancy and childhood and become mature bone only during puberty.

3 *On my baby's head there is a depression and it feels soft. What is this?*

This is a fontanel. The word is French, and can be translated as a "small fountain." A baby's head has two fontanels: a large square one located between the forehead and the parietal bone, and a small, triangular one on the back of the head about a hand's breadth above the neck. The bones of the skull have not yet grown together at these two places. This is also the case at the skull sutures; they can be felt as slight depressions. Many parents are concerned that the child's brain is not yet protected by the bones of the skull in these places, but they don't need to worry. A tough membrane (the dura mater) protects the brain at the fontanels. They will gradually close up: The small fontanel usually ossifies within three months, and the large one generally by the first birthday. The fontanels provide important information about a baby's brain growth.

4 *Our baby has been diagnosed with an umbilical hernia. What does this mean?*

An umbilical hernia is a bulging of the peritoneum in the vicinity of the navel. With newborns, there is a natural opening in the stomach wall for the umbilical cord; this generally closes in the first year of life. But until that time this is a weak point in the abdominal wall, which can intrude into the peritoneum. From the outside, this bulging is visible as a small (nut-size) or fairly large (tangerine-size) bump; in serious cases it can be even larger. From the inside, the intestine fills the bulge. When the abdominal wall is tensed or pressed, and especially when the baby cries, the breach in the area of the navel protrudes. Usually an umbilical hernia is not painful, and it closes up by itself in the first three years. If you notice the hernia becoming hard or dusky, call your pediatrician immediately because the intestines may have become trapped in the outpouching and an emergency surgery is indicated. Some cultures use belly wraps or place a coin on the umbilicus to try to reduce it; however, this practice is not recommended because it makes it difficult for parents to notice if the bowel has indeed become trapped in the hernia.

5 *Our baby is always restless toward evening, starts to cry, and wants to suckle at my breast without really drinking. What's going on?*

Many babies have an established time for their "crying hour," usually between 6:00 P.M. and 9:00 P.M. Your baby will calm down most quickly if you remain calm. Take the baby in your arms and use physical contact to show that you are there. Often a tummy massage helps babies to calm down. This racket usually vanishes when your baby reaches the age of three months. For more tips on how to deal with this problem, refer to the section on colicky babies (page 59).

The Third Month

In the course of the third month, the neck muscles become so powerful that lying on the stomach is no longer so uncomfortable. Generally, the baby can hold herself up on her forearms and hold her head up for a few seconds. This is good because the world looks totally different from this position. If the baby doesn't want to do this any more, she will quickly make that known by fussing loudly.

How Your Baby Develops

At first the hands were clenched in fists, but they keep loosening up, and after lots of practice, some babies can run their hands over their stomachs at the age of three months. They take pleasure in turning their hands, using one hand to hold the thumb of the other, and putting them into their mouth. The baby discovers how her fingers feel and understands that "these fingers belong to me."

Play with Me!

If your baby has had this *aha* experience, it's time for finger games. These develop not only the agility of the baby's hands but also her ability to speak. So it's no wonder that your child likes to join in with you to combine the vowels *a*, *e*, *i*, *o*, and *u*. With some practice, your child will begin to make guttural sounds!

On the Back and in Good Shape

Now your baby is very active at times while lying on her back: She flails powerfully with her arms and thrashes with her legs—and has fun doing it. Gradually your baby will decide in which position she wants to lie. When she's lying on her stomach, she may roll over onto her back—even if it's by accident. Henceforth the baby will be so mobile that you have to be really careful on the changing table. From now on, don't let your baby out of your sight while you are changing a diaper.

Hello, World, Here I Am!

The balance organ, more precisely the semicircular canal filled with lymphatic fluid inside the inner ear, plays an important role in stimulating the sense of sight. It allows the baby to correctly understand the information he takes in through his eyes. So if you let a ball bounce in front of your child's eyes, the balance organ inside the inner ear informs the brain that it's the ball that is bouncing, and not the baby's head or entire body.

Now the baby continually tries to interact with his surroundings. Many mothers do not understand why their child stubbornly focuses on other people. As soon as the baby recognizes his mother, father, or another person he has grown to like, he may project joy from ear to ear and wave about in wild joy with arms and legs. That's how your baby shows what he wants: He no longer wants to be alone. He may begin to cry when he's bored. But once you pick him up, his world is back in order. Your baby can also communicate without words, provided that you understand the signals. And the baby uses his voice more consciously; he cries loudly when he's angry or hungry, and cries pitifully if something hurts. When he feels good, he laughs joyously, and he whines when something's not right.

115

Playful Encouragement for Baby

A Room with a View

Train your baby's vision and at the same time show the baby where she lives. Simply pick up your baby and go for a little tour of the house. Explain what's in the picture on the wall, water the flowers together, or stand in front of the mirror with the baby. And there is a lot to see from the baby stroller: The swaying of the trees or the dance of the leaves in the wind.

The Itsy Bitsy Spider

This song and the accompanying finger movements are right at the top of the hit parade for all babies and playgroups. Baby will get to see your fingers in action when you make them move through the air as you sing the song. Babies enjoy the lively movements and the melody—and soon can take part. Here are the lyrics:

The itsy bitsy spider
Crawled up the water spout (fingers crawl
   up baby's arm)
Down came the rain (wiggle fingers down
   from head to waist)
And washed the spider out (throw arms to
   sides)
Out came the sun and dried up all the rain
   (raise hands above head, make wide
   circle for sun)
And the itsy bitsy spider
Crawled up the spout again. ("climb" up
   the arm again).

Handball and Soccer

Tie a beach ball or a balloon to a string and let it dangle over your child. At first the baby will merely follow it with her eyes, but soon she will try to grab it or kick it with her feet. When your baby manages to grab the ball, she will try to put it into her mouth, which is very typical for children at this age.

Cute finger puppets stimulate baby's vision.

Shaking down Plums— a Classic Finger Game

Use your right hand to explain to your child each finger of your left hand or your child's hand. Grasp each finger in sequence and say: *This is the thumb, this one shakes down the plums* (index), *this one picks them up* (middle finger), *this one carries them home* (ring finger), *and the littlest one eats them all up* (little finger).

Swing Game

Babies love to swing. As you swing back and forth to varying degrees they like to sit facing you on your lap. It's also lots of fun for babies to be rocked back and forth in a baby swing. While baby is in the swing, you can engage him by playing games such as "peek-a-boo." Just remember, a baby in a swing should always be supervised.

Back Training

Your baby still finds it exciting to look at the world while lying on her stomach— from the "bird's-eye view." Of course, the little bird can't sit up high, but that doesn't

Beach ball or balloon—balls are favorites among discoverers both large and small.

matter much to the little ones. You can help your child to raise her head a little higher by sliding your forearm under her chest as she lies on her stomach. The baby is more comfortable lying in this position. You can also roll up a blanket or a towel tightly and place the roll under the baby's chest.

117

Questions and Answers

1 *My baby is already four months old and still keeps his fists tightly clenched. Is that bad?*

Basically a baby should be able to open his hands and bring them close to his mouth and face. If the baby keeps his hands clenched, gentle pressure on the surface of the hand may help them to open. The second question is, how is the baby's muscle tone at the neck (that is, is there improving head control)? Third, how is his feeding progressing? If the fisting is intermittent, and is not present all the time, then your child is developing more motor control and simply needs a little more time. If you are worried about the baby's progress in head control, feeding, and using his hands, then the doctor will have you bring your baby back in at about four weeks. If the baby has stayed persistently fisted, your pediatrician will refer you to a neurologist who can determine the cause of the abnormal tone in your baby's hands. After several evaluations, both the pediatrician and neurologist can refer you to a physical therapist for additional management of your child's fisting.

2 *My baby has a head full of cradle cap. What can I do about it?*

With cradle cap (a type of seborrheic dermatitis) the scalp is afflicted with scales that look like dried, crusted milk. This normally is harmless and is the result of the immature sebum production in the scalp. Cradle cap, which is dry and scaly, is thus inconsequential from a health standpoint and is mostly a cosmetic problem that many parents still try to improve. This condition can become so severe that the skin of the entire head becomes scaly. This is not only noticeable but also in many cases unsightly. Still, you should always exercise care in removing cradle cap because it adheres tightly to the scalp. Try the following: Carefully rub your baby's head with a little baby oil and let it work overnight. The following morning wash the baby's head with a mild baby shampoo. Some of the cradle cap will come off even without significant rubbing. Clinging, stubborn scales may be removed with a soft brush. Caution is still called for if the cradle cap becomes wet and gives off a yellowish secretion. This could be the initial stage of an atopic eczema (see page 56) or infection, which should be treated by a pediatrician.

3 *My baby always turns her head to the same side. What can I do about this?*

Some babies may have strong preference for one side over the other. This should be checked by your pediatrician if the condition persists, for this could mean that your child has shortened neck muscles on one side. This is called torticollis. Your pediatrician might also suggest other reasons for your baby's preference to turn to one side. Once these conditions are ruled out, try to speak to your baby only from the unused side and try to get the baby's attention. Speak to the child or sing a song, show the baby a toy or something else just as exciting. Surely your baby will become curious and turn her head to look at you. Do this exercise several times a day, and soon there will be no more favored side. But be alert: If your baby absolutely doesn't want to change from her favored side, talk to your pediatrician. A precise examination can make sure that there are no serious neurological conditions causing this problem.

4 *Does my baby need a light at night in order to sleep?*

The short answer is no. Babies do not automatically sleep better when there is an artificial light in the room. On the contrary, the source of light may at first keep them awake. The relaxing hormone melatonin is produced in the pineal body in the brain, but only in sufficient darkness. If the windows are not blocked off, the moon and stars provide enough light in the room. The familiar things that a baby likes to feel in his bed don't have to be visible to the eye. Experts continually note that the parents' desire to use a nightlight goes back to their own childhood. Because they were afraid of the dark as children, they transfer the desire for a light to the baby. But if the child's room is pitch black and you can't see your hand in front of your face, a small nightlight in the wall socket will provide a little spatial orientation. Or leave the door open a crack to let in a little light. This light is mainly for your benefit rather than the baby's.

How Your Baby Develops

At this point, your baby's favorite toy is his own hands. Lots of babies now hold their hands over their face, put their little fingers into their mouth, and fold their hands on their stomach. This is the time of grasping, and the coordination between mouth and hands becomes more precise.

Everything Has to Do with the Mouth!

Babies examine everything they take in their hands—preferably with the help of their mouths. It doesn't matter if this is their own finger or Mom's thumb, a tissue, building blocks, or a teething ring—everything receives an initial investigation in the mouth. This is good, because it allows your baby to become familiar with the surroundings: What does this thing taste like? What does it feel like? Is it hard or soft, warm or cold? Will it try to run away? But they don't just examine objects closely. Everything that doesn't move away is now worthy of investigation—even if it's Mom's or Dad's nose. Everything that won't fit into the mouth is examined more closely by licking. Many babies are now so curious that during the "long" waiting time at nursing they will suck Mom's cheek, earlobe, or chin. The result is usually a little smooch mark.

Training for the Senses . . .

Now the fingers are used more consciously in playing—and are a welcome substitute for the pacifier. On the one hand, most babies already have tried sucking their

The Fourth Month

Now the baby's own hands are a major attraction: They are so warm and soft, so mobile—and always ready to grasp things! Your baby is increasingly aware that the hands belong to him. Still, there is more and more fun in using the voice for trilling at the wildest pitches. When Mom and Dad are happy about the display, that's a good incentive . . .

thumb inside the mother's womb, so they are already intimately acquainted with their fingers. On the other hand, the fingers are always available and have a pleasant temperature. Many parents are not enthusiastic about the baby's finger sucking, for they believe it is unhygienic. But putting things into the mouth and sucking are important experiences.

One prerequisite for a good sense of smell is a nose that works properly—so it's also good for the baby to develop his sense of smell. So with every gulp of milk and every spoonful of baby food on the tongue, scent molecules enter the baby's nose and provide corresponding feedback to the brain: "This tastes good" or "This doesn't taste good." It is scientifically known that the nerve endings in the mouth provide three times better information than the touch sensors on the hands.

. . . and Speech

Now your baby practices a lot with his mouth: He babbles and croaks, making new sounds with his tongue. The baby now enjoys shouting and forms unique breathy sounds by pressing the lips together and forcing the tongue through: this produces consonants such as *m*, *b*, and *w*.

Increasing Mobility

When you place your baby on his stomach, he can now support himself well on his forearms. Many babies now show an astonishing ambition when they discover something interesting in their field of view: They try everything possible to get closer to what they have seen. This spans

TIP	GETTING ADVICE

You should consult your pediatrician if your baby exhibits one or more of the following characteristics at the end of the fourth month:
- ➤ Your baby remains in one position for a long time.
- ➤ Postures and movements are largely one-sided.
- ➤ While supported in a sitting position, the baby cannot hold his head up for more than a minute.

the range from simple swimming motions to wild thrashing with arms and legs. Still, your baby prefers to lie on his back because that requires less effort. When the baby is helped into a sitting position, he holds his head up very well and can turn it to all sides. The back also straightens more and more. When you hold the baby horizontally over your head, he stretches out his arms and legs and lifts his head.

Checkup Number 4

This checkup usually occurs at four months of age when weight and height are recorded again. But at this point the main concerns are your child's mental and motor development: What is his muscle tone like? How well can the child hold up and turn his head? Do his eyes follow an object? Does the baby react to sounds? Can he bring his hands together in front of his face? The second set of immunizations will be due at this visit.

Playful Encouragement for Baby

A Gentle Baby Massage

Massaging you child can give her a sense of security, relaxation, and love. Scientific studies have shown that healthy touching encourages additional release of growth hormones. In addition, the heart and circulatory system, including circulation to the skin and muscles, are stimulated. The entire digestive tract is also stimulated, and that is particularly good for babies who experience gas. Massaging can also lead to a particularly close relationship with the baby, and that has a very positive effect on the healthy development of bonding. Most importantly, you don't need any special training to give your baby a massage, for the main thing is tender stroking and loving touch. The few moves that make up a gentle baby massage are easy to learn. You can either buy a guide or attend a nearby baby massage course. There you will get instruction in a warm room (around 77°F/25°C) on how to use a little oil and your hands to treat your baby to a gentle massage.

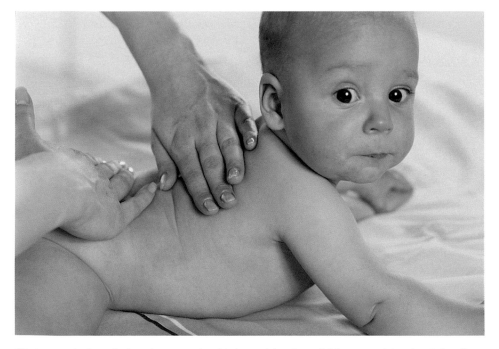

"Being touched, stroked, and massaged—this is nutrition for a child. . . . Nutrition that is love."
—*Frédéric Leyboyer*

Mom, the Wonderful Voice

Stimulate your baby's sense of hearing by showing her how many sounds and pitches there are. It's up to you whether you toot through a hollow cardboard tube for paper towels, talk through a funnel, or simply whistle a melody. But these three example show this doesn't require a lot of effort. Babies find it amusing when people change their voice while speaking to them—speak loud and forcefully, and then softly in whispers, and then maybe shrilly. Show the baby what wonders your voice holds. You probably will get an amazed look from your offspring, who is appropriately surprised at her mother . . .

What's That?

Show your baby several age-appropriate toys and demonstrate what you can do with them: The little spoon is small and cool; you can use it to pound on the table, and it fits just right in the mouth. The plastic teething ring is warm and soft and goes around your fingers. Building blocks are angular and hard and can be stacked on top of one another.

Dry-land Swimming

Playing on her stomach is now more fun for your baby. Take advantage of this fact and notice how the baby is beginning to move more and more from this position. See for yourself: Put your watch, a puppet, some other interesting toy a couple of hand's breadths in front of the baby's face. The baby will immediately try to grasp the toy. This is strenuous and thus the best type of baby training.

Fly, Baby, Fly . . .

Grasp your baby by the hips and lift her overhead with extended arms so that the baby hovers over you like a plane. When you hold your baby in this hovering position for a while, she enjoys the new bird's-eye view. If you also walk through the house in this position, the baby will yell with glee.

Laughing Is Healthy

The object here is to trigger a laugh in your child. Some babies love to be tickled gently, and others love to "fly" through the room. Still others dissolve into laughter when they are bounced around in a sitting position on your lap. Find out what your child likes—and repeat the fun as long as it gives your baby joy. Laughing also relaxes a baby's muscles and is refreshing.

Tell Me a Story!

Babies who hear lots of stories learn quicker and speak with fewer errors. So whatever you do, let your baby participate and keep speaking to her. Tell the baby who you telephoned, describe what you have to do today, or what's for lunch. The more stimuli you provide the baby with now, the more talkative she will be later on.

Questions and Answers

1 *Although I am still nursing my baby, I would occasionally like to offer him a bottle. But he just doesn't want to take the nipple.*

Try out some specially shaped nipples that are available on the market. Manufacturers keep trying to duplicate the shape of the human nipple as closely as possible. But there are still some stubborn babies who prefer to experience thirst or hunger than drink from a bottle. Then your only choice is to try again later. Sometime the day will come when even these bottle resisters will accept the bottle without a fuss.

2 *There is baby food on the shelves of the supermarket with a label that says, "After the fourth month." But I would like to continue breastfeeding until my baby is six months old. Does he already need baby food?*

No! In the first five to six months there is nothing better for your baby than mother's milk, which is best suited to the child's needs and is easily digestible, or formula based on mother's milk. During this time it will provide everything your baby needs. Only after this time are baby foods a necessary addition to the diet. So don't be led astray by the cunning of the baby food manufacturers; the time is not yet right.

3 *My baby sticks everything she can grab into her mouth. Should I worry that she will pick up germs or bacteria?*

That depends. Basically, your baby should not grow up in a sterile environment. Many mothers (especially first-timers) would like to wrap up their baby in soft cotton and kill all germs around the child with disinfectants. But this doesn't always make sense. Germs will stimulate your baby's immune system and strengthen her constitution. In other words, it won't hurt your baby if she plays with toys that other children have previously held in their hands. She can even put into her mouth a spoon that has fallen onto the floor. But care is advised if your baby likes to suck on the fingers of visitors. Don't hesitate to ask your guests to wash their hands before contacting the baby. Parents should wash their hands, especially after going to the bathroom or changing diapers. Also, in a random meeting, don't hesitate to ask strangers to refrain from stroking the face of your baby as she sleeps in the stroller.

4 *My baby keeps dropping his pacifier. Do I have to wash it off every time it falls onto the floor?*

If the pacifier lands on a clean floor, it doesn't need to be disinfected immediately. As long as you can pluck off a ball of fluff or a hair and there is no other visible contamination, the baby can put the pacifier back into his mouth. Only when the pacifier falls into dirt, sand, or onto a dusty floor must you rinse it thoroughly in clear water. Never "clean" the pacifier by sticking it into your own mouth and licking it clean—the germs in your mouth (especially candida) would harm your baby more than a little dust from the floor!

5 *Our older child has a cold. Is it alright for the child to pick up the baby, or should we forbid all contact?*

It's generally true that every infection that a baby goes through strengthens her immune system. So it doesn't make sense to wrap infants up in soft cotton and use overblown hygienic measures or prevent contact with other people. On the contrary, scientific studies have shown that children whose immune systems have always had to deal with germs and foreign proteins such as pollens (children who have grown up on a farm, for example) are noticeably healthier in the long run and suffer much less frequently from allergies than children who have grown up in nearly sterile living quarters. As for your question, the answer is a bit more complex: It is not necessary to keep a sibling with a cold from contacting the baby because both children live under the same roof. So the child can carefully hold the little sibling after washing his hands. You should simply make sure that the older child doesn't breathe or sneeze directly onto the baby, or lovingly kiss or lick him. One notable exception is the premature infant or infant with special health needs. These babies can be very susceptible to infections and should be protected from older siblings and visitors who have viral illnesses. There will be plenty of time for this type of attention once the cold is over.

6 *Our baby is happiest sitting in the swing or the baby seat and looking at us. At three months, how long should she sit in this position?*

As long as your baby is not mobile or cannot put herself into the desired position, the swing is an ideal lookout position. Since the angle can be adjusted, your baby can get a good view. But be careful: don't let your weeks-old baby lie in it for more than thirty to sixty minutes at one time. The same is also true for the baby's car seat. The older your baby becomes, the longer she can sit in the seat. At around six months she can easily spend an hour in the baby swing.

7 *My baby continually drools, so his top is always wet. What causes this?*

You can bet that your baby is teething. The teeth grow for many weeks in the jaws, and that gives the babies an itch in the gums. So babies continually stick their fingers into their mouth because it reduces the itching when they bite their fingers. The fact that your child's saliva flows copiously is a neat trick of nature. Because the baby continually has his fingers in his mouth and the gums itch, extra saliva dribbles from the mouth and carries germs away with it.

How Your Baby Develops

Some particularly crafty little ones also do things in reverse and turn from lying on their back to lying on their stomach—and this is amazing progress. But not all babies are so speedy. Don't be discouraged if your child still shows no interest even at seven months in rolling from stomach to back, and vice-versa. All children take whatever time they need. And this has absolutely nothing to do with "being normal" or "not being normal" but only with your child's individuality.

All Senses Engaged

Your child's senses keep developing further. She is so alert that she can tell what kind of a mood you are in by the tone of your voice. Her eyes, too, are always on the lookout, and she investigates everything that comes within reach. And now, for your baby, being a participator is everything—preferably during meals, too.

Head Up

During these weeks, many children manage to hold their heads up very well. If you can put your baby into a sitting position and keep her stable with support, she can hold her head up for several minutes. When you put the child on your lap and move her from side to side, she can keep her head perfectly balanced.

The Fifth Month

Your baby has now perfectly mastered lying on her stomach. Depending on how agile and active your little dry-land swimmer is, it may happen that the baby rolls from the stomach onto the back during these weeks. The baby may find the experience frightening. But what may originally have happened by accident will gradually become routine.

Give Me Your Hand . . .

When you hold out your hands to your baby, he clamps on tightly. He may also be able to hold on so tightly that you can pull him up from a prone to a sitting position. Don't pull on the wrists as you do this. Incidentally, many children already prefer the right hand for grasping. If your baby often uses the left hand, it doesn't yet mean that he will be left-handed. Children can still change to either side. But even if your child shows that he will be a lefty, you should never attempt to retrain him by forcing him to use the right hand. Forced changes may lead to developmental problems later on.

Stand up!

The legs also demonstrate the first interest in standing up. If you hold your baby securely under the arms so that his feet touch the floor, he can stand for a couple of seconds on his own two feet, push his toes against the floor, and extend his legs.

TIP | SITTING

Your child can learn to sit independently only if his neck and trunk muscles are sufficiently developed and the nervous system is able to coordinate strength, muscular activity, and balance with one another. This will happen if your baby is exposed to a variety of physical activities such as rolling, spending time on his tummy, and performing weight bearing on wrists. If your child can do this, he can be placed in a sitting position with one hand supporting him.

Sharp Antennas

Your child is not only progressing physically but also developing his capacity to perceive things. The child can tell your mood by your facial expression and tone of voice; he also feels whether you are stressed out or happy, irritated or relaxed.

Playful Encouragement for Baby

Mirror, mirror in the hand, which toy's the best in all the land?

Ordinary Toys

Your baby's predilection to put everything into her mouth continues unabated during these weeks. Your baby doesn't care if she has an expensive toy—the main thing is that it tinkles and rattles. Ideally, the "toy" is so light and handy that the baby can change it from one hand to another. Examples that meet these criteria include an empty yogurt container with no sharp edges, a soft glove, a simple wood ring, or a small, unbreakable baby mirror. All toys in the United States must go through safety testing. Items are designated or marked safe for children younger than three when there is no choking hazard present. Always look for safety warning labels on toys.

Introducing Rituals

Already some repeated actions can be turned into significant rituals. You share with your baby an outline of the day's events, and she knows that when Mom or Dad repeats the same behavior patterns, she has to play by the rules. For example, if you put your baby to bed at night, it makes sense to always sing or hum the same lullaby. That way she knows that when this melody comes, it's time for sleep.

Coo-coo

Play hide and seek with your baby in such a way that you always remain visible. To make your baby happy, all you have to do is hide your face behind your hands, or a piece of paper for a moment. When you then come out of your hiding place, the joy at seeing you again is sure to be huge.

Tongue Play

It's fascinating for babies to see what parents can do with their tongue. They stick it out, make it dance on their lips, hide it quickly inside their mouth, wag it up and down . . . If your baby is one of the tongue-game aficionados, put on a little "tongue play" and watch how your child tries to imitate you!

Up High

For many babies, there is nothing better than carefully being whirled through the air. Try it! Your baby is now so robust and strong that she can sniff some different air from a higher altitude. Most babies laugh out loud with delight when held aloft—and gain confidence because such little games continually show them that they are always held securely and safely. Be careful, however, when lifting babies in the air to prevent whiplash or other injuries.

Umbrella Show

Sit down with your baby on your lap. Now open up a large umbrella and tell your baby a little about rain, the sun, and the moon. The child will be captivated and look up with you and listen to your words.

A Little Help in Turning Over

Does your child really want to turn over from the back to the stomach, and vice-versa? Then you can motivate your baby with the following tricks to move from lying on the back to the stomach: when your baby is lying on his back in front of you, put a ring toy into one of his hands. When the baby has the ring in his right hand, motivate him through some action (rustling, ringing, or the like) to look to the left. Now grasp the ring and pull gently. Now if your baby wants to, he can turn onto his left side or all the way over onto his stomach without great exertion.

Questions and Answers

1 *Does it make sense to take my baby to baby swimming lessons?*

The term *baby swimming* is misleading because, of course, no baby learns how to swim in this type of course. Babies won't be able to do that until they are older. Baby swimming lessons are much more of a play group that takes place with babies and mothers in water at a pleasant temperature. As for your question, yes, a baby swim group makes sense because it's tremendous fun for many babies to splash around in the water with Mom or Dad. You will learn how to hold your child in the water and reduce any possible fear of the water. Babies become comfortable in the water and learn to splash, kick, and blow bubbles. They also learn how to put their heads under water, with supervision. Moving back and forth in the water massages the baby's skin, increases body awareness and relaxes and strengthens the muscles. Water stimulates agility and develops the child's senses.

2 *What do I have to be aware of while visiting a swimming pool?*

Generally the baby should be at least nine or ten weeks old before she is taken into a swimming pool, and she should be able to hold her head up. As for the duration, you should spend a maximum of thirty minutes in the water with your baby. Diapers prove useless for babies in the water: they soak up water, become heavy, and hinder more than they help. Most pools require specially made swimming diapers for that fit closer to the body. These can be purchased at any baby shop. You should be aware that even though chlorine helps keep the water clean, many babies react to it with dry skin, and sometimes with red eyes. Finally, a baby lotion applied within a couple of hours helps protect the skin from drying out. Better yet, look for a pool where the water is not purified with chlorine but with one of the new chlorine-free systems, which your baby's skin will appreciate. Do you have a preemie and want to know when you can start baby swimming? Check with your pediatrician.

3 *What's up with the theory that finger games make babies smart?*

It sounds strange, but it's true! Finger games refer to play activities that emphasize the child's hand coordination and fine motor skills. These can involve stacking blocks, playing toy instruments, and manipulating puzzles. Scientists maintain that babies learn to speak earlier when their parents frequently play finger games with them. It is continually observed that the ability to speak first occurs when a baby develops a certain degree of dexterity. One reason for this could be that the speech center in the human brain lies close to the one that's responsible for fine motor control.

4 *My baby is now four months old and doesn't make the slightest effort to grasp anything with her hands or reach for things. Should I be worried?*

Possibly. There are children who are not yet ready to "grasp" their surroundings, but prefer to look at their surroundings from a passive position. This is not necessarily a problem. Simply keep offering your child new objects (a stuffed toy, a large spoon) and encourage her to reach for them. Your baby will surely learn to like finding out what she can do with her hands. If your baby doesn't take the objects in her hands, this may be an indication of a developmental problem and you should bring this up with your pediatrician at the next visit.

5 *Is there a rule about how many bowel movements a baby should have?*

Just as digestion functions individually with adults, that's the way it happens with children. One baby will fill his diaper one or more times per day, but other babies will experience one evacuation every few days without suffering from stomach pains or constipation. There is one broad guideline: Everything between four times a day and once every two to three days is normal.

How Your Baby Develops

When your baby is lying on her stomach, she probably already reaches upward strongly with extended arms. Her hands are open. If you gently lift up the side of the pad on which she lies, she pushes against it to maintain her balance. While lying and sitting, the baby can easily hold her head erect and turn it from side to side. But at this time, most babies can't yet manage to get from the prone to the sitting position by themselves.

Count Me In!

The time when your child participates more actively in her surroundings will come gradually. Communication is no exception: the child now says consonants and vowel combinations out loud and likes to enter into conversations—favorite syllables include "ga-ga," "da-da," or "ba-ba." To the great joy of all mothers, the first "ma-ma" won't be long in coming . . .

The Sixth Month

Now your child reaches deliberately for everything that's interesting. If you hold a toy in front of her face, she eagerly reaches for the object, examines it, and manipulates it with both hands. She grips the object with the entire surface of the hands, using the fingers and the thumb. The baby brings her hands together and then puts them into her mouth.

From Fall to Fall

Once your baby has the object of her desires in her hands, she thoroughly inspects it, turns it, twists it, and of course puts it into the mouth. The toy is playfully passed from one hand to the other. If the object inadvertently is dropped, the baby watches it fall with great interest. Most little cuties have so much fun at this game that they usually drop the item again right away.

I Have Something to Say!

The childish speech becomes increasingly clear—and loud. It's entirely possible that your baby will prattle along while you are engaged in a conversation. In the meantime, the child is able to string together short syllables such as "ga" and "da." If your child has arrived at this stage, you probably won't have to wait much longer for the first "ma-ma." Researchers have determined that babies who are sung to or are told lots of stories learn to speak more easily than other babies.

Many Benefits of Humor and Music

When you joke around with your baby, she squeals with pleasure. When you come anywhere near the child, she talks to you because she wants you to chatter some more. Another pleasure at this age is baby songs. Children can already squeal up and down the scale. Babies often give this musical performance in the mornings after waking up.

Bring on the Baby Food!

In the next few weeks your child will probably experience her first baby food. The appropriate motto for this stage could be "Everything's a mess at first." Don't be surprised if much of the baby food that you carefully spoon into the mouth wells back out: your baby now has the laborious task of learning the difference between sucking and chewing. At first the tongue often pushes more food out of the mouth than rearward toward the palate, from

TIP | TRAINING THE SENSES

Your baby's perceptions are also increasing: When the baby is in a good mood, she always wants to be involved and see everything. When you eat, she prefers sitting on your lap to watching from the highchair. But, be careful: Anything within reach is subject to her inspection. Allow your baby to explore as much as she wants (under your watchful eyes and supervision, of course), for this is training for the senses.

where it is swallowed. This takes patience: Most babies need only a few days to get used to a spoon and baby food.

Checkup Number 5

At six months, the doctor will check if the child's mobility and agility correspond to his age. Can the baby turn onto his stomach by himself? Can he lie on his stomach and hold himself up steadily on his forearms? Does the baby intentionally grasp for toys? Can he hold an object with both hands and transfer it from one hand to the other? Can he grasp his own foot and bring it to his mouth? How does the baby react to strangers? In addition, the child's hearing and brain functioning will be checked. The doctor will also discuss the child's nutrition with you. You will discuss how well breastfeeding is going, and when you should start supplementary feeding. The third set of immunizations will be due at this point.

Playful Encouragement for Baby

Discovering the World

What does water feel like? How about grass under the feet? How does a brush scratch, and what does a rattle sound like? Your baby has now turned on all "sense antennas" and is ready to discover new things. Now you are needed because only with your help can the child continue training the senses. If the season permits, you can hold your baby barefoot on the lawn. If the grass tickles the soles of the feet, the child will want to find out what it is. Equally exciting is a footbath. All you need to do is fill a small basin or a baby pool with warm water and hold your baby's feet in it. But be forewarned: The footbath may be so much fun that the baby will splash around a lot. You could get wet!

Finger Dances

Children love finger games in which they listen to a rhyme or a song and learn about their body at the same time. Here's one great verse you can use: *A man goes up the stairs* (use two fingers to walk up the baby's arm), *knocks on the door* (carefully tap the forehead), *knock-knock* (gently tug on the ear), *the nose man is all done* (tug lightly on the child's nose).

Swinging Games

Swinging games accompanied by a song are always favorites. How fortunate that there are many of them that you can modify as you wish, so there are no limits imposed on your creativity. One modern classic is the following swinging game, in which you place your child on your lap in such a way that he can watch you. Hold the child securely under the arms and rock him back and forth to the following stanza—start slowly at first and then get faster:

Big clocks go tick, tock, tick, tock . . . (Rock your baby back and forth slowly and deliberately in time with the verse.),
Little clocks go ticky-tocky, ticky-tocky (the rhythm speeds up and the baby is rocked in time),
And the little pocket watches ticky-tacky, ticky-tacky, ticky-tacky . . . (Now rock the baby left and right at a faster pace.)

Smooth or scratchy, hard or soft? Let your baby feel the newness of her world.

134

Researchers have determined that babies prefer playing immediately after eating and in the evening. Use this knowledge and plan your playtime accordingly.

Church tower clocks go bong, bong, bong, bong . . . (Rock the baby forward and back in time.)
Cuckoo clocks go coo-coo, coo-coo . . . (Move the baby up and down.)
And the egg timer goes ss-ss-ss . . . (Rub both hands from the baby's head to his toes—as if sand were flowing over his body.)

Where Does the Mouse Run?

Here's another favorite: Seat your baby on your lap and carefully tickle his entire body. Explain to the child that your hands are two little mice that run back and forth over his body so they can play hide and seek.

From Hand to Hand

Encourage the coordination of both hands by putting something interesting into one of the child's hands. Does it stay in one hand or migrate to the other? You can also propose a trade. Ask your baby to swap an object he already has in his hands for a different one. Will the baby trade? Everything that rustles, crackles, or makes noise works well.

Foil Rustling

Are you familiar with a rescue foil blanket? This is a large sheet of foil that is standard equipment in auto first-aid kits and is available in auto parts and camping stores. It not only gleams silver and gold but also rustles marvelously when you crumple it up. Spread out the foil on the floor and let your baby play with it. Many children can't get enough of it—it rustles and crackles so wonderfully that they fairly wrap themselves up in it. The good thing about the foil is that in contrast to aluminum foil, it is rip-proof, and therefore absolutely safe for babies.

Rescue foil: inexpensive, (nearly) impossible to destroy, and frightfully fascinating.

Questions and Answers

1 *As soon as our baby sits at the table, she grabs everything that crosses her path. Is this a sign that supplemental feeding is now appropriate?*

Don't let your baby's grabbing upset you. Parents always think that their baby is ready for supplementary feeding when she tries to grab bread and noodles at the table. In fact, your baby is expressing her interest in the surroundings with her hands and feet. So she will go after a glass of beer, a ballpoint pen, or the remote control with the same passion. Thus, the baby's reaching for the plate has nothing to do with the maturity of her digestive tract; it merely shows that she is actively participating in family life. If you intend to breastfeed for the full six months, you should remain committed. Still, you needn't hesitate to put a hard piece of bread or a rice cake with no sugar or salt into the baby's hands when she is seated at the table with you.

2 *Is it true that babies start getting teeth at six months?*

It can happen that the first little teeth break through at this point. Experience shows that the two lower incisors are the first ones, followed by the upper incisors. But if your baby doesn't "grow" teeth quickly, you needn't worry. It is perfectly normal if it takes a few more weeks or even months for the first tooth to appear. In fact, some children are still toothless on their first birthday.

3 *My baby has no desire to turn over. What can I do so he will practice the movement and enjoy it?*

Place your baby on his back on a blanket or a towel. Lift the blanket on one side so that gravity helps him gently roll onto his stomach. Don't worry if one arm gets wedged under the stomach. Your baby will automatically pull his hand out from under his upper body so he can hold himself up on both forearms. However, if your child is reluctant to roll one way at 6 months and both ways at 8 months, it is important to discuss this with your pediatrician during the next visit.

4 *Big brother keeps sticking his own pacifier into the little one's mouth. Is this bad?*

Yes. Make sure the older child stops doing this because the shared pacifier transfers bacteria and viruses. The same, of course, applies to adults: a pacifier only goes into the mouth of the child it belongs to, and must not go into any other mouth—not even for a moment to lick it clean.

5 *How soon can I take my baby for a ride on a bike?*

Taking an infant younger than twelve months in a bicycle child seat, trailer, sidecar, or any other carrier is not recommended. In fact, some states, like New York, prohibit it. That explains why you will not find a child helmet on the market sized for a tiny tot. You certainly do not want to ride with a bare-headed child, and in some places it is illegal. Several states have laws against taking children younger than one year of age on a bicycle, even with a helmet. For an official U.S. government view, the Consumer Product Safety Commission has information on age-related guidelines for ride-on toys.

6 *My baby is sometimes cross-eyed. Is this bad, and should I do anything about it?*

Do nothing in the first year of life because the parallel orientation of the eyes has to become established first. The mobility of the eyes is examined at every checkup so that improper alignment can be detected in a timely fashion. If it is constant, it should be checked by three months. Additionally, if one eye points inward, upward, or to the side at the end of the sixth month, your pediatrician will refer your baby to a pediatric ophthalmologist (eye doctor). Without treatment, these issues, if persistent, can turn into visual impairment.

7 *The stores sell baby jumpers. What are they for?*

Baby jumpers are a type of swing in which the child sits in a basket with his legs sticking out. The whole device hangs on a spring so that the baby can hop up and down when his feet touch the floor. The problem is that the children in these jumpers don't have much support. In addition, they do not promote the baby's own development of muscle balance and can delay learning to walk. It is tempting to "park" the baby in the jumper, which may lead to fewer learning opportunities from exploration and interaction.

How Your Baby Develops

Many babies manage to roll from their backs to their stomachs by the end of the seventh month. The world looks very different from this position. They feel the carpet, see what is close enough to grasp on the floor, and see Mom in all her size from top to bottom. This viewpoint may seem "normal" to us, but it is the beginning of a new, exciting part of life for baby.

Little Explorers

While lying on her stomach, your baby will soon try to grab anything within reach. She gets so excited that she flails with hands and feet, as if she were dry-land swimming. This movement strengthens the muscles and shows that the baby wants to use all available muscles to reach her goal—a clear sign that her spirit of discovery has awakened. If your baby holds an object in one hand, she can hold it shoulder-high for around three seconds while she supports herself with the other arm.

You Are Mine!

This is the time when many babies realize that they have feet—and that the feet are equipped with toes that move! Now the baby curiously tries to reach one foot while lying on her back; this works best if there are no clothing and diaper to interfere. Once the baby finally gets the foot, this object of desire too is put into the mouth. While the parents are mostly

The Seventh Month

Most babies discover their feet in the seventh month—they move so nicely, are easy to grab, and sometimes find their way into the mouth. Your baby will also take great pleasure in standing on his own two legs: Babies dance back and forth, bend their knees, push back up again, and carefully attempt to take their first steps.

impressed by this trick, the baby happily sucks on its toes. This is how the baby finds out what her feet feel like.

Careful: Baby at the Table!

As soon as your child sits at the table, nothing is safe any more! Everything the child sees can be interesting, especially plates and silverware. Once these objects of desire find their way into the baby's hands, he will inspect them in the mouth—and sooner or later they will end up on the floor. By now your baby has grasped the connection between letting go of something and falling—and now feels that this knowledge needs practice (see side bar).

Help, Mommy's Gone!

This is the time that your baby will start to realize that you are gone as soon as you leave the room. In the past, the baby perceived the parents when they were in the vicinity; if they weren't there, the child didn't miss them. This changes overnight: Your child notices that he can no longer see you when you leave the room. At the same time, he senses that you still exist. As soon as he realizes this, he feels distress, for he misses you and wants you back. He also knows that he can't run after you. The baby wants you because you are familiar. What better way to get you back than to call for you loudly!

> **TIP | UP AND DOWN**
>
> If your baby loves to drop things and squeal with delight when you pick the object up again, you should play with the baby for a while: Remember that the child doesn't drop things to irritate you, but rather so that you will play with him. This way, important playful nerve connections are being established in the brain.

OK to Be Shy of Strangers

The shyness stage occurs around the seventh month. This means that babies may react shyly and cautiously with strangers, or may even begin to cry as soon as people approach, speak to them, or try to pick them up.

Little Chatterboxes

Babies love to "chat" when they are in a good mood, things are going well, and they are playing by themselves in their familiar surroundings. This chattering often involves entertaining themselves with their whole repertory. Vowels, strings of *r*'s, fricatives, and labial sounds are run together and spoken more or less loudly or used in conversations with Mom and Dad. It might come out something like, "eeee, hi, hi, hay, e-pa-pa, da-day, ma-mam-mam . . ."

Playful Encouragement for Baby

Encouragement to Lie on the Stomach

Children who still prefer to lie on their backs rather than rolling onto their stomachs may need a little encouragement. Try the following motivational trick: Tie a string to a building block or a large wooden ball (preferably with a hole in the middle for tying and large enough so your baby can't swallow it). Using the string, hold the object at eye level next to baby's head until he notices it. As soon as the baby becomes interested, he turns his head in the direction of the object. The gaze is usually followed by an arm—and with a little luck the baby will roll onto his stomach.

Learning to Take

At the fifth checkup, the doctor checked to see if your child was able to hold an object in one hand and pick up a second item. You can practice this. Give your child a large wooden ball and let the child examine it briefly. Then give the baby a second object, such as a small rattle. At first, the baby may appear irritated; he may not understand what he is supposed to do with the object. But soon the baby will reach for it with the free hand.

Fishing for Toys

Lie down on your stomach across from your baby so that your heads are about 3 feet (1 m) apart. Then bring out some object that your child is likely to find interesting (this may be a rattle or a kitchen spoon). Hold it in front of your baby's face just out of reach. The baby will flail with arms and legs to get to the object.

Up and Down, Up and Down . . .

Put your baby onto your lap and give her a little ball—preferably one that bounces well and is easy to hold. After your child has had a good look at the ball, drop it. The child will watch it with interest—and it's especially fun when the ball bounces several times on the floor. If you use a "Super Ball" for this game, use one that's big enough so there is no danger of swallowing it.

Getting Acquainted

Keep letting your child get acquainted with the harmless objects of daily life. If you are working in the kitchen, the child can lie in the playpen or on a blanket on the floor and watch you. It's ideal when you explain what your are doing: emptying the dishwasher, boiling water, washing vegetables. Your baby will gladly listen and watch you. This way the child comes to know the environment using the eyes and ears—and the fingers, if a spoon or a whisk happens to "fall down" for his inspection.

Where Am I?

Hiding games are always a hit, and they are easy to do, for everything that the baby cannot see is not there. And the child is even happier when the vanished person suddenly pops up again. Sit down in front of your baby and put a cloth over your head. Your baby will look at you in surprise and wonder what's going to happen now. When you pull the cloth off your head, laugh, and say, "Peek-a-boo," your baby probably will burst out laughing. Your baby can also "hide." Put a silk scarf or a thin, clean cloth over the baby's head and ask, "Where is my little dear?" Then pull the cloth off the baby's head and greet her by saying, "There she is, I found you!" Hiding games like this are not only fun, but they are also a playful way to help the child get used to minor separations. Your baby will also like it when you hide familiar objects. Simply put a stuffed animal under a cloth and ask the baby where it went. The baby will look at you excitedly and be happy when you remove the cloth.

Encouraging Child Contacts

Even if your child doesn't yet play with other babies, regular contact with other children of the same age has a very positive effect. Children are very aware of whether the person in front of them is an adult or a child, and the little ones can already communicate cleverly. This is a good age to visit a play group with your child. The play group is a plus for many mothers as well. There they meet other mothers and compare notes. How do you locate a play group? Ask around at daycare centers, church groups, or women's clubs.

Where'd Mommy go? What may seem dull to us is pure excitement for babies.

Questions and Answers

1 *My baby is not very shy around strangers. Does this mean that the baby doesn't feel close to me?*

Every child feels shy with strangers to some degree. And that's good because this is an important and meaningful step in development that your child must go through. It's just that the degree to which your baby shies away from strangers can vary. If your child is not too shy with other people, it may be because she is already used to people who are not part of the close family circle.

2 *I have started to give supplemental feedings and would like to give my baby something to chew from time to time. How about baby crackers?*

Generally baby crackers contain lots of sugar and white flour. Thus, they are carbohydrates with minimal nutritional value, and they are absolutely unnecessary. If you feel like giving your baby something to bite, go to a health food store to buy whole-grain snacks. An easy between-meals snack is rice cakes made from puffed, whole-grain rice (with no sugar or salt). Take advantage of the fact that your child doesn't yet have any knowledge of sugar—except for the little sweet milk sugar in mother's milk or formula. Your baby won't (yet) miss the sugar, and you can put it off for a while longer—and the longer, the better. You should give your child hand-held edibles only when you can remain present. The little ones can easily choke and, in the worst case, suffocate.

3 *As soon as anyone but me approaches our baby, she acts shy—even with Grandma. How should I act?*

At this stage, most babies smile only for Mom—and with luck also for Dad. That's how your baby shows her love and trust: Mom is now rewarded for all her loving attention in the previous weeks and months. Your baby loves you—she is not afraid of you, she trusts you completely and absolutely. Sure, it's sometimes difficult to explain that to outsiders. Explain to the people your baby is afraid of, that the baby is now going through an important phase, and that the shy behavior has nothing to do with them personally. Soon the baby will be over it, and your child will beam at Grandma. And another thing: accept your baby's wishes if she's not happy in Grandma's arms and wants to go back to you. Grandma will just have to be patient a while longer. In the future, Grandma can spend more time with the baby and win back her favor.

4 *Ever since we began supplemental feedings, our baby has had a sore bottom. What can we do?*

Take another good look at your baby's menu: Is he getting too many fruits and vegetables that contain a lot of acid? This group includes citrus fruits such as oranges and tangerines. But kiwis, bananas, grapes, some types of berries (especially currants), and tomatoes could also be responsible. Diluted fruit juice, which is void of nutrients, could also be the cause. Instead of these juices, get your child used to non-carbonated water. If you want to give your baby diluted fruit juice from time to time, look at the ingredients. It should contain at least one part water to one part juice; three parts water to one part juice would be better.

5 *Can I give my baby tap water to drink?*

Most homes in the United States have safe drinking water for newborns. But if your water supply comes from a well, or if you live in a very old house with lead and copper pipes, you should have your tap water analyzed. If the test indicates that your tap water is of good quality, there is no reason not to give it to your baby. Otherwise, you should use purified bottled water that contains less than 1 mg/liter of fluoride. Water is an appropriate drink for older babies (four months and older) who are thirsty rather than hungry (such as in hot weather) so it should be used as a supplement to milk feedings instead of as a substitute for nutrition. If you have questions about how much water is good for your baby, speak with your pediatrician.

6 *Ever since we have been giving our baby supplemental feedings, she has suffered from constipation. What's the cause?*

Consider your baby's menu, which may contain at least three starting points. First, your baby is getting foods that cause constipation. These include carrots, grated apples, and bananas. If this doesn't apply, check the second possibility: If you are blending cereal-milk-baby food with infant formula, maybe you are not observing precisely the recommended amounts. The last and most probable reason is that your baby is not taking in adequate fluids. In this case, make sure your child drinks a lot at every mealtime (at least $1^{3}/_{4}$ oz/50 ml per meal of baby food). If the child absolutely refuses to take water from a bottle, you can serve it in a small, unbreakable cup and help the baby drink from it. You can also spoon the fluid into the baby's mouth while you are feeding baby food.

How Your Baby Develops

Toward the end of the eighth month, nearly all children manage to roll from their stomachs to their backs and vice-versa and to hold themselves up on their hands. With luck, you can also see the "supine garden gnome" position: When the baby is getting onto his stomach, he remains lying on one side and supports himself on the lower arm. In this position, the upper leg is used for balancing.

The Next Step to Sitting and Crawling

The prone sitting posture is a warm-up for sitting up directly. The baby continually succeeds in stretching out the arms while lying on his stomach and lifting his entire upper body. Eventually the bottom may also push upward. This accidental "four-legged" stance is the warm-up for crawling.

Let's Get Out of Here

Your baby now works harder on moving in the desired direction under his own power. But the movements are still quite rudimentary, so we can scarcely speak of creeping or crawling in the traditional sense. When your baby stands on his legs, he starts to bounce up and down: He bends the knees and goes halfway or all they way down to a squat, and then pushes off with a little momentum and bounces upward. Bouncing up and down is great fun for most children. Don't hesi-

The Eighth Month

In this month, there's nothing much new in terms of movement—the eighth month is more of a "transitional" phase. Your baby takes the time necessary to practice and refine things previously learned. But there's a lot going on inside your baby's mouth: either the child will soon experience the breakthrough of the first tooth—or instead of a toothless smile, there may already be one or more sparkling teeth . . .

tate to help your child stand on his feed. With practice and time, your child will develop standing on his own two feet.

Sit up!

Now the stomach muscles also get some intensive training. If you extend a finger to each of your child's hands as he lies on his back, he may clamp on to them with all his strength and pull himself up as if he were doing a chin-up until he reaches a sitting position. In so doing, the child holds his head in alignment with his back, and his legs stretch out loosely on the floor. If you carefully let go of your baby in this position, he can sit up unaided for a few seconds.

An overview of the baby teeth: The numbers on the right indicate the sequence of appearance; the ones on the left indicate the months in which they break through.

The First Teeth

Your baby has been continually sticking his fingers into his mouth for several weeks and months, biting them, and producing lots of saliva—the teething process is going full-steam ahead. Perhaps your baby is an early teether and there is already at least one tooth gleaming inside the mouth. Generally, the first tooth appears around month eight; the two lower incisors are the first, followed about four weeks later by the upper incisors. But here, too, exceptions are the rule, so with or without teeth your baby is completely within the norm.

Solidifying What the Baby Has Already Grasped

When you give your child two small objects, such as building blocks, play figurines, or balls, he may simultaneously reach for a block with each hand and hold them both for a few seconds. In the sixth month, the first block got dropped as soon as he picked up the second one. This is another milestone in the baby's life: Your child has mastered coordination on both sides. This means that now your baby can concentrate on both hands at the same time, even if only briefly. Here's something else that's noticeable: When you give your child a flat toy (such as a small, thin book), he doesn't reach for it with the entire hand, but with bent index fingers and extended thumbs. This will allow him to pinch objects and is known as the pincer grip.

Playful Encouragement for Baby

String Games

Once your baby has mastered the pincer grip and can grasp small objects with extended index finger and thumb, the time for string games has arrived. Tie a 3-foot (1-m) piece of string to a toy duck or dog. Give your seated child the other end of the string and have her pull on the sting to see what happens on the other end. Soon the child will recognize the connection between the action she performs (pulling on the string) and the reaction (the toy dog comes closer). Don't forget to supervise your child at all times when playing with a string—although it is unlikely, there is a choking hazard.

Asking Questions

Your baby loves all of your questions—no matter how dumb they may sound. For example, sit in front of your child and ask, "So where is your tummy?" If your tickle the child on the stomach and say, "Theeeere it is!" your baby will chortle with delight. Of course you can also ask about the toes, the nose, and the ears; it's guaranteed to get a laugh. At the same time, these little tickling games will help your child learn language more easily. If you program this game into the daily routine, after a couple of weeks your baby will point to the correct body parts on her own—to the satisfaction of the parents, when this "performance" turns out right.

Patty-cake, Patty-cake

Patty-cake is an absolute children's classic. Sing the song to your baby, and clap your hands in time; your baby will love it. And very soon your baby will also clap along as soon as she hears the first verse. Make the gestures with your hands to illustrate patting, rolling, and putting the bread into the oven.

Patty cake, patty cake, baker's man,
Bake me a cake as fast as you can.
Roll it and pat it and mark it with a _____
 (initial)
And put it in the oven for _____
 (name) *and me!*

When your baby understands that she can
make something move, a new phase begins.

Sorting Large Pegs

Your child surely loves pegs! They are long, light, angular, great to hold, and can be put into containers or large holes. Give your child a container with large colored pegs and watch as the baby examines them piece by piece. Be sure to supervise your baby at all times while playing this game.

Hand Games

Give your child various objects to grasp— soft and hard, round and angular, large and small. At eight months, your baby should be able to "rake" with fingers an object and pick it up flat. (Be sure to keep all dangerous objects out of baby's reach.) Your baby will also probably be able to pass a block or other "shaped" object from one hand to the other. Your baby may also possibly be able to pick up tiny objects with thumb and finger. (Remember to keep dangerous objects away from baby's reach.) This is a noteworthy accomplishment as it signifies that manipulative play will be developing shortly!

Whispering

Talking softly and whispering are high on the baby hit parade at this age. If you whisper something to the baby, she will attempt to answer at the same volume— in baby talk, of course.

Simply ingenious—ingeniously simple. There's a reason that children like big pegs so much.

147

Questions and Answers

1 *If I'm not paying attention, my baby puts everything into his mouth—from building blocks to tissue paper, scraps of paper, and leaves from houseplants. What do I need to be aware of here?*

First of all, it's important that your baby not find any dangerous small items on the floor (e.g., marbles and coins). They can be dangerous if the baby swallows them—and the consequences can be even worse if the baby breathes them into the windpipe and they get stuck. From a hygienic standpoint it doesn't matter if your baby sticks a crumb from the floor into his mouth or sucks on his sock. You should, however, make sure that the rooms in which the baby is kept on the floor are as free as possible from traffic with street shoes. Otherwise, the baby could come into contact with dirt. Since the dirt or gravel in flowerpots usually contains lots of germs, you can cover the pots with plastic overlays (usually available where plants are sold). Or you can cut a leg from an old pair of nylon pantyhose and pull it over the pot from below. Then simply wrap the upper part tightly around the plant, tie it in a knot, and you're done. Outdoors you can hardly prevent your child from trying sand, nibbling grass or daisies, or licking a rock to see what they taste like. Usually all you have to do is rinse the baby's mouth out with water. But you have to be careful with cigarettes, plant parts, and berries, for they can be harmful to your child. If your baby ever eats unknown plants or berries, you should call your local poison control center to ask for advice.

2 *Our baby was measured again at the last checkup. Is there a guideline for how big the child will eventually grow to be?*

Yes, there are guidelines. It is possible to estimate your child's eventual size using various rules of thumb. Here's one of the rules: Add the height of both parents and divide the result by two. For a girl, subtract $2\frac{1}{2}$ inches (6.5 cm), and for a boy, add the same amount. The result shows the likely height as an adult, with a tolerance of plus or minus $3\frac{1}{2}$ inches (8.5 cm). These figures are of course very imprecise, but they communicate how closely growth in height is connected to genetic factors. There is another way to estimate the height of your child. Look at a growth chart and plot your child's length as measured at regular intervals. If the child's height regularly is above the average growth curve, you have a tall baby; if it's continually below the curve, you have a short one.

3 *I continually read that a baby can sit up at six months. Mine is nearly nine months old and can't yet get up into a sitting position unaided when lying on her stomach. Is this normal?*

It's true, we often hear or read that at six months a baby can sit up independently and already has two teeth. However, this is not the usual case. Babies generally can sit up by themselves around nine months. Sitting in this instance means that the baby can use her own strength to get into a sitting position after lying on her stomach or back and then sit up for a while without support. But exceptions confirm the rule, and every child has her own pace. Nevertheless, exceptions should be checked out with your pediatrician.

4 *The first tooth is in! Do we now need to start dental care for the baby? If so, how do we do it?*

Yes, start, by for example, gently dabbing the tooth with a cotton swab. With the first teeth you should get a special child's toothbrush. The bristles for the little ones are softer and shorter than with the usual adult toothbrushes. At first, all you have to do is brush the teeth once or twice a day after meals (especially before going to bed). Another option is the so-called finger toothbrush in the shape of an elongated thimble, with short, soft bristles in the upper third. This greatly facilitates early tooth care; you can get these in well-stocked drugstores. Toothpaste is not necessary in the first year of life when the baby has just a few teeth. But if you have an early teether who has six or more teeth in the first year, you can use a baby toothpaste without fluoride. Starting in the second year of life, you should brush your baby's teeth with a fluoridated toothpaste. By the way, there is a widespread fallacy that baby teeth don't need any extra care since they eventually fall out anyway. On the contrary, because the enamel is significantly thinner than that of the permanent teeth, cavities can develop more quickly. In addition, they are important placeholders for subsequent teeth and thus are closely involved in the development of the jaw. Be sure to discuss with your child's pediatrician what might be appropriate for your baby.

5 *Our child shows absolutely no signs of taking things in her hand. Why is this?*

First of all, you should not give up, and you should keep encouraging your child in fun ways to hold things. Offer the child an interesting toy in the form of a fingernail brush, a large spoon, and similar items. If the child still shows no interest in taking them, you should consult your pediatrician for a thorough checkup. Since you surely have taken the child to all scheduled checkups, it would be quite rare for some trouble with the motor skills to crop up now, in the eighth month.

6 *When can my child begin to sit in a high chair?*

The short answer is as soon as the child is able to sit up unaided. This is a clear sign that the child's back muscles are strong enough. But this doesn't mean that your baby can hold himself upright when you pick him up from lying on his stomach or back and set him down. The baby must be able to move from a prone to a sitting position under his own power; with most babies, this happens around nine months. Until this time, your baby can participate in daily life in the baby seat adjusted to the highest angle.

The Ninth Month

Here's how things stand for nearly all babies: Even children who so far have not been able to get into a sitting position under their own power will manage to do so in the coming weeks. Empirically, around ninety percent of all babies can do this by nine months. And something is going on with endurance, too: When you place your child onto a flat surface where she can stretch out her legs, she can sit up unaided for at least a minute.

How Your Baby Develops

In order to sit up, babies first turn from their back to lying on their stomach. From there they get into the position of the "supine garden gnome" (see page 144). While lying on their side, many children push upward so that they sit on their bottom by themselves. The first time most babies are surprised at what they have accomplished. This also means that from now on your baby is more maneuverable and agile on the changing table. Make sure he is always supervised!

A Totally New Perspective

Once your baby has managed to get into a sitting position, he is usually ready to investigate and learn new things. Hands and fingers are now his best tools. The initial grasping reflex has transformed into intentional grasping for objects. Toward the end of the ninth month, your child refines this skill further. For quite a while he has been able to use the thumb and bent fingers to grasp and inspect small items such as wool threads, the cap to a water bottle, or a crumb from the floor.

What's in There?

All kinds of containers and boxes, which hold exciting things like wood balls and building blocks, are of great interest. At this age, babies learn that a smaller object is in the box—and that it can make a great noise when you shake the container.

"Amazing," the baby is probably thinking. And then the child will enjoy to the fullest investigating the contents.

Look What's Falling!

Another important skill comes to light in these weeks and is applied consciously: dropping things on purpose. Drop a building block drop in front of your baby's eyes and allow it to hit the floor with a big noise (but don't throw it); your child probably will imitate the action. That way he learns to open his hands intentionally—and enjoys being responsible for the noise. At about the same time, your baby will understand that there is a connection between cause and effect. What does this mean? When your child drops a building block, shortly thereafter you can hear it hit the floor. If you pull the cord of a music box, the music plays momentarily. The baby understands: If I throw the block or pull the cord, the result is either a bang or music. So the baby will try to drop the block or pull on the music box. This understanding represents one more important step, because now your child finds it interesting to keep busy all by himself for a couple of minutes—at last he is capable of moving something.

Mobile at Last!

Toward the end of the ninth month, most children learn to low-crawl from the "dry-land swimming position." They crawl forward with wiggling motions in the legs. But many crawl backward: They have so

INFO | CHATTERBOX

Did you know that you can encourage your child to babble? Babies now enjoy putting two similar syllables together. Generally this has been going on for a few weeks, but now you will hear him repeat a sound twice. This means that your baby manages with increasing frequency to put together two similar, very clearly pronounced syllables. The most common syllables are "ma-mma," "da-dda," and "dee-dee." To encourage your baby to babble, you should speak with him and repeat his answers.

much strength in their arms that they push themselves backward with seemingly little effort. Forward or backward, the goal is to become mobile. Generally children don't low-crawl for very long (rarely longer than two months), so low-crawling can be classified as a transitional phase between dry-land swimming and crawling.

Playful Encouragement for Baby

Putting Cups Inside One Another

All kinds of cans, boxes, buckets, and all other containers that hold some object inside are now extremely interesting. Give your child various cups or boxes in which you have put some small items. The boxes and other containers needn't have a cover, but of course it's much more interesting if your child first has to take off the lid (which should be easy to remove) to investigate what's inside. Here are a few examples of how you can easily make this "toy" yourself: Put a rattle, a small ball, or a stuffed animal into a shoebox with a lid. Close the top and show your baby how it rattles when you shake the box. Also show the baby how to open the lid. Once the child's curiosity is aroused, he can use his own hand without Mom or Dad's guidance to explore inside the carton. . . . Another great favorite is a set of small plastic cups (cup pyramid) or buckets in various sizes that fit inside one another and can be stacked up into a tower.

Crumpling

Children are all attention when something rustles—whether the rustling is from foil (see page 135) or from a shopping bag that Mom is emptying in the kitchen. There are lots of materials that rustle and crackle when worked with the fingers. Let your baby play with different types of paper— for example, with an empty bread wrapper (which can also be blown up and twisted shut at the top), paper towel (which is also great for a "snowball fight"), or a foil first-aid blanket (which not only rustles nicely, but is also rip-proof and harmless for the baby). These are available at low cost at camping supply stores, or you can pilfer one from your auto first-aid kit.

Babies have been delighted with the baby pyramid for generations, for the cups can be put inside one another, set up—and knocked over!

Ring, Little Bell

Little bells ring beautifully when shaken. They are handy and perfect for investigation by a child. Ideally, give your child two or three little bells that ring at different pitches. The more different tones your child gets to listen to, the better the training she receives for the sense of hearing—without, of course, creating overstimulation. Put a small bell into your baby's hand for precise observation and tactile exploration. Perhaps the child will even want to ring the bell—with your help. You can also hide the bell in a cloth pouch and shake it in front of your baby's eyes. What does it sound like now? Where is the noise coming from?

Temperature Differences

The following exercise is beautifully suited to stimulating the sense of touch and providing a sense for different temperatures: fill a (not too small) bowl with warm water, and a second one with cold water. Place both bowls in front of your child and let her feel the water. Of course, this exercise is best done in the summer when the temperature allows the child to sit in just a diaper outside. The child will be stimulated by something "swimming" in the bowl—such as a squeaky duck, a teething ring, or a colorful plastic fish.

When Mom rings the bells, that's exciting enough. But when the baby wants to become active, the ringing will never stop.

Questions and Answers

1 *My baby snores so loudly I think she has a cold. How can I help the child to breathe more easily?*

Here you have to make a decision. There are stuffy noses with a continuous, runny discharge, and stuffy noses that are really congested, sometimes so severely that the child can breathe only through her mouth. Treating a runny nose and congestion requires patience. Usually the condition goes away in a few days, and you should help the nose get rid of the secretions as quickly as possible. This works well if you regularly put drops of saline solution into your baby's nose using a dropper (both available in a drugstore). Treatment of a stuffy nose is called for when you have a sense that your baby can scarcely take in air through her nose. In addition, when your baby has a stuffy nose, you should be sure that the air in your baby's surroundings is sufficiently moist. You can accomplish this with a humidifier. If you are inclined to try herbal remedies, a freshly diced onion also is effective when placed inside a porous pouch and hung over the baby's bed. The effective ingredients in the ethereal oils cause the mucous membranes to shrink. You will find further information and tips starting on page 272. Be advised that there is a strong correlation between chronic snoring and sleep apnea. If snoring persists, it should be discussed with a healthcare provider.

2 *My daughter has been diagnosed with labial synechia. What does this mean?*

This involves a harmless sticking together of the labia. There is a visible parchment colored line between the small, stuck-together labia. In extreme cases, the entire vaginal opening can be closed with the exception of a tiny opening for passing urine. The result may be that the urine drains poorly from the urethra and builds up inside. The treatment for labial synechia is simple and effective: estrogen ointment is applied to the little labia twice a day. In most cases a small opening will be visible after a few days, and after two to four weeks, the condition will disappear.

3 *Precisely what is meant by foreskin constriction?*

With a foreskin constriction (phimosis), either the foreskin of the penis is too tight or it is stuck to the glans. The result is that the foreskin cannot be retracted over the glans. In newborns and infants, a phimosis is entirely normal. Don't attempt to force the foreskin back. This could lead to small injuries and tears in the foreskin that would not only be painful, but could also scar. This scar formation can lead to a worsening of the condition. Usually the foreskin can be retracted easily no later than age three. But the situation is different with a phimosis, which interferes with proper urine discharge. In this case, the head of the penis swells up like a balloon when the youngster urinates because the urine now collects in the front tip. In this case, you need to consult a pediatrician.

4 *My baby has an infection in the bed of one nail. What can I do about it?*

An infection of this type results when the nails grow into the skin. The nail bed becomes red at some point and swells so that germs can get in fairly easily and cause an infection. You should always see the pediatrician for infected skin. In serious cases, treatment with antibiotics is necessary.

5 *My child continually has cold feet because he keeps pulling his socks off. Is this bad?*

No, as long as the feet are not ice cold. Many babies feel that their freedom is restricted when they have socks on. They feel safer when they conduct their expeditions through the house barefoot. But if you determine that your child's feet have become ice cold — regardless of any yearning for freedom — you must protect them. Either put on pants with attached feet, which will constrict his feet unpleasantly, or some special baby shoes, which your baby may not be able to get off quite as easily. However, always give preference to socks if you have a choice. The baby's feet are still too young for street shoes with thick soles. If you use shoes, you should choose soft leather ones with flexible soles that can be put on securely. Remember the role of shoes is to protect the feet.

6 *Is it true that my baby feels afraid when she has to sleep in a big bed?*

Yes, a comparatively large bed with lots of room to move around can make your child uneasy. This makes sense. During pregnancy, the baby lived inside her warm, dark cave; things were quite tight in there during the last weeks. But this limitation gave the baby a sense of security. Every time your unborn child moved and stirred, she felt something warm and familiar. This means that your child is comfortable with a feeling of constriction, but not wide-open spaces. That's why it makes sense to have the baby sleep at night in a cozy little bed that doesn't allow too much freedom of movement. This has also been proven by studies that showed that babies sleep better when they feel boundaries. In some native cultures, such as the North American Indians, babies are wrapped up very snug even today; with their arms at their sides, they are encased in several blankets and thus have a feeling of being sheltered (also see page 38).

The Tenth Month

A new perspective opens up. Toward the end of the tenth month of life, most babies have progressed so far that they can move around by themselves and can pull themselves up on anything that provides support. This can be the bars of the playpen, the living room table, the leg of a chair, or Mom's or Dad's legs. The theme is now upward. Congratulations, little discoverer!

How Your Baby Develops

If your baby has low-crawled around the house in the past few weeks, she may already have attempted getting up on all fours. In so doing, the child stretches out the arms, lifts up the bottom, and rocks a little unsteadily on hands and knees. But some children are so steady in this position that they actually crawl, but it often still looks somewhat uncoordinated. Others simply enjoy the rocking position—they are not yet ready to crawl. But the chances are good that it won't take much longer to get started crawling. For most babies finish their low-crawl phase by the end of the tenth month.

As soon as your baby gets onto all fours, the next step is already pre-programmed: The baby pushes rearward out of the hand support into a sitting position.

Sitting with a Straight Back

It's possible that your baby is using chair legs, playpen bars, and all kinds of grips to move independently from a prone to a sitting position. Once in this position, your baby enjoys the view and remains sitting longer in order to play. It's amazing how straight babies hold themselves. You practically never see a rounded back. Now your baby is happy, for she finally has freedom of choice: She can choose to remain seated or do something different by getting onto all fours and move along by crawling or low-crawling.

Standing with Mom or Dad's Help

When you offer your hands to your baby, she probably is happy to hold them tightly and pull herself up into a sitting position. Since your baby is now exercising her muscles every day, especially the thigh muscles, it's getting easier to stand. But the joy doesn't last very long because she gets tired and then sits down—until the next attempt, this time a few seconds longer than the previous one.

The Main Thing: Small and Decorative

The objects and things that attract a baby's particular attention now become smaller. Your baby especially wants to investigate small, fancy items—and this curiosity absolutely must be satisfied. One favorite thing is touching eyelashes—on Mom, Dad, or a doll. Your baby points to the object of her desire and takes it in a pincer grip, that is, with index and thumb, to inspect it more closely. The interest in small things becomes much clearer—fuzz balls are inspected and discarded, crumbs are discovered and . . . eaten!

TIP | QUESTION GAME

By now your baby understands so many words and sentences that she can react to them intentionally. For example, if you ask about a commonly used object or a person the baby knows ("Where is Daddy?"), the baby turns her head in the appropriate direction and searches with her eyes. Perhaps the little question and answer game won't yet work, but it will once you try it several times in succession.

Good Coordination on the Trail of Tiny Things

The so-called double coordination has now progressed so far that many babies can bring their hands together several times in a row while holding a building block in each hand. And now they are in a position to examine one block more closely while the second one remains in the other hand.

Playful Encouragement for Baby

Now your child has begun, or is about to begin, making his own way around. Support your baby on his way to independence with gentle help, and especially with lots of praise for the new things he learns.

A Gentle Carrier

If your baby repeatedly attempts to get up onto all fours, but can't lift his bottom, you can provide some help. Fold a cloth diaper or thin dishtowel in thirds lengthwise to produce a "belt" 4 to 6 inches (10 to 15 cm) wide. Lay this under your baby's tummy and hold both ends over the child's back. Now carefully lift the child up with the belt so that he gets onto all fours. This way the baby can get a feel for the new position. Note: If your child tries to "practice swimming" in this position, it's still a little too early. Try the exercise again in a couple of days.

Up with Your Belly!

Sit on the floor with your legs stretched out and close together. Lay your child face down diagonally across your thighs. Use one hand to gently hold the baby's bottom steady and slowly move your thigh upward an inch or so. When you put your legs back down, your baby will try to hold himself up with his hands on the floor.

Mommycrawler

Once your baby learns to crawl, it's great fun to crawl on all fours on Mom or Dad. All you have to do is lie on the floor. Your baby will head in your direction and crawl over you. He may even take a break en route by sitting on your stomach or the middle of your face. This unaccustomed rest area is usually amusing for everyone present, and the baby is happy to be the source of the fun.

Clop-Clop

Baby's manual dexterity and visual perception can be trained by giving him an object for each hand. Take two objects in your hands (e.g., two wooden balls or plastic cups) and tap them together. Most babies find this exciting and immediately imitate the action for quite a while.

It's Fun to Eat by Yourself

Most babies have by now been long accustomed to a supplementary diet and a spoon, and really would like nothing more than finally taking hold of the spoon themselves. This is trying for many parents because only half the baby food finds its way into the mouth, and the rest lands on the face or splatters nearby. The steps of "wanting to eat independently" and later on "being able to eat independently" are important milestones on the road to self-reliance. You should not stand in the way of your baby's progress, but rather be happy about her new skills—and institute some damage control. Just get used to the fact that the majority of the baby food will miss the mark and be prepared to deal with it; bibs and washcloths are washable. Make an effort to support your baby's great progress.

Banging Pots

Noise—especially self-generated—sounds great to baby ears. Your child will listen with interest to noises and tones and try to figure out where they are coming from and what's producing them. Let your baby make some noise by making available one or two kitchen spoons and a pot. At first both of you can pound on the pot together. Or you can get a second pot and a different beater, such as a wire whisk. Then there are no further obstacles to making "music" together.

It's quite difficult to hit the pot just right to produce a lovely noise. When it works, it's a source of great joy.

159

Questions and Answers

1 *My child is very mobile, crawls all around the house, and investigates everything she can get her fingers onto— even the wastebasket. What should I do?*

A baby's field of action increases markedly with the onset of the crawling age. All at once the whole world seems to open up to the baby. Lots of "exciting" things are finally reachable—including those things we are not particularly fond of seeing in the baby's hands, such as flowerpots and soil, toilets, trashcans, street shoes, and similar items. If your baby misappropriates these things, you should take the following two considerations to heart. First, be consistent, and polite but very firm with your child. For example, if the child opens up the wastebasket and digs around in it, explain, "No, that is not for you!" Then put the child back into a play area or some other place. Give the child a toy so that she has an alternative to the wastebasket. Second, whenever possible, avoid transferring your feelings of disgust to your child. Interjections such as "yuck!" are meaningless because the child doesn't connect them with anything unpleasant, and may think you are playing a game. By the way, it's a real accomplishment later on, say in the second year of life, to keep your cool when some other things find their way into the baby's mouth, such as certain crawly critters.

2 *My child always wants to eat by himself, but this turns into an absolutely rotten mess. Is this something I have to go along with, or is it better for me to simply feed my child?*

Let's put it this way. Your child will be grateful and will soon reward you if you give him a chance to practice. For practice makes perfect in this instance. In other words, the more patience you exercise, the quicker the messy phase will be over. A child who never touches his food and is not allowed to feed himself won't know what spaghetti or tomatoes feel like. And you can be sure that every baby wants to know what warm baby food, cold fruit slices, running water, firm pretzels, cooked noodles, and bread with a spread feel like. The child wants to test the nature of these foods with the hand and the mouth. Then the child can form his own opinion about them and store the information in his brain.

For babies, eating isn't just about allaying hunger; it's also about satisfying the thirst for knowledge. Still, there is one *but*. A child must, of course, also eat to take in nutrients. So make sure that your child has a chance to experiment between meals and still take in enough food. Give your child his own spoon with which to eat, and feed him at the same time with a second spoon; that way you can be sure that some baby food actually lands inside the mouth. If you have a sense that your child is full and only playing around, terminate the meal and remove the plate— even if your child protests.

3 *I heard that necklaces and amber are supposed to facilitate teething. What's this got to do with it?*

Many cultures consider amber to be a natural analgesic that can help calm a baby without resorting to over-the-counter drugs or remedies. Amber really is fossilized resin, not a stone, and thus is organic and warm to the touch. Aficionados of healing stones swear on the curative, harmonizing effects of amber, which is supposed to help with such things as teething problems. The effectiveness of amber in teething has not been scientifically proven. However, parents should be careful and make sure the amber does not pose a choking hazard.

4 *In this day and age do babies still fall from the changing table?*

Unfortunately, yes. One study conducted between 1995 and 1999 found that 1.7 percent of all accidents involving children up to the third year of life involved falls from a changing table. At the time of the fall, 81 percent of the children were no more than one year old. The most prevalent injuries were bruises. At the time of the accident, 60 percent of the adults involved were facing the baby. In nearly all cases the children were restless, or the parents were pressed for time and not as vigilant.

5 *My child sweats a lot while drinking. What does this mean?*

It's difficult to give a clear answer to this because in most cases, there is no plausible explanation. In fact, many children sweat— especially while drinking milk from a bottle or sleeping—so much that their hair and body become damp. If your baby is always drenching his shirt, you should notify your pediatrician. The doctor will make sure there is no underlying disease. If the check-ups so far have been unremarkable and the child is developing in an age-appropriate way, the increased sweating is not a cause for concern.

The Eleventh Month

Now the next round begins. Once your baby manages to get into a standing position, the first step is not far behind. Of course, the start into a life of mobility is easier with lots of praise and support from Mom, Dad, and the rest of the family. Open your arms, offer your baby your hands, and, if the time is right, the child will accept your invitation . . .

How Your Baby Develops

Is your house already childproof? If not, you should take care of this quickly. Experience shows that 90 percent of babies make the home insecure on all fours no later than the end of the eleventh month. This includes nearly all children who are truly crawling: They move forward on hands and knees with diagonal coordination, as the experts refer to it. This means that the child moves forward using an outstretched arm and the diagonally opposed thigh (crosswise): left leg and right arm, right leg and left arm. The better the baby's balance the more deft and agile the crawling.

Fall Over? Not Me!

Of course, so much exercise makes a child tired, and from time to time a break is needed. The baby sits on her bottom from the crawling position and remains upright, with a straight back. This sitting position is sometimes so stable that your child instinctively supports herself when you lift up the front of her legs. The child pushes the palms of the hands against the floor to provide resistance, for she doesn't want to fall over. That's fine! That way sitting reaches its developmental zenith in the first year of life.

Step by Step

As in the previous month, the baby continually strives to pull himself up from the sitting position into a standing position by holding tightly onto a piece of furniture. Every day the baby becomes fitter and more agile. When the baby finally stands on his own feet, at first he holds on tight. But gradually the child begins to move back and forth sideways. The really brave ones then dare to take the first steps, still following along the table or the sofa. Parents who now hold out their hands to their child usually experience their child's first attempts at walking. At first the steps are still hesitant and with legs far apart. But it won't take much longer for the steps to become more secure through continual practice.

Little Masters of Things

Gradually your baby masters not only her feet, but also her toys. The child finds more and more pleasure in taking objects in her hands, simply to toss them away or drop them. It seems that there are several fun factors at work in this game: the noise caused by the fall, the knowledge of being responsible for the noise, and, not least, other people's reaction—for usually the observers laugh at this behavior (at least at first). Another favorite activity for the child (but not for Mom and Dad) is to use the forearm to sweep everything off the table in front of the child.

The First Words

Your child's ability to speak also develops further in these weeks. At the age of eleven months, many children have progressed so far that they can say a few proper words—a favorite is the word *hot*. Nearly all babies

INFO | **NAY-SAYERS**

The baby not only can express herself more effectively but also can understand quite a bit. The child knows, for example, what you mean when you say "no" to some action. As soon as the child hears the word, she interrupts her plan and holds still for a moment. The child checks out the situation— looks at the "nay-sayer" and considers the next step. Should she simply proceed as if nothing had happened? Or protest loudly? In any case, your baby knows what "no" means: Mobile, active babies hear it several times a day. This is also why babies can say "no" before "yes" and learn to shake their head earlier than nodding.

now babble in their baby talk, and often their words are so clear that the people who know them well know precisely what they mean. So often a "brrr" is used for car, a "ba-ba" for ball, or a "pa-pa" when the father or another man comes through the door.

Playful Encouragement for Baby

Messy Play with Hands

Many mothers at first flinch when a messy play session is planned for a play group. But you shouldn't hesitate to let your child take part. There is nothing more appealing to children than splashing with both hands in a container of cream or finger painting. The little ones' motto is *I can spread things with my hands.*

You Give to Me and I'll Give You . . .

Give your child a variety of things—for example, a kitchen spoon, a ball, or a hairbrush. As you hold out the item, explain what you have in your hand. "Look, this is a ball. Do you want it?" As the child takes the object from you, encourage your child to swap some other items for it. That way the objects move back and forth between the two of you.

Ball Pool

Your child also will want to visit to a ball pool, a large container (e.g., a small inflatable swimming pool) filled with little balls in which your child can "swim" and play. This type of "pool" stimulates the children's sense of touch. In the summer, the ball pool can naturally be replaced by a wading pool filled with warm water, preferably along with a playmate. Here's another thing that babies love: a pile of fresh, dry, clean leaves. Most children inspect every individual leaf and stem and edge with a love for detail.

Emptying Drawers

When you are preparing something in the kitchen and your child diligently empties cupboards, your baby probably thinks "the main thing is to be involved." To keep your work within reasonable bounds and your baby from damaging dishes, set aside one drawer (or a cupboard) with harmless contents for the child. Plastic bowls, kitchen spoons, freezer containers, and so forth are ideal. Now your child can take things out and put them back, play, and make noise—and enjoy being near you.

Towel Train

Spread a large towel or a bed sheet on a smooth floor and place your child on the far end facing in your direction. Now pull on the front end of the cloth (so gently that your seated baby doesn't fall backward) and play locomotive conductor as you pull the passenger (your baby) through the house. Since the towel or sheet wobbles, the child must try to maintain his balance and remain sitting. The "train trip" is even more fun when other children come along for the ride and Mom or Dad must pull hard.

Here, This Is for You, and Thank You

Hold out a commonly used toy for your child and say invitingly, "Here, this is for you." After a moment, hold out your hand and ask for the item back. When you get it, say, "Thank you." That way your child learns these important words early and in a playful manner.

Feeling and Touching

A baby's hands are his most important instruments of touch. The palms of the hands contain many important nerve connections that can be trained. Give your child a variety of objects and materials—from soft to hard, from smooth to rough, from warm to cold. There are no limits to your imagination: Cold can be a stone or a metal spoon; warm, a water bottle filled with warm water or a freshly rinsed saucepan lid. You can easily make "touch-sticks" (see right) at home. These are round dowels (or empty paper towel rolls) covered with various materials (e.g., terrycloth, sandpaper, or smooth foil); they are great for playing with and feeling. If the weather is warm enough, your child can also sit barefoot in the sandbox or on a lawn. The child can use the soles of the feet to see what the ground feels like.

Questions and Answers

1 *Sometimes my baby's eyes are crusted totally shut. What causes this, and what can I do?*

This may involve a stenosis (constriction) of the tear duct. Typical symptoms are crusty eyes with a thick, yellowish secretion. The secreted tears flow slowly through this innate constriction and become thick. To treat, use a clean cloth and warm water to wash the eye regularly. In so doing, it's important that you always wipe from the outside toward the inside. But if there are further symptoms such as red eyelids and an eyeball colored with reddened veins, or a stuffy nose, bacteria may be the cause. In this case, consult the pediatrician, who can help your child with antibiotic eye drops.

2 *How do I childproof our house?*

If you want to check how childproof your house currently is, briefly assume the perspective of your child as she crawls about. How? Get down on all fours and crawl around your house. That way, many potential sources of danger will become visible for the first time from this viewpoint. Although not meant to be a comprehensive list, here are a few tips you should consider in any case:

➤ Secure all wall sockets that your child can reach with childproofing aids you can buy at a hardware store.

➤ Whenever possible, conceal electrical cords behind furniture because children like to pull on them to see what will happen. Tie up cords to blinds and draperies so baby won't become entangled in them.

➤ Install childproofing devices on windows and balcony doors. Keep climbable furniture away from windows.

➤ Close off staircases with special gates (various types are available at hardware stores and baby shops).

➤ As a safety measure, remove all door keys so that your child cannot inadvertently turn them and lock you out. For safety, deposit a second key with neighbors or friends outside the home.

➤ You can get protective grates for kitchen stoves that keep your child from getting burned on hot burners or pulling down pots with hot contents.

➤ Cleaning compounds, medications, and cigarettes (and ashtrays) must be kept out of reach.

➤ Sharp corners and edges (such as on a glass tabletop) can be fitted with protective caps from a hardware store.

➤ Drawers and cupboards from which the child mustn't remove anything must be locked with safeguards or strong rubber bands. Keep dresser drawers closed (and if possible safety-latched) so the baby won't climb on them or pull the dresser down on top of him.

➤ Keep electrical appliances and breakable household goods (glass and porcelain) on tall shelves or in cupboards.

➤ Secure to the wall small pieces of furniture that stand alone, such as bookcases and CD racks, so they can't fall over. Little ones not only use these furnishings to pull themselves up, but they may also try to climb on them.

➤ Make sure there are protective grilles or other barriers in front of fireplaces, heaters, radiators, or floor furnaces. Unplug space heaters when not in use.

➤ If tablecloths hang over the side of table and are not well anchored, remove them until baby knows not to pull on them.

➤ Put away (poisonous) houseplants and cover the dirt (see page 148). It may be a good idea to keep all houseplants out of reach.
➤ Fix loose, sliding carpets with adhesive tape; they can cause babies to take a real tumble.
➤ Make sure there are no small items that your baby could swallow lying on the floor.
➤ Be eternally vigilant. No matter how carefully you childproof your home, remember you can't make it totally accident-proof.
➤ To avoid slipping, allow your child to walk on a smooth floor only with bare feet, non-slip socks, or training shoes.
➤ Avoid using tablecloths because your child will certainly grab on tightly and perhaps pull plates and hot food right off. When possible, avoid eating and drinking hot things while you have your child on your lap.

3 *My child will soon be a year old, and doesn't make the slightest effort to sit up. Should I be concerned?*

As long as development has so far proceeded normally on other fronts, you needn't worry. Often there is a delay in motor development that is passed on through a family. Ask the child's grandparents. It usually turns out that the parents' development was also delayed. Still, a thorough neurological examination by a pediatrician is appropriate to make sure everything is alright.

4 *Which houseplants are poisonous and can harm my baby if she eats a piece of them?*

There are a few cherished houseplants that are poisonous to people—especially for small children and babies. Avoid the following plants, or keep them out of the baby's reach: Dieffenbachia, Wine Cup Primrose, Belladonna Lily, Philodendron, Poinsettia, Amaryllis, and Calla Lily. Search the Internet under "poisonous plants" using any common search engine to get more information. Non-poisonous plants include rubber trees, hibiscus, Flaming Katy, gloxinia, spider plant, and African Violet. Also, there is no reason for green plants to be in the child's bedroom. Plants attract dust (danger of allergies), and their soil is a good culture for mold. Of course the same rule applies to plants outdoors. Make sure your child doesn't put leaves or berries from poisonous or unknown plants into her mouth. The same goes for mushrooms growing in your pot or backyard.

5 *Is a baby monitor really so important that it's "basic equipment"?*

That depends on your living situation. If your baby sleeps on the top floor and you are listening to the radio or watching television one floor below, a baby monitor can be an important basic accessory. Basically, the device gives the parents security by keeping "an ear" right next to the baby's crib. As soon as the baby makes a noise, wakes up, or cries, the parents are in the know. But this security can also have some drawbacks. On the one hand, there's no sense in running to the bed for every little peep. Give your baby a little quiet time to wake up. He will sound off loudly if things are no longer fine without you. Before buying a device, get as much information as you can.

The Twelfth Month

Is your house still not childproof? Then it's high time to change things, for your baby will shortly be heading out on exploratory missions. Most babies pull themselves up to full height shortly before their first birthday, appear to achieve some stability, and set out on their way. Tables and chairs are still used for support, but soon the child makes the first independent step into life.

How Your Baby Develops

Now your baby seems to pull herself up effortlessly on large objects to get into a standing position. As soon as the child stands on her own two feet, she takes off. She wanders the length of the sofa, goes around the table, or walks around the chair. As long as there is someplace to hold onto securely, the child feels safe. Most babies are able to walk by their first birthday if someone holds their hand. The very mobile ones among them have already taken their first steps alone. Under no circumstances should you lift your child by her forearms because the radius (forearm) bone could pop out of the elbow joint.

Enthusiastic Climbers

If you have stairs in your house, they should be blocked off by now. Many babies are magically attracted to stairs, and they go in just one direction: up! Whenever possible, you should give in to her desire to climb. With every step that she climbs, she strengthens her muscles and her self-confidence. At first, she will climb systematically, one step at a time. If you offer her your hands, she may try to go up the stairs in succession. In a few weeks, she will discover the banister and try to hang onto it securely while going up the stairs. Still, you should never let your baby climb stairs without supervision. But it would be wrong to make the stairs totally off limits and continually keep your child away from them. The sooner and more frequently your child can practice going up and down stairs, the more secure she will be. Most children instinctively turn around and climb down the stairs backwards and feet first.

A Ball, Please!

At one year, most children are able to recognize and grasp objects when encouraged to do so. For example, if you put a ball into the center of the rug and ask your child to bring you the ball, the child probably will crawl or walk to the ball, pick it up, and hold it out to you while radiating happiness. With a little luck, the child may even bring you the ball—but that's almost too much to hope for . . .

The Sixth Checkup

The sixth checkup with a pediatrician should take place no later than the end of the twelfth month. In addition to the basic examination, such as measuring the circumference of the head, body length, and weight, the following points are also on the program: How does your baby react to strange people? Is the baby still afraid of strangers? Can the child play alone for a short while (start of the detachment phase)? Does the child move in order to get objects that are beyond reach? Does the baby hold one object and let another drop? Does the child point at objects with

> ### TIP | MINI VOCABULARY
>
> Your baby knows her name. If you call her, she immediately understands that you are referring to her. Still, the child's vocabulary is limited; yet, she knows exactly which things are designated by the few words she knows. For example, the child can say, "brrr" and mean a car, a motorcycle, or an airplane. For most babies, "bow-wow" means not just a dog, but all four-legged animals. And it's always amusing when the baby says "pa-pa" to every strange man.

a finger—for example, a doll someone holds up? How good is the child's "vocabulary"? Can he say double syllables and babbling sounds and string of syllables ("me-me-me," "da-da-da")? Does the baby get onto all fours and then into a sitting position? Has he mastered the pinch grip—and thus the ability to grasp a small object using the bent thumb and index finger? How are the motor skills? Can he pull himself up all by itself, or does he already walk when held by both hands? Does your child react with eye contact—for example, does he let an object drop onto the floor and look at you as if to ask, "Did you see or hear that?"

Playful Encouragement for Baby

Up, Up, and Away

Climbing is now a favorite activity. There are no limits to this—provided that you never leave your child unsupervised. For example, you can supervise your baby as she climbs stairs, stepladders, and playground equipment.

Singing and Whispering

Your child likes your voice, which is why you should sometimes use it in as many pitches as possible. This usually works particularly well when you are in a good mood. Perhaps you feel like singing. As for singing, when you sing a song aloud for your child, you should make your voice louder and softer. It will be most exciting for the baby when you nearly whisper the lyrics.

What Kind of Animal Am I?

Babies learn the most by imitating things. This means that you have to model things such as how a cat crawls and meows. At first perhaps your child will look at you with some irritation, but he will then attempt to imitate you. The more often you do this game, the more quickly your child will make the connection between the movements and the noises he imitates and the real animal. And the next time the child sees a cat, he may say "meow," and you can confirm, "Yes, that's a cat, and it says meow."

Setting Limits

You have been rearing your child for almost a full year. Even though your child still looks small, you should not hesitate to rein her in and set some limits. For example, there are things that simply don't belong in a child's hands. And there are words whose meaning your child should know at this age—for example, *no*. Experience continually shows that the more consistently parents enforce established rules of play, the sooner children will accept them.

Have confidence in your child. The little ones can often do a lot more than we adults at first give them credit for.

Taking a Bath

It's always great fun to splash in the water. Fortunately, there are some neat water toys, plus some simple and inexpensive things such as plastic cups, plastic cans, and spoons that will give your child lots of enjoyment in the bathtub. Try giving your baby an ice cube while he's in warm bath water. The child will use his hands and feet to investigate and determine the difference in temperatures. Hold the ice cube in his hand, and let it slide into the water. He can marvel at how transitory many things are . . .

No Strings Attached!

Everything that's attached to a string or that hangs from a chain and can be pulled along excites your baby's interest. So attach a cord to a wooden ball with a hole in the middle, or tie together a chain of large building blocks. You can also tie a line onto a stuffed animal. Whatever you choose, most babies find it highly amusing to pull a cord and a wooden ball, a chain, or an animal toy behind them and watch what's following them. Here's another idea that promises success: Put a pull toy as far away from the baby as the length of the string allows. Now the baby has to pull the animal as far as possible. Then you move the animal a distance away, the baby pulls it closer, you move it away . . .

Playing Soccer

For babies, it's wonderful to finally be able to walk. But the joy is just as great when they realize that they can also play soccer with their feet! When the ball rolls across the room, the baby squeals with delight. For more fun, set up empty plastic bottles in a row and let your baby knock them down. They are very light and clatter so beautifully when they fall over.

Tell Me a Story!

Children love stories! Ideally, you will incorporate stories into your daily routine as a ritual, for example after dinner and shortly before going to bed. Full and tired, freshly diapered and in their sleepers or pajamas, little children like to cuddle against Dad's chest or in Mom's arms.

Round, soft, and good for rolling—balls are always welcome. And as soon as the little ones start walking, they try kicking the ball!

171

You can't tell your baby enough stories! And the time is well spent, for children who listen to lots of stories and are read to speak earlier and better than children of the same age who have not been read to.

If you can tell a nice story using simple words, it's even better. Of course, the story and the word choice are less important than the cuddling and the fact that your child knows, "I am secure and sheltered."

Going for a Walk

Now your child is really on the go—and there is nothing more enjoyable than a hand she can hold onto while discovering the world. Whenever you feel like it, you should walk your baby through the house or explore the world outside. But make sure the child's arms are not stretched too far over her head. Your baby has the best hold when your hands are around hip-high on the child; this is uncomfortable for you, but it's best for your baby.

Personal Experience

Larissa (34), mother of Hannah (15 months) and Elena (35), mother of Maya (15 months) went to a play group once a week with their daughters.

Play Groups—A Benefit for Children and Parents

Larissa: In the first few weeks the babies are still very small and just lie there. Still, we can stimulate their senses of touch—with toys or simple objects of everyday use.

Elena: I was grateful for the songs, movement games, and, of course, the ideas on how to stimulate babies in age-appropriate ways. For example, the suggestion of placing a baby on her stomach on a mirror so she can see herself . . .

Larissa: Or to put them into a splash pool where they could take a dip in chestnuts or shredded paper. They tried lots of things that you really don't do at home—because it's simply too demanding for a child, or because you simply didn't think of it. A play group really makes sense because it's great for babies to meet others of their age. I got a lot out of it, too. This was the first group with mothers and children of the same age as my daughter.

Elena: In this session, you got stimulation for the babies, plus you got rid of your concerns and saw that most things are totally normal, and practically every mother is confronted with similar problems.

Larissa: Another neat thing in our group was that there weren't just first-time mothers, but mothers with several other children; they were able to give some tips and report on their experiences.

Elena: They also shared many other things—for example, the proper way to carry a baby, how to encourage lying on the stomach, what to do if a baby shows no interest in crawling, how breastfeeding and supplemental feeding work, and so forth., The meetings were helpful for me as a mother and for my child. I could really see how much good it did Maya to go there. Her father also often notices this in the evening. On those days, Maya soaked up everything, and all her senses were stimulated. Maya sometimes looked as if she wanted to tell me, "Hey, look where we are, this play group is great."

Larissa: The older they became the more attentive the babies were to the group. We now see this very clearly when we get together privately once a week. Our children already know each other and have made friends. Same with the mothers.

Questions and Answers

1 *Sometimes I really would like to put my child into the playpen. Will that do the child any harm?*

No, critics see the playpen as a "baby jail" and believe that the child will suffer severe psychic harm if he has to stay in the playpen. But it doesn't have to be that way. Of course most babies find things much more exciting in Mom or Dad's arms or on Mom's lap. But every parent has moments when he or she doesn't need to be carrying a baby. For example, when the only way to get the housework or cooking done is without the baby, when the parents have to make a quick trip to pick up something in another room or to answer the door—or simply take a shower in peace. Look at the playpen in a positive light as a little play corner that can be outfitted attractively with stuffed animals, building blocks, and toys. And perhaps your baby will find it very agreeable to play alone for a while. But it's absolutely taboo to use the playpen for "long-term parking." Twice a day for thirty minutes at a time is a good guideline.

2 *My child needs a first pair of street shoes. What should I look for when I buy them?*

Shoes are needed really only when the child can stand and walk on her own feet—and when you want to walk outdoors with the child. Shoes are unnecessary in the house and in the baby stroller. A baby's first pair of shoes are to protect the feet and fit comfortably. The shoes should be soft and light. It's best when the shoe can be opened up as wide as possible so it's easier to slip on and off the foot. Leather shoes have an advantage because leather is able to breathe, is soft, and adapts to the shape of the foot. The size can be determined only by having the child's foot measured for length and width in the shoe store. The shoes should be bought about a half-inch (1 cm) longer than the size of the foot. The foot needs this distance to unroll inside the shoe, and for growth. Our recommendation is always to try several types of shoes. Also, small children have a reflex that causes them to roll up their toes as soon as someone pushes on the shoes from the outside. That's why it's difficult for a layperson to tell if a shoe fits well or not. The salesperson will know just what she has to look for. Always bring the current pair of shoes and have them checked to see if they still fit or have become too small. This is a service that the store should provide; a child's foot grows an average of three sizes in the first year of walking, which for the happy salespeople means three pairs of new shoes!

3 *As a layperson, can I tell when a shoe is too small?*

Indications that shoes are too small can include difficulty in putting the shoe on (but this can also be the result of poor design), or toe tips that have been rubbed red by the shoes. You need to be careful with making sure your baby's shoes are big enough; otherwise, he won't want to put shoes on anymore. In any case, you should ask your salesperson at the shoe store.

4 *Should I go to a play group with my child?*

Play groups involving around six to ten parents with their children are basically a good setup. The parents benefit because they can compare notes with other parents, and the children have fun because they are with other children of the same age. Maybe you can even get into a directed play group in which an experienced parent and/or instructor prepares some type of program. You can get information on play groups in your area by contacting local community or church organizations or your pediatrician. Talking to other parents may also prove successful.

5 *In a few days my child will be a year old, and she still doesn't have a tooth. Should I be concerned?*

Admittedly, this is exceptional, but it's not a cause for worry. By the time of their first birthday, most babies are the proud owners of two to eight teeth. Give the first tooth a little more time; in rare cases, this may be a sign of a general or dental developmental problem. But usually there would be other signs, such as a fontanel that hasn't closed up, generally slower growth in height, or the inability to sit up at one year. But as long as your child's motor skills are appropriate for her age, there is no cause for concern.

6 *My child is really bowlegged. Is this normal?*

Yes, up to a certain point. Up to the age of about two and a half, all children's legs are fairly bowed (the knees don't touch). The reason for this leg position is located in the region of the thighbone: With babies and toddlers the upper part of the thighbone is turned so far to the front that the result is a wide gait. As toddlers grows, and spend more time walking, they often become knock-kneed. The knees and ankles don't align until puberty. Therefore, therapy is rarely required for bowleggedness. As long as your child stands securely on both feet and walks, the doctor can determine if your child's legs have the expected bowleggedness or if the child has a faulty position. For the time being, you can let your child walk around barefoot.

175

Baby's Nutrition
in the First Year

Nutrition is important! It is the fuel for our life's engine. But what's the right way to feed your baby? Some mothers breastfeed. If this is not possible for some reason, you need an equivalent substitute. After six months, during which your baby gets nothing but milk, the age of baby food begins . . .

Mother's Milk—Baby's Elixir of Life

There's no doubt about it: When you breastfeed your baby, you are giving her the best possible start in life. The World Health Organization (WHO) also concurs in this finding, and it has evaluated over 3000 studies on breastfeeding. The purpose was to answer the question: What's the best length of time to breastfeed?

WHO found that at least six months of exclusive breastfeeding, with no supplementary food, is good for babies. But the first food from a spoon doesn't simultaneously mean the end of breastfeeding. On the contrary, breastfeeding can continue as long as baby and mother wish—along with age-appropriate baby food.

The Best Right from the Start

The best food for the first six months of your baby's life is mother's milk. But for newborns, breastfeeding means more than simply nutritional intake: the closeness and skin contact allow your baby's confidence to grow and demonstrates your affection.

(Practically) Everyone Can Breastfeed

Experience shows that 95 percent of all mothers are able to breastfeed their baby. That forces the question of why they don't all take advantage of this opportunity. There are many reasons. On the one hand, there are health reasons. For example, the mother may have to take medications for a chronic illness. And some mothers must return to work soon after giving birth. If breast pumping doesn't work well, they switch to the bottle. But many women forego nursing because they have been taken in by false information, for example, that breastfeeding is harmful to the breast. Or they get no encouragement from their own family to nurse. A mother or mother-in-law may announce that nobody in the family has ever been able to nurse, so there's no need even to try. The partner's influence should also not be underestimated. Breastfeeding in public makes some men uncomfortable.

No wonder it's difficult for so many women to nurse confidently.

Breastfeeding as a Conviction

During pregnancy, you probably considered whether you wanted to breastfeed. Just in case you haven't yet decided, it would be great to be able to thoroughly convince you of the advantages of nursing. Mothers who make a conscious decision to nurse and who have the necessary background information have more patience and willpower to get through the potentially difficult startup time.

Milk Production and Breastfeeding—How It Works

Nipples have tiny openings at the tip—the outlets of the milk ducts. All along these ducts there are countless milk vesicles

TIP | OFFERING THE BREAST RIGHT AWAY

In the first thirty minutes after birth, most babies are wide awake, equipped with a strong sucking reflex, and instinctively on the lookout for the mother's breast. Use this opportunity and give in to your child's longing. If your baby was born full term and in good health, there is no reason not to wait until the child has had a swallow from both breasts before taking care of the routine examination or the bathing. This is one of the most intimate moments between you and your baby—enjoy it.

179

INFO | THE BEST REASONS FOR BREASTFEEDING

➤ **The best match:** Mother's milk is automatically the best match for the needs of a growing baby, and it provides perfect nutrition. The many long-chain unsaturated fatty acids in mother's milk help the brain and central nervous system work to capacity.

➤ **Always available:** Mother's milk is available at any time, always at the right temperature, and always handy even while on the move.

➤ **Immune protection:** Mother's milk protects against diseases because it contains the important immunoglobulin A (IgA). The immunoglobulin A content is particularly high in the colostrum (also known as first milk, foremilk, and immune milk, colostrum is milk produced during pregnancy and early days of breastfeeding, i.e., a few days after giving birth). But after this initial enriched feed, IgA declines and remains constant so that your child benefits from this important immune protection during the entire breastfeeding time.

➤ **Reducing risk of allergies:** Breastfeeding limits the likelihood of allergies, asthma, and eczema, and can lessen their severity.

➤ **Prevention:** Children exclusively breastfed are less prone to become overweight later on. Even the danger of contracting the metabolic disease diabetes mellitus (type 1) goes down by 45 percent when the baby gets only mother's milk for six months.

➤ **Confidence:** Breastfeeding gives the baby a feeling of security and closeness with the mother, which fosters confidence.

➤ **Cancer prevention:** Women who have breastfed are less susceptible to contracting breast or ovarian cancer. Many studies confirm this.

➤ **The cost factor:** Women who breastfeed save around $85 a month on baby food.

➤ **Tooth protection:** Sucking at the breast favors jaw development and prevents improper tooth alignment.

➤ **Relaxation:** Breastfeeding also involves remaining calm. No wonder that it also makes babies calm. Breastfeeding gives mothers a chance to pull back from the hectic daily routine and enjoy some peace with the baby.

arranged in clusters; they are hollow and can hold milk. Their delicate wall consists of milk-forming cells that pull the water and all other ingredients for milk out of the mother's circulatory system and store them in the vesicles. Each of these individual milk vesicles is surrounded by tiny muscle cells. When they contract, they empty the milk vesicles. The hormone oxytocin is responsible for this contraction. When it transfers the stimulus to the muscles around the milk vesicles, the muscles contract and squeeze the milk already present into the lacteal ducts. Right before reaching the nipple, the milk flowing from all the lacteal ducts collects in tiny reservoirs, the so-called milk lakes. The baby uses a wave-shaped movement of the tongue that starts at the front to strip the milk out of the milk lakes. If there were no reflex for giving milk, that is, the squeezing of the milk out of the lacteal vesicles via oxytocin, the baby would come away empty-handed. For sucking alone would not be enough to extract the milk from the fine lacteal ducts and milk vesicles.

When Does the Milk Flow?

No milk would flow without the so-called milk letdown reflex. Here's how it works: As soon as the child begins to suck, the mother's brain secretes two hormones: the milk-forming hormone prolactin and the milk-releasing hormone oxytocin, which reach the lacteal gland through the circulatory system.

Demand Controls Supply

How does your body know how much milk it has to produce and have available for your baby? It's simple. Milk production depends on your baby's needs. The more frequently the baby is given the breast, and the more she sucks, the more prolactin (which stimulates milk production) and oxytocin (which triggers the milk release reflex) are released so there is that much more milk available for the next breastfeeding. So nursing is a wonderful interrelation between mother and child: The breast produces milk, the child empties it, and thereby stimulates renewed milk production.

Breast Care

A nursing breast really doesn't need extra care. It's more important that the breast avoid stress in addition to the nursing. This means that you should avoid exposing your breast to excessive cold (such as swimming in cold water or wearing thin clothing in the winter). Don't wash the nipple any more than usual with soap, for that can cause sensitive skin to dry out and crack slightly. A couple of drops of mother's milk spread over the nipple after nursing and allowed to air dry are the best care for your nipples. Be sure to keep your nipples as dry as possible. A continually warm, damp environment, caused, for example, by non-porous nursing inserts, can harm you and favor a breast infection. A better choice is nursing pads , which let air pass through and help keep nipples dry. Also, you should wear a nursing bra that fits properly, doesn't squeeze or stretch, and can be opened with one hand.

INFO | BREAST SIZE

A small breast doesn't mean that it can't produce much milk. Regardless of size, the number of lacteal glands is about equal in every breast. The difference in size is due to the amount of fat tissue, which is solely responsible for breast size.

181

Sucking at mom's breast is much more than simple nutrient intake: Feeling, smelling, and tasting Mom is the greatest joy.

Mother's Milk Satisfies Needs Best

What kind of milk should it be? This question is justified because the colostrum shortly after birth is completely different in composition from the mature mother's milk that's produced after a few weeks. Why? Nature matches it precisely to the baby's needs and always delivers just what's required.

Stage 1: The Colostrum
Colostrum is produced even during pregnancy and is available immediately after birth. Colostrum is fairly thick, yellowish in color, and looks a little like cream. In fact, it contains less fat and carbohydrate, but much more important protein than transitional and mature mother's milk do. Colostrum is rich in minerals, vitamins, and immunoglobulins and is very nutritious. Even in small quantities, it supplies newborns with adequate nutrients in the first few days. The colostrum also stimulates the baby's digestion and thus facilitates speedy excretion of the bilirubin and meconium (see page 52).

Stage 2: Transitional Milk
The name is indicative of its function. Before the female body changes over from producing colostrum to making mature mother's milk, it creates a transitional milk (also transitory milk) for a period of about two weeks. It appears to be a combination of colostrum and mature mother's milk, which soon supercedes it.

Stage 3: Mature Mother's Milk
In consistency, mature mother's milk is more watery, even though the fat content has doubled over that of colostrum. The lactose (milk sugar) content has also risen again—thus, mother's milk has a slightly sweet flavor.

Nothing More Versatile
Even during a breastfeeding meal, the mother's milk adapts to the baby's needs: The first swallows that the baby takes are thin, watery, and intended mainly intended to satisfy the baby's thirst. Then after a brief moment flows the so-called hind milk, which is richer in fat and makes the baby full.

Good Stuff Inside

Here is a brief summary that clarifies not only how with time mother's milk changes from foremilk to mature mother's milk but also the major, important differences with cow's milk.

➤ Energy: Mature mother's milk and cow's milk deliver about equal amounts of energy.

➤ Protein: Cow's milk contains three times as much protein as mature mother's milk; in addition, it contains much more hard-to-digest casein than mother's milk. A child's kidneys are not able to excrete this excessive quantity of protein. Thus, giving undiluted cow's milk can lead to kidney problems in infants.

➤ Carbohydrates: In addition to milk sugar (lactose), mother's milk provides more carbohydrates. The so-called bifidus factor is important; this is a carbohydrate that contains nitrogen needed by certain (beneficial) bacteria in the intestine. Milk sugar also provides quick energy and encourages the growth of the child's brain.

➤ Fat: Mother's milk is rich in essential fatty acids (linoleic acids) and contains the fat-splitting enzyme lipase.

➤ Minerals: Cow's milk contains many more minerals than mother's milk. Unfortunately, infants can't excrete the excess minerals taken in with the milk.

➤ Vitamins: Mature mother's milk and cow's milk are relatively low in vitamin D. Thus, a supplementary dose is recommended as a preventive measure for rickets (see page 40). This applies especially to breastfed children because mother's milk contains very little vitamin D. Infant formulas, on the other hand, are enriched with vitamin D. The content of water-soluble vitamins depends greatly on the mother's nutrition. Mother's milk also contains vitamins A, E, and C.

➤ Trace elements: Mother's milk contains some important trace elements in significantly higher quantities than cow's milk, for example cobalt, manganese, and copper.

The Most Important Breastfeeding Tips

Everyone can breastfeed! That's true, at least in theory. Still, breastfeeding can have its pitfalls, as many mothers have quickly found out. Here are some tips that will make it easier for you to get started.

INFO | WHAT THE DIFFERENT TYPES OF MILK PROVIDE

per 3.4 oz/100 ml	Colostrum	Transitional Milk	Mature Mother's Milk	Cow's Milk
Protein	.08 oz/2.3 g	.03 oz/1.6 g	.03 oz/0.9 g	.12 oz/3.3.g
Lactalbumin	*	*	60 %	18 %
Casein	*	*	40 %	82 %
Fat	.10 oz/2.9g	.13 oz/3.6 g	.15 oz/4.2 g	.13 oz/3.6 g
Carbohydrate	.19 oz/5.3 g	.23 oz/6.4 g	.26 oz/7.3 g	.16 oz/4.6 g

* Not present in measurable quantities.

183

➤ Offer the breast early: Enjoy the first moments together with your baby. Hold the baby in your arms, feel her skin. Give your baby time to rest up. The signals are very clear when the child is ready to suck your breast. Help the baby to find the nipple. Let her suck from both breasts. If your baby is not yet ready, don't be disappointed. Simply hold the baby lovingly in your arms and try again later.

➤ Proper positioning: Your nipples will escape injury in the long run only if your baby is positioned properly (see illustration on page 193)—and this turns breastfeeding into pure fun.

➤ Frequent breastfeeding: Breastfeed according to need. That is, offer your baby the breast whenever she wishes, even at night. Don't try to establish a rhythm from the outset. This way the milk comes in more gently, and milk production adjusts to the need.

Nursing Positions

It makes sense to practice several breastfeeding positions, for each one of them empties a different area of the gland tissue. Your baby always empties the area of the breast where its lower jaw is located.

The C-grip

C-grip describes the handgrip used: When you place your fingers together and bend them slightly while spreading your thumb, the hand forms a C shape. Place your right hand in this position on your left breast, or the left hand on the right breast. When you hold your breast in this way, with the index finger about an inch (2.5 cm) from

the nipple, the breast and nipple are in the best shape for the baby to suck. From now on, get comfortable and relax. If you and your baby are a good breastfeeding team and the milk is flowing, there is no reason to huddle over your baby with tense shoulders and bended back. Incorporate a (breastfeeding) cushion or an armrest into your position. A stool for your feet is worth its weight in gold. Any time you have a feeling that you are using your shoulders to hold your baby, you're sitting

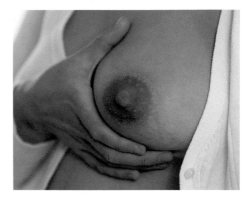

When you present the breast with the C-grip, it's easier for the baby to latch onto the nipple and areola.

Nursing while lying down is easy on the body, especially the pelvic floor.

in the wrong position. Your body should be loose and relaxed. Adjust your position until most of the baby's weight is on your thigh or a nursing pillow and you can take your forearms away. That's the only way you can nurse with a straight back.

Breastfeeding While Lying Down (on Your Side)

It is easy on the body, especially your pelvic floor, to breastfeed while lying down. Simply get comfortable on your side, support your head on a pillow, and bend your knees slightly. Place the baby on his side close enough to you so that his mouth is higher than your nipple. Stabilize the child by placing a pillow or a rolled-up blanket at his back. You can use your free hand to offer the baby your breast with the C-grip.

Breastfeeding While Sitting (Cradling Position)

The most commonly used breastfeeding position is sitting. It is very important, however, that you are able to support your forearms. The baby will not become too heavy over time only if you can move your arms away. A chair with armrests is ideal, or else you can get by with a nursing pillow. It's just as important to provide support for the baby's body. Hold your baby in your arms so that she's facing you and lying on her side. If you want to offer the right breast, lay the baby's head in the crook of your right arm. Now draw the child to you and guide her to the breast. Don't bend down to offer the breast to the baby or you will have to stay in this uncomfortable position. After getting the child into position, shore her up using a

Nursing while seated is even more comfortable when the baby's body is supported by a (nursing) cushion.

pillow or a nursing cushion so she can lie at this height and relax as she drinks.

Holding the Back While Breastfeeding (Side or Football Hold)

Here the baby is not lying in front of you, facing you with her stomach, but rather her body is held to the side under your arms with the legs pointing rearward. This position also has its advantages: It is recommended for women with large breasts because it's very comfortable, and it's a good one after a cesarean, for this position does not place any weight on the scar. In addition, this grip empties the gland tissue toward the shoulder. Place two or three large pillows next to your hips and lay your baby on them so that her upper body

Important: While holding the baby's back, make sure there is enough room for the legs.

is under your arm and facing forward, with the feet toward the rear. Hold your baby's back with your forearm, with your hand supporting the head. Now you can use the C-grip with your free hand to offer your breast to the baby. The baby's body must lie close to you.

The Most Important Questions About Breastfeeding

Anyone who tries to nurse a baby for the first time has lots of questions: "How can I find the best nursing position for me?" "How frequently should I nurse?" and "Does my baby get full?" are just three among many questions. Here are the answers:

What's the Best Nursing Position for Me?

There is no single breastfeeding position that is always right. Choose the nursing position that best corresponds to the feeling of tension in your breast. If your breast feels tight and hard on the inner side, the cradling position is ideal. If you sense tension in the outer regions of the breast, the back grip is appropriate. If you nurse at night or are still exhausted from giving birth, you may prefer lying on your side. In any case, you should try out all positions to be ready for any possibility. It also makes sense to keep changing nursing positions even if you have no breast problems, for that will prevent problems before they occur, since the breast is emptied in a different area each time.

What's the Right Way to Use a Nursing Cushion?

Many types of nursing cushions (also called breatfeeding support cushions) are heavy and massive, and others are featherlight and very soft. Regardless of the model, they all should help you position your baby at the right height. When using the back grip you may be able to bend the pillow in half and place it at your side folded in two. For the cradle grip it's helpful to fluff up the nursing pillow to make a perfect armrest, with the slightly thinner part over your stomach. You can lay the baby on this. If you are breastfeeding while lying on your side, place the nursing pillow behind your baby's back for support. The cushion offers many possibilities; simply try them out. It is perfect when you find a comfortable position, which means that you don't have to hold or lift up your baby during breastfeeding, and instead the baby lies there well supported.

INFO | THE OPTIMAL POSITION

Your baby is lying on his side and facing you directly. The baby's mouth is at the level of the nipple so that he doesn't have to turn his head to drink. The baby's ear, shoulder, and hip form a straight line. You present your breast using the C-grip. Touch the baby's lower lip with the nipple to stimulate him to open his mouth wide. Promptly draw your baby to the breast when his mouth is open. Your baby is drinking properly when the upper and lower lips are bent outward, for then he has the nipple and areola in his mouth. The nose and chin are touching your breast. Your child is drinking audibly and visibly—the muscle movements are detectible even in the temple area.

How Often Should You Feed?

How often you feed depends on the child's hunger and how frequently you wish to empty your breasts. Generally, you should feed on demand, that is, whenever the baby is hungry. The old fairy tale about new milk on top of old milk producing stomachaches is passé. Today we know that the protein in mother's milk is so easily digested that breastfed children become hungry faster than bottle-fed children. But be wary, however, because a child is not hungry every time he cries.

How Do I Release My Baby from the Breast?

Ideally, the baby will release the breast once he has drunk enough. But it may happen that you need to remove the baby from the breast. In so doing, carefully insert your little finger between the corner of the baby's mouth and the breast to break the suction. Now you can easily take your baby off the breast.

How Do Babies Show That They Are Hungry?

Because babies perceive hunger as real pain, they begin to cry loudly if their early hunger signs are misinterpreted. But it shouldn't come to this. If you are with the child, you will notice that she first smacks her lips quietly, moves her head back and forth, or puts a finger into her mouth.

If your baby absolutely refuses to let go of the breast or is not positioned properly, you can gently use your little finger to release the baby from the breast.

187

Also sticking out the tongue, intensive sucking on the little fist, and licking the lips are clear signs. If you now place your baby at the breast, she is not yet so hungry and excited that she greedily snaps at the nipple. Now she opens her mouth wide and allows herself to be placed properly.

Must I Always Feed My Baby from Both Breasts?

At first, always let your baby drink from both breasts because that helps the milk production start up more effectively. It often happens that the baby completely empties the first breast, but just "samples" the second one. The next time you breastfeed, start with the breast with which you previously ended. Then this one will be completely emptied, and so forth. After your baby has drunk the first breast dry, you should interrupt the feeding and burp the baby. Another helpful point: To keep from becoming confused about which side to start with next time, you can tie a piece of yarn to this side of your bra. Once supply and demand even out, it makes sense to offer the baby just one side. For every time the baby is breastfed, milk production is stimulated.

How Long Should a Breastfeeding Take?

As time goes on, your baby will make it increasingly clear how long she wants to drink. After a few days, most babies settle in at around twenty minutes per side. Of course, there are also chuggers and meticulous connoisseurs. Normal drinkers and connoisseurs will always get the fat-rich hind milk, but the chuggers may miss it.

Babies learn quickly: As time goes on, they learn to suck more effectively so that they get the hind milk even if they drink for a shorter time.

How Do I Know That My Child Is Getting Enough to Drink?

While breastfeeding, many mothers are concerned that their baby may not be getting enough milk—aside from weighing the baby before and after breastfeeding there is hardly any way to check the quantity of milk. But there are a few points that provide security: A baby who gets only mother's milk has five to six wet diapers in twenty-four hours. The urine is colorless (not yellow). The stool from mother's milk is mustard colored and may be runny or grainy. It may appear two to five times a day in the first four to six months and less frequently thereafter.

Note also the weight gain, which should fall within the following ranges for healthy babies:

➤ One through four months: $4\frac{1}{4}$–$7\frac{3}{4}$ oz (120–220 g) per week
➤ Four through six months: 4–5 oz (115–140 g)
➤ Six through twelve months: $2\frac{1}{8}$–$4\frac{1}{4}$ oz (60–120 g)

In addition, you will know by your child's appearance and behavior that he's getting adequate mother's milk. Does the child appear full and content? Is the baby active and lively? Is the skin color rosy? Are the eyes clear and shiny? Does the baby have good muscle tone? Then the child is generally developing marvelously.

I Would Like to Use a Breast Pump; How Do I Go About It?

There are several types of pump for extracting mother's milk from the breast. We can refer to one type as hand pumps; they must be used manually, with no electrical current. They are a good choice if you want to pump fairly small quantities from time to time. It's considerably easier with an electric pump. There are at least two basic models:

➤ The smaller variety is very handy; it has a small motor that is surprisingly strong. It's ideal for when you are on the move.
➤ The larger milk pump is also very strong and well suited for pumping regularly at home.

Mom's nearness always helps—even when your baby is not entirely comfortable during a growth spurt.

Growth Spurts— What Can We Expect?

Dutch researchers have discovered that babies repeatedly go through phases when they need more food than usual, arc restless, and especially are growing well. In the first six months, these growth spurts occur around the fifth, eighth, twelfth, nineteenth, and twenty-sixth weeks. You can find more information on this in the front flap of this book.

189

Personal Experience Report

**Sandra (31), mother of
Lilly (5 months)**

Initial Troubles Breastfeeding

*During my pregnancy I was firmly resolved
to breastfeed because I know that mother's
milk is the best thing for the child. I also
considered breastfeeding to be extremely
practical. I didn't like the idea of preparing
a bottle in the kitchen with a screaming
child in the middle of the night, and not
knowing if I was preparing too little or too
much, if it was too hot or too cold, too
runny or too thick. Unfortunately, in the
hospital I didn't get a chance to put Lilly to
the breast right away. She had amniotic
fluid in her lungs, which had to be suc-*

*tioned, and that took quite a while. After
that, I got to hold her, but didn't put her to
the breast. Maybe we forgot. I became aware
of it for the first time only a week later. In*

*the first couple of days after the delivery,
Lilly was not interested in my breast. She
suckled a little but that's all. My midwife
and sisters thought she didn't require much
at first and that a couple of drops were adequate. But after three days, we could see
that Lilly was becoming dehydrated: Her
lips were dry, and the fontanel was slightly
sunken. That's when we realized that Lilly
needed more fluid. And she was given liquid
from a bottle in the hospital. And a pacifier
to boot.*

*A short time later, it occurred to me that
maybe Lilly had drunk from the breast, but
couldn't form a vacuum, for she didn't place
her lower lip on the breast properly. So on
recommendation, I tried nipple shields.
These are specially shaped caps that slip over
the nipple. They make it easier for the baby
to suck, for she has more in her mouth. That's
how the drinking went. So we kept working
on it at home. But I wasn't really so happy
with it because when I nursed Lilly away
from home, I found the caps uncomfortable.
A few weeks later, I was advised to contact a
breastfeeding coach. She invited me to come
to the "open nursing group." Sure enough!
The advisor determined that I had previously
been positioning Lilly incorrectly. When she
was lying down, Lilly stretched her head so
far to the rear that she couldn't open her
mouth wide enough. So I changed the nursing position. Additionally, I gradually got
Lilly used to my skin and placed her at the
breast more frequently—without nursing
caps. After eight weeks of nursing with the
caps, I have finally been able to enjoy direct
physical contact with Lilly.*

Breastfeeding Problems— All Fixable!

Be happy if everything is flowing along smoothly as you begin breastfeeding. But if there are occasional problems, you needn't become discouraged. There is a solution for every problem.

Milk Let-down

Between about the third and fifth day after giving birth, the milk comes into the breasts. As soon as the baby sucks on the breast, the mother's brain releases the two hormones oxytocin and prolactin. They stimulate milk production and flow and initiate milk production.

Dealing with Milk Let-down

This is very important: You must give your baby the breast regularly. Help the baby find the nipple since sometimes the breast is so full that this is difficult. In this case, you should attempt to express a little milk before putting the baby to the breast. This works best if you first dilate the vessels and lacteal ducts with heat. Place a warm wrap onto the breast or take a warm shower. Release the greatest pressure by first stripping out a little milk. Gently run your fingertips from the base of the breast toward the nipple so that a little milk can flow out. Now you can gently express as much milk as you wish so that your baby can latch onto the entire nipple and areola. After breastfeeding, you may cool down the emptied breast with air or a cold pack to keep more milk from collecting (cold constricts the vessels). If the milk lets down in great quantities over time, the balance will change.

When Will Things Get Better?

These conditions will change in two or three days. Thereafter the baby and the breast are used to the increased demand, so the milk quantity becomes more regular.

Special Case: The Milk Is Not Flowing

It frequently happens that the breast is full and painful, but the milk is not flowing. In this case you should resort to the following first-aid program.

Think about why the milk is not flowing. What's not working? How can you get rid of this pressure? Often a conversation with a lactation specialist or lactation coach will help. Speak plainly about any problems. Try to get the milk to flow using heat applications and massages.

Many lactation specialists or lactation consultants know how to open up the milk ducts with a gentle massage and the proper pressure technique so that the stored milk begins and continues to flow. La Leche League can also provide you with breastfeeding support and the advice you need. Information can also be found on the website for the International Lactation Consultant Association (ILCA) at ilca.org.

Concave, Flat, and Inverted Nipples

None of these nipple shapes is a reason not to breastfeed a baby. You simply need to exercise a little more patience and stick-to-itiveness when you breastfeed.

Dealing with Special Nipple Shapes

Pharmacies sell nipple shields that can be used to project very flat or inward-turning nipples outward. These cups are to be placed onto the nipple about an hour before nursing. A slight vacuum builds up through body heat, and the nipples become erect. When you nurse the baby, you should get into the proper position and remove the cups immediately before putting the baby to the breast. Most babies can then latch onto the nipple. If you have difficulties, be sure to get help from the lactation coach.

INFO | NICOTINE IS TABOO

Studies have shown that smoking can interfere with milk production. Two weeks after giving birth, the daily milk quantity of people who smoked at least ten cigarettes per day is 20 percent lower than in the case of non-smokers. Four weeks after birth the smokers produce only half as much milk as non-smokers. Even passive smoking has a negative effect on milk production and harms your baby. This is a time to work on quitting for both you and your baby's health.

Sore Nipples

Sore nipples and small tears occur mainly as a result of improperly positioning the child for nursing. This is always a sign that you need to change something in the breastfeeding position. Ask your breastfeeding coach.

Dealing with Sore Nipples

If you feel discomfort after putting the baby to the breast, you should gently release the vacuum and reposition your baby. Make sure that the baby has opened her mouth wide before you put her to your breast. It is very important that the baby really has the nipple and areola in her mouth. If the baby simply sucks on the nipple, it will soon bleed. And then the only effective treatment is applying a natural breast cream and keeping the area clean and dry. But this can be avoided.

After breastfeeding, let the leftover milk and baby saliva air dry on the nipple; they soothe and help your little injuries to heal. Use only nursing bra pads that allow plenty of air to flow through. Also, lanolin and special (unfortunately very expensive) breastfeeding inserts made from hydrogel have also proven their worth. Both products are available in pharmacies. Most importantly, in spite of all problems, keep breastfeeding. If breastfeeding hurts too much, you can switch to a good breast pump for a day or two. Make sure to get some help from a breastfeeding coach.

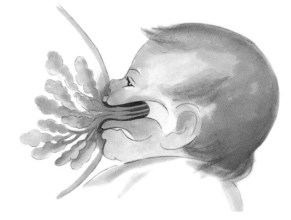

Your baby is brought to the breast in the proper position when she surrounds not only the nipple, but the entire areola, with her lips.

Plugged Milk Ducts

As soon as you have a feeling that milk is backing up inside your breast and forming lumps, you should pay even more attention to the proper breastfeeding position. Place your baby at the breast in such a way that the lower jaw contacts the location of the engorgement because this helps empty this area (see page 184). Try to get the milk to flow by using warm compresses. If the milk cannot flow out, everything gets backed up. This becomes noticeable with a usually red, hard area on the breast that is exceptionally sensitive to pressure. Sometimes a lump can even be felt. This is also not good for you psychologically, for you worry about your baby. There are at least two causes for milk back-up: a clogged milk duct or a bacterial breast infection.

Cause No. 1:
A Clogged Milk Duct

The milk back-up develops slowly, can change location, causes only a minor sensation of warmth (or none at all) in the affected area, and is painful only in the affected spot, not around it. It has no negative impact on general wellness and causes the body temperature to rise to about 101°F (38.5°C).

Cause No. 2:
A Bacterial Breast Infection

This comes on suddenly and involves a specific area. The mother's breast becomes red, hot, and swollen. This type of infection causes severe pain. The symptoms are similar to those of a cold, with temperatures of 101°F (38.5°C) and higher. If a bacterial infection is suspected, it is necessary to contact a doctor.

Dealing with a Milk Backup

With a clogged milk duct, you should place a warm, damp compress on the affected breast before breastfeeding. You might also try gently massaging your breast in the direction of the nipple. Now choose a nursing position in which the

193

baby's lower jaw lies on the affected spot. And even if it's painful, nurse frequently with the affected breast and treat yourself to some rest.

With a bacterial infection rest is also the best recommendation—stay in bed and, if necessary, ask a friend or a relative for help. Get in touch with your doctor right away in case it becomes necessary to prescribe an antibiotic for you. This is not a cause of concern regarding your baby: there are medications that are compatible with breastfeeding, so there generally is no need to discontinue breastfeeding prematurely. You should also continue breastfeeding in the case of a bacterial infection so that the affected area is emptied as completely as possible. In rare cases, espe-

cially if they are not treated, a bacterial infection can turn into an abscess that requires immediate treatment by a doctor.

Too Little Milk During a Growth Spurt

Babies grow in spurts, and then they need more energy (see front cover flap). The result is that most babies will call on mom's breast more frequently during such development spurts. At first, many mothers wonder if they will have enough milk. Yes, it will be adequate; it's just that your baby is consuming more because she is growing. The supply soon increases to meet the heightened demand. Also, during a growth spurt, your baby especially longs for the familiar—and her own mother's breasts.

Healthy nutrition for nursing mothers at a glance: choose grain products, vegetables, fruits, and salads. Sweets should be an exception.

Nutrition for Nursing Mothers

Basically, nursing mothers who have followed a healthy, balanced diet before giving birth don't need to change their nutrition significantly now. The biggest difference is that they now have a slightly elevated energy requirement, but this doesn't mean, "eating for two." Of course producing milk eats away at your reserves, and the little milk drinker saps your energy, but the added nutritional requirement is minor. A woman of average age who is not pregnant and not nursing may need around 2300 kcal per day, and a nursing mother can add another 500 kcal to this figure.

Quality Counts

The quality of the diet is much more important than the quantity. And of course a nursing mother has to eat! Aftercare midwives and breastfeeding coaches continually find that young mothers who have recently given birth are under so much pressure and so busy looking after

INFO | **500 KCAL ARE . . .**

500 kcal more energy every day! This corresponds to about the following quantities that you can eat in addition to your 2300 kcal:
one slice of bread or one roll,
one small potato or one tablespoon of cooked rice or noodles,
one tablespoon of vegetables, one apple,
one cup of milk, one slice of cheese,
one slice of salami, and one tablespoon of oil. And then there are the sweets: four whole-grain cookies, two squares of chocolate, or two dips of ice cream.

195

Right now you shouldn't develop any misdirected ambition for doing housework. Round-the-clock care of a newborn makes it difficult to combine a perfectly picked-up house and a well-adjusted new mother—at least without using up the mother's emergency reserves. So accept help if it's offered!

their families that they forget to take care of themselves.

Energy for Nursing Mothers

Here are a couple of dishes that deliver pure energy to the body and give nursing mothers renewed strength.

Nursing Cocktail

3 tablespoons each yeast flakes, powdered milk, and wheat germ
1 tablespoon peanut, or almond butter
Juice from 1 orange
1 very fresh egg yolk
4 ounces (100 g) natural yogurt
4 1/4 cups (1/2 liter) milk

Put all ingredients except the milk into a bowl and blend. Pour in the milk and mix as desired with a spatula. Drink half of the cocktail in the morning and the other half in the evening. Note: To keep the egg from going bad, keep the prepared nursing cocktail well refrigerated until you consume the second half. You can get all the ingredients in a natural foods store.

Secret Tip: Chicken Broth

There truly is a great power potential in this soup—in which the long cooking time is the key—for it promotes circulation, warms the body from within, and is a good source of energy. Countless physically exhausted new mothers have gotten back onto their feet by eating this soup. So you would do well to prepare (or have someone else prepare) some and keep a supply on hand. It can be frozen in individual portions so that you always have a bowl available whenever you want it.

1 organic soup chicken, 2–3 carrots
approx. 1 1/4 inch (3 cm) fresh ginger
1/4 bunch of celery
1/2 bunch of parsley
2 bay leaves
5–6 coriander seeds
3–4 juniper berries
salt and freshly ground pepper
soy sauce to taste

Wash the chicken and it put into a large pot. Trim and peel the carrots, ginger, and celery and cut into pieces. Rinse the parsley and put it in with the chicken, along with the vegetables. Add enough cold water to completely cover the chicken. Add the spices and bring to a boil. Reduce the heat so that the soup merely simmers. Let cook gently for three to four hours. Strain out the broth. Season with salt and freshly ground pepper and soy sauce. If you like it a little tangier, add a little more grated ginger. *Tip*: The broth will easily keep in the refrigerator for four to five days.

Chicken soup—with or without vegetables— is the perfect power soup after giving birth.

Energy Balls

These nursing balls provide concentrated energy and lots of nutrients. They are easy to make in advance and will last many days in the refrigerator. *Hint*: Ask a friend or your mother (-in-law) to make the energy balls for you.

12 oz (330 g) each wheat, barley, and oats
11 oz (300 g) cooked whole-grain rice
12.5 oz (350 g) cold butter
8¾ oz (250 g) brown sugar (or honey)

Mix the grains together, crumble coarsely, and fry light brown without grease in a coated pan. Mix in a bowl with the rice, butter, and sugar and knead into a dough. Add a little water if necessary. Make ping-pong-ball-sized spheres from the mixture and refrigerate in a plastic bag. Eat two or three balls every day.

Drinks

If you are taking in inadequate fluid this will manifest itself in concentrated urine, digestive problems, headaches—and less mother's milk. Ideally, you should be drinking three quarts of carbohydrate-free mineral water or juices highly diluted with water. You have to drink lots in order to keep milk production on track.

INFO | TEA, COFFEE, ETC.

Most babies tolerate it fine if mom has two cups of coffee or black (or green) tea per day. But if you notice that your child is extremely wound up after nursing, you should examine your coffee or tea consumption.

Alcohol should be strictly off limits for nursing mothers, for the alcohol is transferred in the milk. If you want to toast with a small glass of champagne on some special occasion, you should do so immediately after nursing.

Questions and Answers

1 *Should my baby drink water in addition to mother's milk?*

No, not unless there is some exceptional situation in which additional fluid is required. For example, your baby may need water is she loses a lot of fluid through a high fever or diarrhea. You should speak to your pediatrician first before giving your baby water to drink.

2 *Must I always expect my baby to burp after drinking?*

That depends largely on your baby's sucking behavior. If the baby is an eager, hasty drinker that sucks in lots of air, you definitely should provide him with an opportunity to get rid of the air. Place a cotton diaper or similar cloth over your shoulder. Hold the baby upright in your arms so that the head lies on your shoulder, but don't drape the baby over your shoulder. Gently pat between the baby's shoulder blades with the flat of your hand or stroke the baby's back; it won't take long for the burp to appear. Some babies have no problems with swallowed air, for they drink slowly and deliberately. Simply experiment whether your baby will go to sleep without burping after eating.

3 *What's the story on contaminants in mother's milk?*

A German study found that the high residues of chlorinated hydrocarbon such as DDT, HCH, HCB, and PCB previously noted in mother's milk have been declining noticeably since the mid-1980s. Thus, the national breastfeeding commission in Germany recommends that children be breastfed exclusively until solid food is introduced (that is, for six months). It sees no health risk to the infant if breastfeeding continues further.

It's important that you go on no diets while you are nursing. Since environmental contaminants are stored primarily in fatty tissues, with a diet these would exist in larger quantities in the mother's circulatory system and be transferred with the mother's milk. Here are some other foods that you should avoid as a nursing mother because of their possible contaminants: liver, kidney, wild game (from older animals), long-lived predatory fish such as tuna and shark, plus grilled and smoked products. A more recent study in London (in 1999) found 350 contaminants in mother's milk. Despite these two studies, breastfeeding is still recommended for its immunological benefits, the nutrient benefits, and the mother–baby bonding.

4 *How can I increase my milk production?*

Since your body produces mother's milk on demand, you can increase the milk quantity by nursing your baby more frequently (about every two hours—measured from the start of one feeding to the start of the next one). You can increase production further by increasing your fluid intake to around three quarts (around three liters) a day. You can also stimulate milk production by changing breasts several times during a feeding. Usually more milk is required when your child is going through a growth spurt and temporarily needs more nutrients. But it also frequently happens that your child does not suck long enough or hard enough to stimulate milk production adequately. In this case, it may make sense to pump extra mother's milk for a transitional period.

5 *What's the best way to store my pumped milk?*

Refrigerate expressed milk as soon as you can. If that's not possible, breast milk will stay fresh at room temperature (away from heat sources) for as long as six hours. Pumped mother's milk will keep fresh in a clean bottle in the refrigerator for two days, or up to six months if frozen in a freezer maintaining a 0°F (−18°C) temperature. It's best to freeze the milk in individual portions (e.g., in milk bottles or boiled ice cube trays that you can cover with a lid). Once the milk is frozen, you can repack the cubes in freezer bags and return them to the freezer. Then you can take out just the quantity you need and thaw the cubes. Make sure the cubes are small enough to fit through the neck of the baby bottle. You can also freeze the milk directly inside baby bottles. Before freezing, always let the milk cool down uncovered inside the refrigerator. Be sure to always thaw milk slowly and gently; never boil it. Milk can be warmed by running the bottle of frozen milk under lukewarm tap water. Never thaw or heat milk in the microwave because that destroys important ingredients. Once milk has been warmed, do not freeze it again.

6 *Which nursing pads are better—ones made from wool, silk, or the practical disposable ones?*

The gentlest ones for the nipples surely are the ones made from wool or silk because they let air pass through. The natural material can soak up lots of moisture and pass it on to the outside. Sheep's wool can soak up about 40 percent of its weight in moisture; cotton, on the other hand, only about 6 percent. Disposable pads can't match this 40-percent mark, but they have a built-in protective barrier against possible leakage. Wool inserts have another advantage because they naturally contain lanolin, which not only keeps the nipple supple but also kills bacteria. Some women may be allergic to wool.

7 *Which foods should I avoid while breastfeeding?*

It's best to try out different foods in succession. Nobody can predict what may cause gas in your baby. So you needn't avoid onions and similar foods from now on and throughout the entire nursing time. Eat a variety of healthy foods, as you hopefully did while you were pregnant. Experience has shown that infants who react to the mother's foods are most commonly bothered by gassy vegetables such as cabbage, broccoli, legumes, onions, garlic, stone fruits, and pears. Sometimes the cause may also be cow's milk that the mother has drunk.

The Milk Formula Alternative

Today, people who don't nurse are in a much better situation than a couple of decades ago. The formulas available in the stores are extremely faithful "reproductions" of mother's milk. Still, even though they are a good substitute for it, they will never achieve the

uniqueness and versatility of mother's milk. With formulas there is a basic difference between infant and follow-up formulas, and the choice depends on the baby's age. Your baby will scarcely miss a thing as long as the bottles are filled with lots of love and devotion . . .

The Right Infant Formula

When you look at the infant formula shelves in a well-stocked drug store, super-market, or pharmacy for the first time, you may feel overwhelmed by the quantity of products. It's not just the number of manufacturers that produce this variety but also the number of different types of formulas that are divided into various age groups, needs, and health problems. No wonder you feel the agony of deciding. To help you find your way through the jungle of milk formulas and settle on the right one for your baby, here's an overview of the distinctions among the individual types of milk.

Age-oriented

The first criterion in buying infant for-mula should be that the selected milk type corresponds to the baby's age. You can get your bearings on the two basic groups of infant startup formulas and follow-up milk: Only the initial infant formulas are for the exclusive feeding of an infant with milk formula from birth through the introduction of solid food. Follow-up for-mulas are not suitable as sole food sources for babies, for they don't meet the little one's entire nutritional requirements. They are formulated in such a way that they are to be given only in parallel with solid food.

The Basis: Cow's Milk

Most infant formulas are manufactured from the basic food cow's milk, to which vitamins and minerals are added. The goal of all these is to approach the contents and quality of mother's milk. The greatest dif-ference between cow's milk and mother's milk is in the quantity and composition of the protein: The protein content of cow's milk is so high that it will harm the baby if it is fed in pure form. Therefore, it is reduced for infant formula and adjusted to match mother's milk protein (60 per-cent lactalbumin, 40 percent casein; see page 183), which is much more digestible for babies.

Quality Control

Infant formula is subject to strict legal guidelines that every manufacturer must observe. The contents and possible conta-minants are continually checked. That way your baby gets the energy and nutrients he needs for healthy growth.

What Else Is in There

DHA (docosahexaenoic acid) and ARA (arachidonic acid) are fatty acids found in the fat of breast milk. DHA is found in high concentration in the brain and eye of the developing fetus, particularly in the third trimester. These substances are supplemented in formula because of their possible role in promoting brain development.

Nucleotides (which are the building blocks of genetic material) are also supple-mented in infant formula to bolster the immune system.

201

Iron is also added to infant formulas. Iron is necessary for the production of red blood cells. The American Academy of Pediatrics recommends iron-fortified formula for all infants who are not breastfed.

What Types of Formulas Are Out There?

Probiotic formulas have recently become available in the United States. These formulas add to the milk a healthy bacterium, *Bifidobacterium lactis*, which is found in the digestive system of breast-fed infants. Research has shown that probiotics can reduce the incidence of viral diarrhea, lower the risk of food allergy, and improve infant colic. Some manufacturers offer a USDA-certified organic formula.

➤ Follow-up formulas are designed for infants between nine and twenty-four months who are already eating solid foods. The child's healthcare provider will be able to advise you about whether a formula of this type is necessary. Regular cow's milk is not recommended before one year of age. Formulas are sold in ready to feed, liquid concentrate or powder form. The various forms are equivalent in nutritional value but vary in terms of cost and convenience.

➤ The ready-to-pour formulas are the easiest, as the liquid formula must only be poured into a bottle of your choice to be ready for use. Any formula left in the container needs to be stored properly.

➤ Concentrated liquid formulas are less expensive than the ready-to-pour ones but a little more time-consuming to prepare, as the concentrated liquid is diluted with equal parts of water to make the finished formula.

➤ Powdered formula is the least expensive option, but it is the most time-consuming and messiest to prepare. It is reconstituted by adding a specified amount of water. Besides the reduced cost, another advantage of powder formula is that it doesn't need to be refrigerated until it's mixed.

Your baby needs nothing but milk until the end of the sixth month.

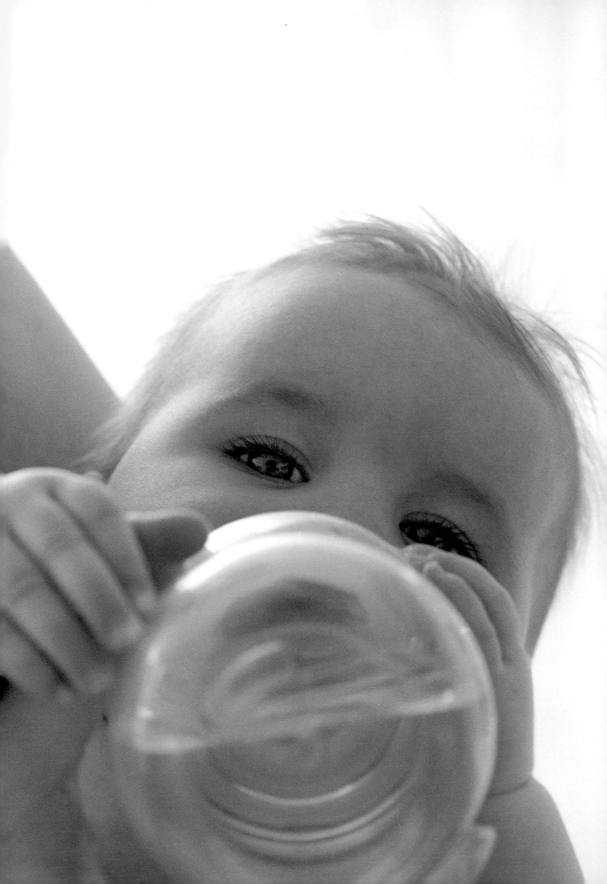

Special Infant Formulas

In addition to the normal infant formulas, there are special ones for children with allergies or food incompatibilities and metabolic disorders.

Hypoallergenic Formulas for Babies at Risk for Allergies

Exclusive breastfeeding for six months is ideal for children at risk for allergies, that is, children with one or both parents and/or siblings who have allergies. This gives the child the best possibility of avoiding or at least minimizing allergies. If this is not possible, it is recommended that these babies be fed with what's known as hypoallergenic formula. With this formula, the protein in the cow's milk is broken down into such small protein building blocks that the baby's body doesn't easily recognize it as foreign protein. Thus, this infant formula is also said to be low in antigens. Depending on the manufacturer, the milk protein is broken down into a number of component parts so that the formulas are distinguished by degree of hydrolysis. The reduced content of potentially allergenic materials (antigens) of these formulas is no sure protection against an allergy to milk protein, however. In relevant studies, only a reduced tendency was detectable in babies at risk.

Milk Formulas for Special Situations

Despite the best planning, it frequently happens that some babies can't tolerate regular or hypoallergenic formula and develop allergies. In these cases, the following milk formulas usually help.

For Babies with an Allergy to Cow's Milk

These products are used when babies already have an allergy or cannot digest cow's milk (see also, box on page 206). They are only for special medical conditions and should thus be fed under the regular supervision of a pediatrician. In these special formulas, the cow's milk protein is split even further than with the hypoallergenic formulas so it is not recognized by the body as an allergen. Unfortunately, these products taste a little more bitter than hypoallergenic milk—and yet babies generally get used to them.

Soy-based Formulas

Soy formula contains a different protein (soy) and a different sugar (glucose or sucrose) than milk-based formula. Sometimes a soy-based formula is used to treat intolerance of cow's milk; in comparison

INFO | A MATTER OF TASTE

When the protein in milk such as hypoallergenic or special formulas is broken down very fine, the taste suffers because they always taste slightly bitter. It is important that you not let your baby first try any good-tasting alternatives. That's the only way the baby will drink the bitter milk without a fuss. You should never sweeten the formula.

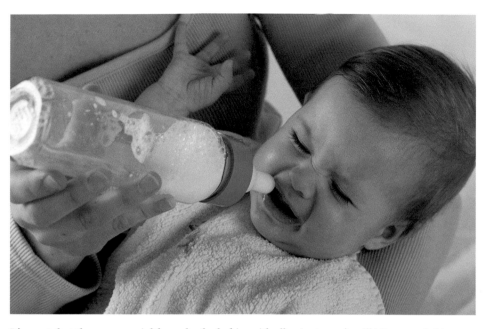

It's great that there are special formulas for babies with allergies to cow's milk! But most babies are quick to catch on to the fact that this milk doesn't taste as sweet as regular milk.

to products with broken-down protein, they are not only tastier, but also significantly more economical. But it's important to know that there is what's known as a cross allergenicity. This means that the protein from cow's milk and soymilk are so similar that children who can't tolerate cow's milk have a 25 percent risk of an allergic reaction to the soy protein. But soymilk is absolutely unavoidable with disorders of milk metabolism and lactose digestion.

It is important to note that in contrast to hypoallergenic formula, soy formulas are not useful in preventing allergies. Additionally, long running studies show that adults who were fed with soy formula as infants display an increased tendency toward allergies.

Milk from Other Mammals
By itself it's a clever idea to choose milk from some other animal, such as goats, sheep, and horses, if cow's milk is out of the question. However, these too are usually unsuited to babies with allergies because their composition is still very different from mother's milk. Because they are similar to cow's milk, they are just as indigestible for babies who are allergic to cow's milk—not to mention the problems in getting these other types of milk.

Alternative Milk Types
We frequently read that infants can be fed using other types of milk—such as rice, almond, or fresh corn—however, nutritionists warn that these types of milk are totally inappropriate for infants as an

205

INFO There are many different formulas available for infants that have trouble digesting standard formulas. For instance:

➤ Lactose intolerance
➤ Milk allergy
➤ Fussiness or gas
➤ Frequent spit-up

Consult your pediatrician for recommendations specifically geared for your baby.

exclusive food source. Depending on the composition, there is usually too little protein, and/or the child's body cannot effectively utilize that type of protein. There is also a lower vitamin and mineral content, so it's no surprise that infants who are fed exclusively with these substitutes suffer from aggravated growth disorders.

All About Bottles

Bottles, nipples, formula, sterilizer . . . Is that it, or is there something more? If you are to have everything ready when you come home with the baby, you should now think about what you need as you get ready to go out shopping.

The Bottle

Glass or plastic—that is the question! For each of the bottle types, there is a devoted fan club with convincing arguments.
➤ Glass: The contents remain warm longer, the bottle is more esthetically pleasing, and it remains clean and clear even after many washings. Unfortunately, glass is heavier and breakable. As a result, the infant won't have the strength to crumple the bottle or heave it out of the bed. Realistically, there is a greater danger of breakage in preparing the formula or washing the bottle.
➤ Plastic: This material is practically indestructible, but with time it also looks less appealing. Even though plastic bottles can be washed as thoroughly and germ-free as glass ones, at some point they become cloudy and look messy. That is more of a visual problem, not a hygienic one. Plastic bottles have one great feature: They are light so that babies can hold them unaided later on and bring them to their mouth. There has, however, been some recent concern about PCBs in plastic. As for price, neither type of bottle has an advantage, for they both cost about the same.

The Nipple

Now for the next question: latex or silicone? There are also two basic types of nipples.
➤ Latex nipples are made from pure rubber and are thus natural products. In dealing with babies, this is very welcome, except in those cases where an allergy to latex may be present. But if you choose rubber nipples, you accept the fact that as time goes by they change, become unsightly, and start to get sticky. So rubber nipples should be replaced every four weeks. Additionally, many children are allergic to rubber, and others dislike the typical rubber smell.

➤ Silicone nipples are made from synthetic material and last longer. But they are easy to bite through and thus are less suited to older children (with more teeth). Once a silicone nipple develops cracks, it must be discarded.

Neither type has an advantage with respect to price. And there is no difference in cleaning—both can be kept equally clean.

Nipple Size

Since the baby's mouth is growing, the nipple must grow along with it. Stick to the manufacturer's recommendations. Over time, nipples that are too small can lead to a deformity in the roof of the mouth. The same applies to the size and number of the holes that regulate the flow of milk, or semi-solid food. If the holes in the nipple are too small, the child will tire too quickly while drinking and may fall asleep. If the milk flows out of the bottle too quickly because the holes are too large, the baby can easily swallow wrong and get too much air into the stomach, possibly getting hiccups. For expressed breast milk and ready-to-drink formula, you need a nipple with fairly small holes. For formula mixed from powder or breastmilk that is being fortified with powder (on your doctor's recommendation), a nipple with larger holes is recommended. Nipples for milk being thickened with rice cereal have even larger holes. You should watch your baby while drinking from the bottle for clues as to which nipple should use. If she is gagging, the nipple hole may be too big, which allows too much milk to enter the mouth at a time. If she is straining and not emptying

Plastic bottles have the great advantage of being much harder to break.

the bottle readily, you can assume the nipple hole is too small. Follow her cues and you will soon learn which nipple is correct.

207

Nipple Shape

For a long time, the recommendation was for nipples with an angular, flat underside and an opening on top near the roof of the mouth. This nipple shape doesn't encourage the broadening of the roof of the mouth. One very rare and yet entirely possible long-term side effect is the so-called "Gothic hard palate," which is high and pointed rather than growing rounded and broad. As a result, nipple experts today recommend nipples that are uniformly round and shaped like a tube. They don't stick so far into the mouth. With each swallow, the nipple exerts pressure on the roof of the mouth and encourages it to grow broader. A positive side effect is that later on there will be more room for teeth.

Preparation

In preparing infant formula there are a few rules to observe.

1. Precise Dosage

When you prepare infant formula, always go strictly by the dosage instructions on the packaging. Don't get the idea that you can mix up some extra-tasty milk for your baby by adding another spoonful of powder. If the milk formula is mixed improperly, your baby gets too much protein and fat, and too little water. The result could be overeating, constipation, or diarrhea.

2. Right Temperature

The ideal temperature for prepared infant formula is between 95 and 99°F (35 and 37°C). Check it by sprinkling a couple of drops on the inside of your wrist. The temperature must feel pleasant. You must never serve the milk too hot. Important: As an adult, never put the nipple into your mouth or lick it. That would transfer (cavity-causing) bacteria and/or fungus from your mouth to the baby.

3. Prepare as Fresh as Possible

Prepared milk should be left out at room temperature for no longer than four hours; if it stays out any longer, it should not be used. A particularly bad practice is keeping infant milk warm in a bottle warmer for a fairly long time; it allows bacteria, fungi, and other organisms to multiply very quickly. That will do more harm than good to the formula—and thus to your child.

> **TIP | QUICK BOTTLE**
>
> Anyone who has prepared a bottle for a baby crying from hunger knows unnerving the crying can be. To avoid the problem, try this: Boil a larger quantity of hot water in the morning and keep two-thirds of it warm in an insulated thermos bottle that's used only for the baby. You can use this hot water all day long and night. Cool the remaining water in a clean container. That way you have two sources of water at the right temperature and you can quickly get the baby's bottle ready by mixing them.

Amount of Fluid Intake

For the precise amount of fluid intake for your baby, you should follow the directions on the package. It contains charts that list precisely how much milk your child should drink in the appropriate age group. Your baby will also show you if the amount of fluid intake is right. Full babies appear happy and develop well. One indication can be your baby's weight gain (see the box on page 210). Now, most babies lose weight in the first few days after birth, but once the birth weight is reached again around the second week, it increases rapidly, as the chart on page 210 shows: by the fifth month, most babies have doubled their birth weight, and they have quadrupled it by the end of the first year.

Trust Your Instincts!

You shouldn't place too much emphasis on the statistics. You know your baby best and should trust your instincts: Is your baby feeling fine? Is your baby's skin rosy and smooth? Can you see his muscles? Are the cheeks round? Does he put on baby fat in the traditional places such as the arms and thighs? Is he usually in a good mood and even-tempered? Then small variations from the weight chart are acceptable. Spare your baby the stress of weighing every day. A weight check every two to four weeks is completely adequate.

Cleaning Bottles and Nipples

Hygiene is the top requirement! Since infants are not yet used to germs and their immune systems is still in the practice stage, nipples and bottles must be thoroughly cleaned and sterilized after every usage. Ideally, you will maintain this procedure until your baby is about six months old. Thereafter, you merely need to wash the nipple and bottle after every use and sterilize once a week—unless the baby is sick.

In cleaning, you should thoroughly wash everything in hot water with dishwashing detergent. Bottle brushes and special nipple brushes help reach into the toughest corners (you can get these in a drugstore or supermarket). After washing, all bottle parts (bottle, nipple, cover, and threaded ring) must be rinsed with clean water and sterilized as needed.

Always take time to check the temperature of the bottle. The sensitive skin on the inside of your arm is good for this purpose.

INFO | BABY'S WEIGHT

Here is the average weight gain for babies in the first year of life:

Age/ Month	Increase/ Day	Increase/ Week
➤ 1–3	1.02 oz (29 g)	7.1 oz 203 g
➤ 4–6	0.71 oz (20 g)	5 oz (140 g)
➤ 7–9	0.53 oz (15 g)	3.7 oz (105 g)
➤ 10–12	0.42 oz (12 g)	3 oz (84 g)

Sterilizing Bottles and Accessories

Put all the parts of the bottle (bottle, nipple, and tops, and if necessary, the pacifier) into a pot of boiling water and let them bubble and boil for five minutes. That way you can be sure that all germs and bacteria have been killed. Then let the individual pieces dry on a fresh dish towel. Alternatively, you can use a handy sterilizing device (a vaporizer, not to be confused with the device used when the child has a cold or congestion, available at baby shops), which works with steam.

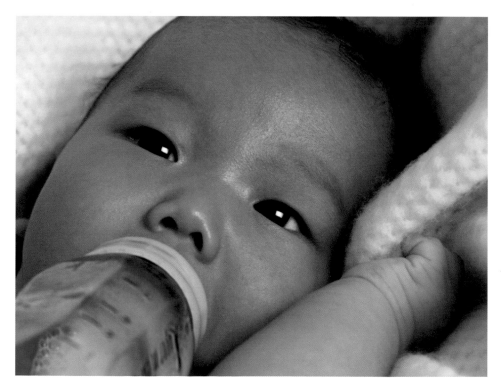

Even when your baby is fed with a bottle, drinking always means taking in energy and attention. Take time and enjoy these intimate moments with your baby.

Questions and Answers

1 *Is it bad for me to give my baby commercial formula from time to time even though I am nursing?*

Bad is not the right term. The fact is that if you have a baby who's at risk for allergies, you should try to breastfeed exclusively because that reduces tremendously the baby's risk of suffering from an allergy. As long as milk from the bottle is the exception, the allergy protection gained from the mother's milk is still in force. Giving your baby both breastmilk and infant formula can become necessary for medical reasons, if the milk quantity fails to increase, or if a baby doesn't take in enough over a fairly long period of frequent breastfeedings. Reasons associated with the mother may be that she has to get back to work and the pumped milk is not sufficient by itself. But perhaps it's just that the father is also taking charge of the feeding so that the Mom can sleep through the night and rest up. You need to be aware that if you frequently give your baby a bottle, he could get used to the easier sucking from the bottle and refuse the breast.

2 *How long can a commercially mixed infant formula be kept in the bottle?*

If possible, you should prepare the bottle only once your baby expresses hunger, and then immediately feed the child. It's also acceptable to keep the formula warm for up to fifteen minutes—but no longer. The lukewarm baby formula is a perfect culture medium for bacteria, which can double within twenty minutes. This danger also exists when commercially mixed bottle formula is kept in the refrigerator. Thus, always immediately discard leftovers (don't freeze them!) and wash the bottle.

3 *I would like to make my own infant formula. How is it done?*

Nutritional scientists advise against preparing infant milk at home. For homemade milk can almost never achieve the safety and nutritional quality of commercial infant formula. There would always be a danger that your baby would lack essential vitamins, nutrients, and minerals. There are also some practically unavoidable hygienic problems (see also page 208).

4 *Is it all right to give my eight-month old baby yogurt?*

Even though there are yogurt products for children seven months and older, you would do better to leave them on the shelves. Nutritional scientists advise against giving other milk products besides mother's milk or infant formula in the first year of life. They reason that if exposed to other milk products, a child could absorb proteins that may predispose him or her to certain allergies. Another negative is the high sugar content of many products. Don't be misled by the spiel "sweetened only with natural fruit juices." This involves quickly digested fruit sugar, which should still be considered a sweet.

5 *Why is it dangerous if my baby falls asleep on the bottle?*

When children continually suckle on a baby bottle or other drinking bottle, fluid is continually inside the mouth. The saliva thus becomes diluted and can no longer protect the teeth. In addition, drinks containing sugar and acids such as fruit juice and milk foster the development of bacteria that are harmful to the teeth, or they even attack the enamel directly.

6 *We are taking a vacation trip by plane with our baby. What's the best way for me to prepare infant formula on vacation?*

The drinking water in many vacation countries can be contaminated, so you should use nothing but non-carbonated bottled mineral water in preparing the bottle.

7 *How long will my baby need to be fed during the night?*

Starting at the end of the sixth month of life, a baby is able to make it through the night without a feeding. Now the baby should be able to sleep around eleven hours at a stretch without eating. Nothing changes with respect to the total number of feedings, for the night feedings should be given during the day.

8 *Is it true that many people around the world can't tolerate cow's milk?*

It's true. Many Asian, some northern European (Finns) and many African peoples can't consume cow's milk because they lack the lactase enzyme, which breaks down milk sugar. So it goes to the intestine and ferments. As a result, they get diarrhea, colic, and gas. The amazing thing, though, is not that most people lack this enzyme but rather that some have it! Almost all adult mammals, including people, are intolerant of cow's milk. Most northern and central Europeans are the exception. One possible explanation is that people who can digest milk well may be descended from livestock breeders who were able to consume the milk of their animals during times of need. However, most babies of every ethnicity are able to drink cow's milk because lactase deficiency is a condition that develops over time, starting after the toddler years. So even if you cannot tolerate cow's milk, your baby almost certainly can.

The First Baby Food

Things have progressed so far by the sixth month that your baby no longer wants or needs only milk. It's time for baby food. This is exciting for many reasons. For one, every beginning is messy. Your baby now must learn step by step to guide the solid food from the lips, over the tongue, rearward into the throat, and then swallow it. Even if your baby isn't totally enthused by the first baby food, it won't take long to develop a taste for it and then grab for the spoon . . .

Step by Step to Supplementary Food

The baby is a half-year old, and for some time everything has been running like clockwork. Mother and child have found a comfortable rhythm for everyone, nights are once again for sleeping, and the baby is developing beautifully thanks to the (mother's) milk. In short, everyone is happy. Then all of a sudden you have to start supplementary feeding. Why do we have to upset the apple cart right now, when everything is going well?

gradually declines and is replaced by conscious chewing and sucking motions. This marks another milestone in your baby's development. Chewing also means that your baby can taste, that she subsequently swallows the food, and that she has learned to give signals when she has eaten enough. Very soon your baby will take up the spoon for the first time. Then the baby will feel big and know that she's one of the family, among the big people.

New Food for a New Stage of Life

Never again will your baby grow at such a fast pace—the birth weight has at least doubled. Starting at six months, babies need lots more energy and some vitally essential nutrients such as iron. In short, the baby's nutritional requirements change—and milk is no longer adequate by itself. And there's another factor: the inborn sucking and swallowing reflex

How Does the Changeover to Supplementary Food Take Place?

Solid feedings should begin when baby's ready, somewhere between the ages of four and six months. Baby's first solid food is often rice cereal—if you are beginning solid foods before the age of six months, rice cereal is all that is recommended. Normally, supplementary food is introduced in three steps. First, the

INFO | WHAT BABIES NEED EVERY DAY

	Age 0 through 3 Months		Age 4 through 12 Months	
	Male	Female	Male	Female
➤ Energy	500 Kcal	450 Kcal	700 Kcal	700 Kcal
➤ Protein	0.33 oz	0.30 oz	0.93 oz	0 .93 oz
	(9.4 g)	(8.4 g)	(26.3 g)	(26.3 g)
➤ Fat	0.93 oz	0.84 oz	1.1 oz	1.1 oz
	(26.4 g)	(23.8 g)	(31.1 g)	(31.1 g)
➤ Carbohydrate	1.99 oz	1.78 oz	2.78 oz	2.78 oz
	(56.3 g)	(50.6 g)	(78.8 g)	(78.8 g)

midday milk meal is replaced. You can begin with very finely pureed carrots, which have a slightly sweet taste and are thus readily accepted by most babies. Once the pure carrot mash evolves into a vegetable-potato-meat mash, it's time to introduce the evening milk and cereal mash, which is followed after a certain time by the cereal-fruit mash that is given at midday.

Step 1: Replacing the First Daily Meal (Midday Baby Food)

The main goal is to make it palatable so your baby will willingly exchange the familiar, beloved breast or bottle for baby food. The problem is that the baby is not familiar with the baby food, and at first

INFO | ALLERGIC TO CARROTS?

For decades babies have eaten carrots in the change to solid food because carrots were considered less allergenic and were known to taste good to babies. Then the frightful news that carrots are responsible for the outbreak of allergies came a few years ago! As a result, a new beginning vegetable was sought and found in zucchini, parsnips, and squash. In the meantime, the all-clear was sounded: Present scientific studies demonstrate no connection between carrots and increased incidence of allergies.

the baby food doesn't make the baby feel full. Of course, there are always some babies who wean themselves quite quickly. However, they truly are the exceptions. Solid food should be introduced slowly so that the child's digestive system—and the breast in the case of nursing mothers—can gradually get used to the changeover.

Here's How It Works

➤ Experience shows that it's best to first replace the midday milk feeding with baby food. Why? It's easy to organize: Perhaps you are preparing something to eat at midday and can also get the baby food ready. Also, there is plenty of time before going to bed to observe how your baby digests the baby food. Specifically, if your baby reacts with vomiting or gas, you have more energy and patience at midday to care for your baby.

➤ Make it easy for the baby to change from the soft nipple on the breast or bottle to the spoon by using a soft, flexible plastic spoon. It's best if the spoon is also flat and rounded.

➤ Start slowly! Begin with one spoonful of rice cereal mixed with liquid (either water or milk) to achieve a smooth consistency. You can work up to three or four spoonfuls within the first four to seven days. Once the baby has eaten this little amount of baby food, you should offer the customary milk (breastfeeding or bottle) so the baby can drink until she feels full.

➤ When things are going well with the baby food, you can increase the portions a little every day. In the first days, the quantity is measured in spoonfuls, but after a week or two, your little one may sometimes

Babies don't need much variety of ingredients or many spices: What they need is good quality and the full flavor of the ingredients.

eat a whole jar (6.7 oz/190 g). But it may also take your baby four weeks before taking in around 7 oz (200 g). It is important to let your baby proceed at her own pace.

Other Important Considerations

If you begin feeding as described at the left, the switch to solid food surely will present no problems for your baby. You should also observe the following points so that the child's digestive tract can gradually get used to the new food.

➤ After your baby masters rice cereal, you can begin to introduce one type of vegetable (e.g., carrots, parsnips, or squash) at a time. That way the child's intestine has time to get used to the vegetable slowly, and you can tell right away if your baby is allergic to it. After a week or two, you can combine a second food with the first one. Potatoes work well. If they are tolerated, you can add some meat after another two weeks (a total of four weeks after the initial feeding).

➤ Offer the first spoonful only when your baby already has half a meal from breast or bottle in her stomach. Then she is partially full and a little more patient with the new situation.

➤ You can place the baby on your lap to feed her. But it's even easier if you strap the child into the high chair, swing or car seat and place her next to you on the table or floor so that you can feed her comfortably. Then you have both hands free if something spills at the beginning.

➤ It makes good sense to put a bib onto your baby—and even more sense to put

217

a hand towel over the baby's legs. You will soon see why . . .

➤ It takes time to do something well! Give yourself, but especially your baby, some time. You have to get used to feeding, and your baby has to get used to the spoon. Because for the baby it's not just the spoon and the baby food that's new, but also the fact that the food has to be moved rearward in the mouth with the tongue and consciously swallowed. Usually the combination of spoon, baby food, tongue, Mom, and child settles in after a few days.

What's Next?

Most babies get used to the baby food after around two weeks. Then you can completely replace the midday meal. This means that you offer no milk before or after the meal of baby food—provided that your baby has eaten about the equivalent of one jar (6.7 oz/190 g).

The best ingredients, cooked with love and served finely blended—that's the way babies like their food!

A Little Swallow for Dessert?

After a complete meal, many mothers also offer their breast—as dessert, so to speak. Nutritionally and physiologically that shouldn't happen, for the baby has taken in enough energy in an adequate meal. The "swallow afterwards" also feeds the baby's need to suck. Of course that is also good— but sooner or later there will be a complete transition to solid food and you are only putting it off with the milk dessert.

Which Vegetable for the Mash?

Basically, all types of vegetables that are rich in nutrients, such as carrots, fennel, parsnips, squash, zucchini, and spinach, are good choices. If your baby likes one of these varieties particularly well, you can stick with it for a while with no problem. It is not necessary to provide variety on the plate every day. On the contrary, in the first few weeks, you should remain true to one vegetable, for the switch from type to

INFO | **PARSNIPS**

Parsnips are a little like carrots in shape, but they are more pointed. On the outside they are yellowish or yellowish-brown; inside they are white to yellow, with very crisp flesh. Their nutritional value is greater than that of carrots and even rutabagas. Parsnips are flavorful, pleasantly tangy, and smell a little like a mixture of carrots and parsley. Since they are easily digested, they are a good choice for infant food.

TIP | **THE MIDDAY BABY FOOD**

Here's a recipe you can use if you want to make baby food yourself:

3/4–1 oz (20–30 g) lean organic meat
3.5 oz (100 g) fresh organic vegetables
1 3/4 oz (50 g) organic potatoes
3 tablespoons fruit puree or freshly squeezed fruit juice (e.g., orange juice)
1 tablespoon oil or 1/2 tablespoon butter

Dice the meat and steam it in a little water until tender. Remove and puree. Wash the vegetables and potatoes, peel or trim them, cube them small, and also steam them soft in a little water. Mash them and mix the meat, vegetables, and potatoes. Stir in the juice and oil. As desired, add a little water to make a creamy mash.

type raises the risk that the baby will develop an allergy. There is safety in the familiar.

Which Types of Meat Are Best?

One good choice is a type of lean, protein-rich and easily digestible poultry. But red meats such as beef and lamb should always be part of the menu because they contain the most iron. At first, stick to one type of meat also. If you prepare the vegetable-meat recipe above at home, you should have the person in the meat department run the meat through the finest plate on the grinder to facilitate making the puree. Then process the meat immediately after purchase. If the meat you cut up is too coarse for your baby—many babies don't like it—you can always fall back on meat preparations in a jar. They are available in various types. The advantage is that you can take out the required small amount with a clean spoon and keep the rest cool and tightly closed for a day or two.

Since the amounts that your baby will eat at first are small, it's worthwhile to increase the ingredients for the adjacent recipe and cook several portions at once. If you divide the baby food into individual portions after cooling and freeze them, you can quickly (but gently) thaw a jar on days when you are pressed for time—and your baby can enjoy the home-cooked meal.

The Exception: Wild Game Is Taboo

Wild game should not be on the menu as the only type of meat, for it may contain many residues. Sausages are also inappropriate for the first year of life, for they contain lots of salt and spices, phosphates (which are suspected of causing hyperactivity), and fat.

Iron: Why It's So Important for Babies

The mineral iron is vitally important for the oxygen-carrying blood pigment hemoglobin, and thus indirectly for the oxygen supply to the cells. So if you want to supply your baby with lots of iron (e.g., in the case of an iron deficiency), you should choose

INFO | MEAT: IS IT NECESSARY?

Meat is unquestionably necessary. Without meat, babies grow big and strong, but things go a little easier for the baby with meat. There are at least two reasons for feeding babies meat:

➤ **Iron:** This is the only critical nutrient in a vegetarian diet. The availability of iron from plant foods is 2 to 5 percent lower than with meat. This means that the body can't make much use of the iron from plant foods. But if meat is present in a meal, iron absorption from plant foods also improves. Even milk and eggs are far behind meat with respect to iron content. In addition, the iron of both foods is less usable.

➤ **Protein content:** The protein content varies from animal to animal, but basically all types offer a valuable amount of usable protein. Animal protein has the greatest biological value. This means that it most closely approaches the protein in the human body in the composition of individual building blocks (the amino acids).

iron-rich vegetables (such as spinach, carrots, fennel, Jerusalem artichokes, and golden beets) and grains (such as millet and oats). Grains also come in convenient flake form (with no added sugar, in natural food stores or well-stocked supermarkets).

A teaspoon of these enriches fruit and milk mashes, and they can also be added to a meat mash.

Vitamin C—a Real "Iron Accelerator"

The human body needs the presence of vitamin C to optimize the absorption of iron from grains. So put one or two tablespoons of orange juice (preferably freshly squeezed) into every vegetable mash. And vitamin C also aids in iron absorption in a vegetable-meat mash. Most infant cereals are iron-fortified. Parents should read labels to avoid giving too much iron to baby! On a practical note, the vitamin C does not necessarily need to be taken in along with the grain. All you have to do is offer your baby a few spoonfuls of fruit juice containing vitamin C (such as apple juice) as a dessert.

Fruit: What's Best for Babies?

Ideal types of fruit to start with are apples and pears. They provide quite a lot of vitamin C and generally are easily digested if steamed in advance. Peel a few apples and pears and remove the seeds; cut the fruits into small pieces and steam until soft in a little water (a few tablespoons is adequate). Then mash finely along with the liquid used in steaming, because of the water-soluble vitamins. This fruit mash can be fed in portions during the day: as a between-meals snack with a spoonful of grain cereal, as a vitamin C dessert at the midday meal, and as a fruit additive to the milk-cereal mash in the evening. In an airtight jar or plastic container it will keep two or three days in the refrigerator.

Gentle and in Tune with Nature

As soon as your baby is used to solid food, you can get more creative in choosing fruits. But you should always choose native fruits that are currently in season. In the winter, apples, pears, and bananas are fine, but in the summer you can use the whole array: Most babies love apricots, nectarines, peaches, blueberries, plums, and raspberries—all in slightly steamed and pureed form. Citrus fruits are not suited for a pure fruit mash; the ones like kiwis have a high acid content and can lead to a sore bottom. Also avoid strawberries, for they often cause allergies.

Fat: Which Fat and How Much Does a Baby Need?

Babies need a fairly large quantity of fat in proportion to their size. It's no wonder, for fat is the primary energy supply, and this is just the energy that babies need for growing. In the first six months of life, babies thus take in up to 50 percent of their total energy in the form of fat—from mother's milk or infant formula. The advantage of fat is obvious: It provides lots of energy rolled up in a small amount of food. Babies reach the point where the percentage of fat in their overall energy usage should fall below the 30-percent mark only after about age two. These figures make it clear how important fats are in the growth of babies. But which fats are best for baby's nutrition?

Good and Bad Fats

Saturated fats, such as coconut and palm seed oils, are not appropriate for babies because they are hard to digest. Pure, cold

TIP | FRUIT FROM A JAR

There is a huge variety of fruit purees in jars. But does pureed fruit from a jar really make sense? Yes, sometimes there simply are no ripe pears or bananas in the stores, and babies really enjoy them. Or if you are on the road with the baby, there is an advantage in having tightly closed jars of fruit that will keep. In addition, the organic quality of the pureed fruits is guaranteed, which is not always the case with fruits from the supermarket.

pressed oils such as rapeseed, sunflower, and corn germ oil are, however, highly recommended for baby's nutrition. Don't buy any plant, table, or salad oils. These usually are a mixture of various types of oil; from a nutritional and physiological standpoint, they are almost always of lesser quality. Butter, preferably made from sour cream, is just as suitable. It is

Fruit compote is very versatile: It gives baby food a vitamin C boost and also tastes good by itself.

generally easy to digest, and it also adds to the flavor of many baby foods. *Tip:* Add both to your baby's menu. Use a good piece of butter in the vegetable-potato-meat mash, for example, and a teaspoon of oil in the evening mash.

Just Perfect

If you prepare the baby mash as directed on page 219, it is nutritionally balanced and complete. No salt, pepper, or other spices or herbs are necessary to enhance the taste. Industrially manufactured products, on the other hand, may lose taste in processing, so manufacturers add salt. Homemade baby food doesn't need that, for it is much more flavorful. Even if your mash seems dull to you, you can't compare your baby's taste perceptions to your own. Your baby is open to all nuances of taste, for she has not yet found out about salt, taste enhancers, and all the rest.

Every start is messy, but mastery requires practice.

Step 2: Replacing the Second Meal (Evening Baby Food)

Next the evening breastfeeding is replaced by an evening meal. This consists of a milk-cereal mash, which will supply your baby with adequate amounts of vitally important protein, carbohydrates, and vitamins.

Which Milk for the Baby?

"Is it OK to give my baby cow's milk before his first birthday? This question is continually on the mind of mothers, and rightly so. Cow's milk critics like to emphasize that nature designed cow's milk for calves, not for human babies. They believe that every mammal should drink milk from its species. In fact, some scientific studies have shown that cow's milk contains proteins that may cause allergies in some babies (see page 183). But most babies will have no problems with cow's milk before their first birthday.

The Compromise: Cow's Milk After the First Birthday

Babies generally are used to supplementary food by their first birthday. Their bodies are now so mature that they no longer need any baby formula and can eat at the table with the adults. As a result, it is often suggested that pasteurized or ultra-heated whole cow's milk can be fed as a "table beverage" toward the end of the first year of life, that is, when the baby starts taking part in family meals. By the way, partially skimmed and skim milk are not appropriate for infant nutrition, for they contain too little fat; raw milk should not be used for hygienic reasons.

TIP | **THE EVENING MASH**

In the evening the mash is so
quick to prepare that it's hardly
worth using baby food from a jar.

¾ oz (20 g) cereal flakes
6¾ fl oz (200 ml) freshly
*   prepared, hot infant milk*
*   formula (or milk from grains,*
*   e.g., rice or oat milk)*
¾ oz. (20 g) pureed fruit
*   (see page 221)*
a couple drops oil or
*   ½ tablespoon butter*

Stir the cereal flakes in with the
milk and let steep a moment.
Stir in the fruit and fat and let
mixture cool.

Flakes or Hot Cereal: A Tough Choice

Whole-grain products are the best choice; they are available as flakes or hot cereals. They have the advantage of dissolving easily in hot milk. Such types of cereals are good for getting started with the evening mash because they contain no gluten; examples are rice, corn, and millet (see sidebar). At first, avoid mashes made from multiple grains, and make sure that these types are pure, with no added sugar or other superfluous ingredients (check the list of ingredients). You can get these products in well-stocked supermarkets (baby department), drugstores, organic food stores, and health food stores.

Alternatives to Wheat

Wheat is quite rich in fiber, vitamins, and minerals, but it's not irreplaceable. In particular, babies who are at a greatly elevated risk of allergies should be given no wheat products in the first year of life. To provide these babies with a balance of all the important nutrients, you can easily switch to gluten-free grains such as rice and millet.

Fruit, Fat, and the Rest

As for the choice of fats, fruits, and how to prepare them, the same recommendations apply to the evening mash as to the one at midday. Here too it is important that fruits or juices containing adequate vitamin C be added so that the child's body can absorb the iron.

Step 3: Replacing the Third Daily Meal (Midday Baby Food)

When your baby tolerates the introduction of the second meal, the evening one, you can gradually replace another breast-feeding meal. This could be the second breakfast in the morning or a snack in the afternoon. This third type of baby food is a cereal-fruit mash. Why? Fruit alone can't be a complete meal for an infant because it provides too little energy. For this reason, always remember to add fat to the mash—regrettably, many parents overlook it. Ideally, the fruit-cereal mash can be ready in the twinkling of an eye.

INFO | CELIAC DISEASE

It often happens that babies develop allergies to grains, especially to wheat. After consuming the grain, the symptoms can range from skin eruptions to stomach and intestinal problems. But this allergy is not to be confused with the autoimmune celiac disease in babies who are oversensitive to the gluten protein contained in many types of grain. The earlier babies are exposed to it, the quicker and the more severe the celiac disease. These children (one child out of a thousand is afflicted) must avoid foods containing gluten for their entire lives; otherwise, they will suffer from an ongoing inflammation of the intestinal mucous membrane. If there is a family history of wheat allergy or celiac disease, you can decrease the risk of developing a wheat allergy by waiting until the first birthday to serve your baby wheat products.

How Much Should My Child Eat?

The indications of quantity in the recipes on the previous pages refer to supplementary feedings starting after the end of the sixth month. At first, it's fine if your baby eats two or three spoonfuls of mash. But once the little ones develop a taste for the mash, it doesn't take long to reach an amount of around 7 ounces (190–200 g) per midday meal. With the cereal-milk mash and fruit-cereal mash, you should mix the same amount as a small jar holds, that is, between 5 and 7 ounces (150–200 g). The switch to solid food should be complete by the tenth month, but this doesn't mean that your baby shouldn't be allowed to continue nursing. It still makes sense for your baby's first meal of the day to be a milk meal. If you still have mother's milk and wish to breastfeed, continue breastfeeding. Otherwise, you can give the child an infant formula in the morning. Whole cow's milk still should be off limits during the first year of life (see page 222).

What Babies Should Drink

In the first four months, an infant normally meets his fluid requirements

When your baby switches to the midday mash, you've made it over all the hurdles involving spoons and splashing. Now all you need is a regular bib, and the spoon feeding can begin.

through mother's milk or infant formula alone. But as soon as the first spoonful of mash finds its way into the baby's mouth, your child needs additional fluid. From now on your baby should have something to drink at every meal.

No Sweeteners

Your baby doesn't yet have any need for commercially made sweetened fruit and vegetable juices. They contain sugar and thus can encourage the development of cavities. Highly diluted juice spritzers are acceptable during meals, but certainly not for suckling on a bottle for a long time (see page 213). Basically, drinks for babies and toddlers must not be sweetened—if the little ones are not introduced to any

INFO | **MIDDAY MASH**

The oil in the mash delivers lots of important energy and helps with the absorption of the fat-soluble vitamins E, D, K, and A, which are contained in the fruit puree.

0.7 oz (20 g) cereal flakes
5.3 oz (150 g) puree made from
mild fruits
½ tablespoon oil or butter

Mix the cereal, pureed fruit, and oil or fat a bowl—and the mash is ready.

225

INFO | YOUR BABY'S FEEDING SCHEDULE COULD LOOK LIKE THIS

	1–4 Month	5th Month	6th Month	7th Month	8th Month	9th Month	10th Month	11th Month	12th Month
➤ **Morning**	Nursing or bottle				Milk-(bread) meal				
➤ **Late Morning**	Nursing or bottle				Snack (e.g., apple, banana, rice cake)				
➤ **Midday**	Nursing or bottle			Vegetable-potato-meat mash					
➤ **Afternoon**	Nursing or bottle					Fruit-cereal mash		Snack (e.g., apple, rice cake)	
➤ **Evening**	Nursing or bottle					Milk-cereal mash		Milk-(bread) meal	

sugary, sweet drinks, they won't miss them.

Away with the Baby Bottle!

It's now time to wean your baby from drinking from a bottle. After the first year, no child needs a baby bottle. Children should be able to eat with a spoon and drink from a cup or a glass. The sooner you start getting your baby used to a glass, the easier the separation from the bottle will be.

Baby's Nutrition Starting in the Tenth Month

The portions change around the tenth month. On the one hand, the amount of mash that your child takes in is increased, and on the other, his nutritional needs

change. Why? Gradually your child is becoming more mobile. He is learning to crawl, starting to walk, and being more active than a few weeks ago. As a result, his body needs more energy.

Power for Active Babies

You can give your baby more energy by increasing the amount of fat that you add to the mash. From now on, for every homemade meal you should stir a tablespoon of oil or a heaping teaspoon of butter into every mash.

The Last Step to the Family Table

So far you have accomplished a lot: You have nourished your baby with (mother's)

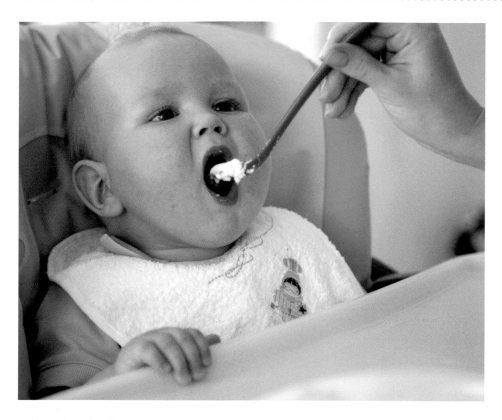

milk and gradually gotten her used to supplementary foods for children. Now you are ready for the next step. At the end of the first year of life, your baby's menu comes even closer to that of the rest of the family. The four or five baby food meals of about the same size that have been given so far gradually change to three main means and two snacks. So the daily routine moves to the family kitchen, and this time you get to enjoy it for more than a few months.

What Do We Need to Watch for When Baby Joins Us for Meals?

Of course, in preparing meals for a small child (and the rest of the family), you must place a high value on the quality of the food. The foods that go onto your table should be freshly harvested or butchered, and when possible of good (organic) quality. The better the quality of the foods you supply to your body, the better it functions. There are, however, many foods that are inappropriate for babies in the first year of life. Since so many foods are allowable, it's not difficult to pass up a few of them. To give you an overview of what could harm your baby, here is a brief list of foods that babies find difficult to digest.

Foods to Avoid
➤ Leaf lettuce may contain lots of nitrate, fertilizers, and insecticides.

➤ Raw tomatoes are relatively difficult to digest.

➤ Vegetables in the cabbage family, such as green, white, and red cabbage, and Brussels sprouts, as well as savoy cabbage, can produce gas in babies. Alternatives that are easier to digest include broccoli, cauliflower, and kohl rabi.

➤ Mushrooms are basically difficult to digest.

➤ Nuts are very allergenic. Also, with nuts there is always a danger that the baby will inhale tiny pieces of nuts into the lungs and suffocate.

➤ Definitely avoid getting your baby used to sweets such as ice cream and chocolate. They generally contain too much sugar, fat, and phosphate.

➤ Unpasteurized honey can contain bacteria (such as clostridium) that cause illness.

➤ Beverages such as soft drinks, cola, fruit punches, and fruit nectars contain far too much sugar, phosphates, and caffeine—everything that children don't need.

➤ Avoid strong spices such as chili pepper and ginger for family meals.

INFO | BENEFITS OF CHEWING

Now your baby should develop the chewing muscles some more. This means that the meals should no longer be pureed smooth. Often all you have to do is mash the food with a fork or a potato masher so that your baby has to chew some. You can also squeeze by hand some small snacks of apple slices or other pieces of fruit for the child, who then can chew on them to her heart's content—under your supervision because of the risk of choking.

➤ No coffee, alcohol, or black tea should be given to the baby—this is obvious.

➤ Many types of sausage are high in fat, phosphates, nitrite pickling salt, and others. So avoid salami, bologna, and pâtés.

➤ Chicken eggs, especially the whites, are highly allergenic, so for the time being they should be avoided.

Personal Experience

Bonnie (34), mother of Leah (5) and John (7 months)

The First Baby Food— Best at Midday

I wanted to start supplementary feeding when Johnnie was just six months old. In the meantime, the breastfeeding meal kept him full for only two or three hours—and I was hoping that he would go back to sleeping through the night if he got a filling mash for his evening meal.

So on the first evening I started by feeding him semolina by spoon. He thought the first two spoonfuls were interesting, but then he was done. The second evening I offered him the mash in a bottle. He absolutely refused it. The third evening, Dad tried it—unsuccessfully. Evidently Johnnie was afraid that the breast was being taken away from him for good—and he howled. The fourth evening all it took was a glimpse of the spoon to start my son bawling. It was clear that this would take a lot of patience.

I gave Johnnie a few days of peace with my breast, and everything was fine once again. But I really wanted a change. So I tried giving him the evening meal (the milk mash) at midday. But Johnnie resisted again. Then I tried baby carrots at midday. Johnnie tried a half-spoonful, but that was all. A friend recommended that I try a mash made from parsnips. I bought some parsnips

and cooked and pureed them. Then I decided to change the consistency. I simply stirred in enough water so that the mash was as liquid as mother's milk. What do you know? Johnnie liked it. In the next few days he took as much as half a glassful. Then I began putting less and less water into the mash until it had about the consistency of baby carrots. Exactly four weeks later my son ate his first complete meal. This experience showed me clearly that patience is the main thing. Switching from milk to mash is a huge change for the little ones, and it takes time and composure. The experience also showed that it makes sense to start the change with the midday meal. For then the baby has had a good sleep and is open to something new.

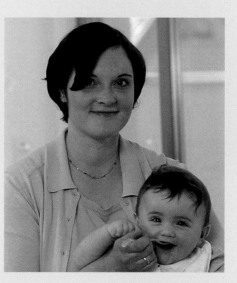

Questions and Answers

1 *What can I do if my baby absolutely refuses to eat her baby food?*

Perhaps your baby is signaling that she is not yet ready to switch to solid food. Up to around the fifth month what's known as the tongue thrust reflex is active. Up to this point, it has been responsible for pushing solid food or objects out of the baby's mouth. So for now continue giving your baby the breast or a bottle and try again after a few days.

2 *The baby food jar says, "After the fourth month." Do I have to begin supplemental feeding starting in the fifth month?*

No, this is a very premature supplemental feeding schedule on the part of the manufacturer, driven by a conscious sales strategy. Mothers can (and even should) breastfeed exclusively, or feed with a bottle, through the end of the sixth month. It takes until the end of the first half-year for the child's digestive system to mature to the point where it can deal successfully with solid food. In addition, the risk of allergies decreases when supplementary feedings are postponed.

3 *Is there any reason I shouldn't use cold-pressed oils in preparing baby food?*

No. If you have a bottle at home, make sure that the freshness date has not expired. Large bottles often are not used up quickly, and the oil can become rancid. So it's better to choose smaller bottles and use them promptly. One disadvantage of cold-pressed oils is their taste; it is much stronger. Use them sparingly so that your baby can get used to the taste. The great advantage to these are natural products is that they are more easily processed by the child's body. Refined oils, on the other hand, are heated to high temperatures. That changes the oils and their original, natural structure, so they are more difficult to digest. In addition, valuable ingredients, such as important vitamins, and especially lots of taste, are lost.

4 *My breastfed baby absolutely refuses to drink from a bottle. How can I give him water or milk?*

If your baby doesn't accept the bottle, you needn't worry, for you can turn a need into a virtue. Spare yourself the detour to feeding your baby fluids with a baby bottle. Instead, gradually get your child used to a glass or a cup right now. It's best to start with a drinking cup with a lid, but without a drip guard, for this lets out the liquid with gentle sucking. If you choose a model with a drip guard, it does have the advantage of preventing spills if the cup is accidentally tipped over.

Children need a little practice and powerful sucking muscles to get water or tea from this type of cup.

There are also babies who reject the cup. The following trick will surely help with these little nay-sayers: During the meal, spoon the fluid into the baby's mouth. It works if you fill a spoon halfway with baby food and then dip it into a glass of water. That way the child gets baby food and water together. Or you can offer a spoonful of water after three of four spoonfuls of baby food.

Sleep, Baby, Sleep …

People spend about a third of their life in the delightful state of sleep. Sleep is even more important for babies than for adults, for the little body needs this rest to process new impressions. Unfortunately, though, not every baby is endowed with consistent sleep behavior.

Gently into Dreamland

Many babies instinctively sleep properly and well, but just as many find it difficult to relax. Oftentimes the parents are at fault. Why? Normally babies show when they are tired and ready for bed. But their baby can pull the plug only if the parents know how to recognize and react to their child's sleep signals. Everyone benefits from this— parents and baby. On the following pages, read how your child shows that she is tired, what makes up a good sleep, and how you can help your baby to find her way into slumber land . . .

Sleep—A Real Elixir of Life

Sleep is a wonderful thing! There's nothing better than simply lying down, stretching out and relaxing, mentally going over the day once again, and taking in another "dreamy" experience in the night. But it's not just the soul that is suspended in sleep—the body, too, achieves a state of repose. Metabolism scales back its activity, and all organs cut back on performance. In sleep there is only enough energy available to keep the body alive. In sleep we store up strength for the coming day and fill up our reservoirs to the brim with energy.

Adequate Sleep— An Absolute Must for Babies

Healthy sleep is important for every human—and vitally important for babies. Because in sleep the entire body grows, and the child's brain also matures in this rest phase. During the day, children who rest too little over a fairly long time or sleep poorly are often fussy, disagreeable, and uncoordinated in their movements. As a result of sheer fatigue, they lack interest and ambition to discover the world, and they are often listless and moody. But in the evening the mood suddenly changes: then they are often more lively, and yet so overtired that despite all efforts they sleep poorly or can't get to sleep at all. This starts a vicious circle that can easily get out of control.

The Need for Sleep— Different for Every Child

Of course, the table that shows the statistical sleep requirements for children in the first year of life simply presents a guideline for how much sleep your baby needs. Every baby has his own sleep needs. Just as one child gets by with less sleep and still spends the day in a good mood, there are others who like to sleep longer.

INFO | SLEEP REQUIREMENTS

Here's an average of how many hours of sleep babies need per day for healthy growth:

Age	Total Sleep Hours	Total Hours of Nighttime Sleep	Total Hours of Daytime Sleep
Newborn	16 hours	8 to 9	8
1 month	15.5 hours	8 to 9	7
3 months	15 hours	9–10	4–5
6 months	14 hours	10	4
9 months	14 hours	11	3
1 year	14 hours	11	3

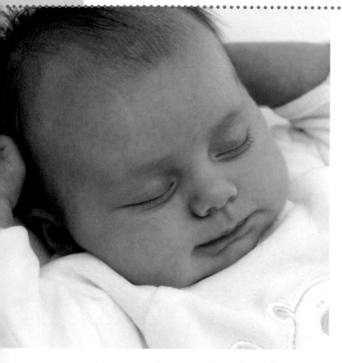

Deep sleep, baby style: breathing calmly, completely relaxed, and so amazingly peaceful . . .

Not All Sleep Is the Same

If you watch your baby while he sleeps, you will see that he goes through various sleep phases. Although he is sleeping, he alternately breathes deeply and regularly, and then quickly and frantically; sometimes the baby starts, at other times he lies motionless; sometimes you can see the eyeballs rolling back and forth under the closed eyelids. There really is a lot going on.

The Sleep Phases

Experts make a rough distinction between two sleep phases: one is deep, non-REM sleep, and the other is REM (or dream) sleep. To understand these terms, we must explain that REM is the abbreviation for Rapid Eye Movement. It refers to the quick movement in the eyes that takes place during sleep.

Deep Sleep (non-REM)

When we adults go to sleep, we generally first fall into a deep sleep. The breathing becomes calm, the heart beats regularly, and the brain rests. Instruments that measure brain waves during this phase register the brain's rest pause as long, large waves on the monitor. Since the central nervous system scales back its activities, it sends few impulses to the muscles. Thus, we don't move much while sleeping in spite of all dreams. Once we are in a deep sleep, it is fairly difficult to awaken us.

Dream Sleep (REM-phase)

Things are quite different after two or three hours of deep sleep, when we enter the dream sleep phase. The term for this phase is accurate: The eyeballs quickly move back and forth beneath the closed eyelids. Additionally, the heart beats more quickly, the breathing becomes more restless, and the body needs more oxygen. The brain becomes active and sends impulses to the muscles, which are controlled by the spinal cord; however, occasionally a twitch is visible in the face or the extremities. In this sleep phase, babies often treat their parents to a so-called angel's smile—that is, they pull up the corners of their mouth and smile in their sleep. Dream sleep is an active sleep phase, from which we can awaken very quickly. While we sleep, we pass through several dream and deep sleep phases in succession.

INFO | **IMPORTANT INFORMATION ON BABY'S SLEEP**

➤ As your baby changes from one sleep phase to the other, she wakes for a moment. Why? She is checking out her location—is everything the way it was when I went to sleep? If it is, that's great, and she moves on to the next round of sleep. But if your baby finds the situation changed, things aren't good. Your baby protests loudly— and she has a right to! Why is Mom's breast or Dad's arm, where the baby was cuddling when she fell asleep, no longer there?

➤ The older the child becomes, the more sleep phases can follow in succession. Consequently, as a child sleeps longer (enters more sleep phases), the sleep is interrupted more frequently because the baby must check out her location between every phase. This means that even if your child sleeps through the night, she is briefly awake several times during the night. So it's important that your baby quickly get back to sleep by herself after every awakening. This going to sleep can be learned—with your help.

Babies Sleep Differently!

Children, too, pass through several deep- and dream sleep phases at night. Sleep researchers have determined that baby sleep occurs somewhat differently:

➤ After falling asleep, newborns first fall into a light dream sleep. This also explains why they wake up fairly easily when you try to put them into their cribs.

➤ Premature babies experience a significantly longer dream sleep phase than full-term newborns.

➤ However, starting with the third month of life, babies first fall into a deep sleep. This further explains why older infants can be lifted out of the car and put into bed without waking; many can even be changed while they remain asleep.

➤ With babies six months and older, deep sleep is not really deep sleep. It can be divided into four steps, the explanation for which would exceed our purposes here.

➤ Sleep is not a steady thing for babies. On the contrary, it takes places in individual stages, where calmer phases alternate with more active ones.

➤ With babies, deep and dream sleep always last the same amount of time. Each sleep cycle (complete deep and dream sleep phase) lasts around sixty minutes.

The Sleep of a Newborn

In the mother's womb, the baby always slept whenever he wanted. He behaves exactly the same way after being born. The seventeen hours of good sleep that a newborn needs in the first month are spread over twenty-four hours, and alternate with brief phases of wakefulness. The infant wakes up because he is hungry. It doesn't matter to him whether it is day or night. The need to satisfy his hunger simply causes the baby to awaken. This produces the regular schedule of "drinking, being awake, and drinking" around the

237

clock. In the first weeks of an infant's life, this cycle usually repeats in three- to four-hour phases.

How Babies Sleep from the Third Month on . . .

It takes a few months for a baby to learn the difference between day and night. And the older the baby is, the more the cycle of sleep and wakefulness changes in accordance with a day and night rhythm. As soon as the third month, the nighttime sleep increases as the amount of wakefulness during the night decreases. Suddenly the situation is reversed: During the day, the baby is awake longer than asleep.

. . . and Starting in the Sixth Month

As early as six months babies are able to sleep for eleven hours at a stretch (without being awakened by hunger). If they wake up at night between sleep phases, they fall asleep again by themselves. A child generally maintains these eleven hours of night-time sleep up to the age of five. Babies get the additional sleep they need during the day: Normally babies up to their first birthday get two hours in the morning and the same amount in the afternoon.

What Babies Need for a Good Sleep

Many things can have a positive or negative effect on your baby's sleep. In addition to external factors (such as a quiet, child-appropriate sleeping place for the baby), the child's psyche plays a major role. Consider that falling asleep is a form of separation. The baby drifts off into slumber land and dreams about her world—without Mom. So to make the transition alone into dreamland, the baby must feel secure. She must be able to rely on the fact that even though there is a separation, she has not been left alone. The baby must know that her parents are there if she needs them. People need to feel this kind of safety and security in order to relax. And to fall asleep in bed willingly and easily they have to be relaxed.

Safety and Security

Security means that your child can rely on your always being there to come and comfort him when he's unhappy. A baby feels secure when he always gets loving attention, when he feels that he has not been left alone, and will always be taken care of. Of course this doesn't mean that you have to carry your child around all the time.

Lots of physical closeness gives your baby the feeling that you accept him and will protect him no matter what happens.

INFO | **AN ESTABLISHED RHYTHM**

Always treat your child to both morning and afternoon naps every day. It would be wrong to think that your child could make up for a missed nap in the following night. On the contrary, the duration of the night sleep doesn't change as a result: the result may simply be difficulty getting to sleep at night, for the child is completely over-stimulated by fatigue.

And the more positive feelings of this type a child experiences during the day, the calmer and more relaxed he will be in the evening when it's time to go to sleep because the child is sure of his parents' love.

An Established Rhythm

Babies are creatures of habit. Established times, clear rules, and limits are important in helping the little ones get their bearings. A baby who knows what's on the schedule and what comes next can relax. For she experiences few surprises that may be frightening.

A Simple Solution

(Healthy) babies are really easy to keep happy. We understand their needs (specifically food, attention, care, and sleep), and can satisfy them quite easily.
➤ When babies are hungry, they need to be given milk.
➤ When they need attention, they long for Mom's (or Dad's) arms and caresses.
➤ When babies are tired, they need rest and sleep.

In short, babies don't have many needs. But they want them fully satisfied.

The Time Frame

The trick is setting aside the time to meet your baby's needs. Most babies find their rhythm by themselves. But there are always some babies who count on their parents for help.

A baby's routine might look like this up to the third month:
➤ Drinking: In the first days your baby may need up to an hour to get full. Over a few weeks, this changes to around thirty minutes.
➤ Being awake: In the first few weeks, babies manage to stay awake for thirty to forty-five minutes after drinking: During this time changing the diaper, dressing, and cuddling can be on the schedule.
➤ Sleeping: After a maximum of an hour and a half, young babies are tired again (older ones last another half-hour). The good mood that has prevailed so far may suddenly change. Now you have to be able to recognize signs of fatigue. Certainly your baby is not hungry now, so don't

offer the breast again. Most babies now sleep around an hour (but many only a half-hour, and others an hour and a half). Then the routine of "drink–wake up–sleep" may start all over. As babies grow older they drink noticeably faster. This requires more stick-to-itiveness on your part while the baby is awake. It is important that you watch for the tiredness signals you baby sends.

Going to Sleep

Now you have to figure out how and when your child best falls asleep. The motto—"An ounce of prevention is worth a pound of cure"—applies here. For when you as parents put your child to bed properly you are spared major sleep disturbances.

Is your baby yawning in earnest? Then it's time for bed. The sooner you react to fatigue signals, the easier it is for the baby to fall asleep.

Recognizing Signals of Fatigue

A newborn can't speak yet, but he is able to communicate. When a baby is tired, he sends out signals to communicate that he wants to sleep:

➤ Newborns soon start to fuss after a meal or while playing. When you pick them up, they use their face to seek shelter at the breast.

➤ If an infant can turn his head, when he's tired he turns his face away from the action. His gaze wanders, and he begins to yawn.

➤ Older babies rub their eyes, pull their ears, twist their hair, or lay their head onto the floor. As soon as your baby shows you that he is tired, you should put him into his bed or cradle. At this point, it is important that you do not try to animate the baby by rocking, singing, or carrying him around. The baby may start to cry because he needs rest and a break from stimulation.

Sleeping Aids: Not Needed

If you interpret your baby's signals correctly and put him to bed at the first signs of fatigue, he won't need any help in falling asleep. Don't even get started with little quirks like the ones described above! Help your baby learn in the first few weeks to go to sleep by himself. The baby is not alone; he has his parents who can comfort him if necessary, plus a couple of stuffed animals and security blankets to help him feel comfortable.

The Start of a Vicious Circle
At first everything is perfectly harmless: The newborn is fed from breast or bottle

TIP | GOING TO SLEEP

Sometimes it's amazing what parents do to make their little ones fall asleep. The gamut runs from hours-long car rides to rubbing Mom's earlobe and stroking the baby's back to the humming of a hairdryer under the bed. But healthy babies are able to fall asleep without help. It doesn't always work because the parents introduce these peculiar rituals, and the babies believe they can't fall asleep without the rituals. That's all there is to it.

and then falls asleep. What a wonderful moment, to hold such a peaceful creature in your arms. At night it also works well when the baby goes right to sleep after a meal. Sleeping babies are pleasant to look at and much easier to care for than crying ones. But frequently the baby won't fall asleep in your arms, but he cries instead, even though he has just drunk. So you need a Plan B here; you need to be able to calm your baby without feeding him again. Parents show great creativity with this—see the sidebar above. Any means is acceptable: riding in a car, vacuuming, bouncing the baby, swinging, singing. It doesn't matter how long or what time of day. The main thing is that it helps. Often it really does work: The baby falls asleep, in the belief that in the future this is how he should fall asleep. The baby has gotten used to this method. And there they are—the gimmicks for going to sleep that appear inconvenient only under closer consideration.

The Trick for a Good Sleep

In the first three months, it is totally normal for a baby to wake up hungry several times during the night. The baby is still too small to regulate his rhythm of wakefulness and sleep to your day-night rhythm. It is also normal for a young infant to fall asleep in your arms after drinking. The baby is suddenly tired, and sucking is hard work. Treat your baby to this brief nap in your arms. However, if the baby wakes up again after a few minutes, don't offer the breast again. If the baby cries, it's surely not from hunger. The child wants a few minutes of love from his parents and to feel the security they provide. Both of these are vitally important, for they build confidence. Then the baby wants a rest—so off to bed with him. Don't confuse crying with hunger.

Step by Step into Slumber Land

The most important goal should be getting your baby to feel secure in her bed and fall asleep on her own as quickly as possible. To achieve this, you as parents need to pave the way. You have to make sure that your baby knows she can rely on you for comfort and attention whenever she's unhappy.

1. Let Her Fall Asleep the Sensible Way

Help your child fall asleep using only the tricks that you care to use over the long run. For example, if your offspring goes to sleep only at Mom's breast, on Dad's

241

stomach, or during a nightly car ride, that's fine for the child, but it's not so great for you as parents. How long will you be willing and able to keep that up? Through your conduct, show your child how people fall asleep—and that can only be in her own bed or the car. So pursue a means to falling asleep that is comfortable for all participants.

2. Provide a Secure Place for Sleeping

A baby always needs the same surroundings for sleeping—at least for night sleep. Often all it takes is a security blanket, a favorite stuffed animal, or a familiar melody to give the child security. Try to keep things in the baby bed as consistent as possible; your baby doesn't need clean sheets every three days, a different mobile, or a new toy. Reliability and familiarity are what's called for.

3. Put the Baby to Bed While She's Awake

Your child can learn to fall asleep by herself only if you put her to bed while she's still awake. Sometime you'll reach the point when your baby knows well in advance that it's almost time for bed—and looks forward to it. Make sure you don't turn yourself into an aid for falling asleep.

4. Avoiding Dependency

Avoid aids that make it easier for your child to fall asleep at the beginning and subsequently produce stress. This could involve a music box that you wind up any number of times (once is enough) or a pacifier that regularly slides out of the mouth (even at night).

5. Establish Rituals

Babies like it when things always happen in the same pattern. They want to know what's in store for them. For example, you can put a sleep sack onto the baby before it's time to go to bed: When the sleep sack appears, it's time for sleep. It also makes sense to sing the same good-night song or say a good-night prayer, play a music box, give the baby a kiss—and be done with it.

6. Separate Eating and Sleeping

The baby should remain awake for a while after the last meal. Depending on her age, at first this may be around ten minutes, and later up to an hour. The crucial thing is learning that drinking from the breast or bottle has nothing to do with going to sleep. Hunger and sleep are different needs.

7. Hold Back as Parents

If at first your baby cries and wants comforting, wait a moment before you take her out of bed and into your arms. Sometimes that initial (sometimes violent) crying is also a way for babies to get rid of the day's stress.

At the Right Time

Babies should learn as soon as possible how to fall asleep by themselves. That's the only way to be sure that you and your child won't later have to struggle with uncomfortable and stubborn gimmicks to get the child to go to sleep. In practice, this means the following:

➤ In the first three months, you simply can't spoil newborns (despite sayings to the contrary). For during this time your baby is dependent on your care, your love,

TIP | CLASSIC MISTAKES

Most sleep problems crop up because
➤ The child falls asleep while drinking.
➤ The child falls asleep in the parents' arms.
➤ The parents want the child to stop crying.
➤ The parents run to the baby bed at the first sound. Perhaps the baby would have fallen asleep again all by herself.

and your attention. So provide as much body contact and closeness as possible. It's perfectly OK if the baby sometimes falls asleep in your arms, carrier or the sling. Still, always put your baby into bed while she's awake when she shows that she's tired. Start your going-to-sleep ritual in the first weeks. In time, babies recognize this as a signal to go to sleep. If the baby starts to cry after a short while, of course you can comfort her. Speak loving words, caress the baby, play the music box. But try to avoid picking her up right away.
➤ Starting in the fourth month of life, you should try to put your child to bed as often as possible while she's awake and it's time for bed. If the baby whines, don't pick her up right away, but give her a chance to comfort herself. The baby has a stuffed animal or a security blanket, her familiar surroundings, and the certainty that in an emergency Mom or Dad is always there.

If It Doesn't Work, What Did We Do Wrong?

There really are only a few classical (parenting) mistakes that cause babies who normally fall asleep by themselves after a certain learning phase to suddenly develop problems with going to bed.

Mistake No. 1: Letting the Baby Fall Asleep While Drinking or in Your Arms

The baby has been awake for a while, and then she begins to fuss. The mother or father gives her something to drink. She suckles peacefully, drinks a few swallows of milk, and happily falls asleep. The parent takes advantage of the opportunity, tiptoes to the baby's bed, and carefully lays the child down. The parent carefully slips out of the room, but before the door is closed, the baby is awake and crying.
➤ Problem: The baby is right to cry. She notices that her aid in going to sleep has been taken away. For the baby, this means that the time for sleep is over, but she is still tired and wants to sleep. The problems is that she needs the former situation, that is, the breast or bottle, in order to go to sleep.
➤ Recommendation: Put your baby into bed while she's awake and help her to find sleep by herself. If she has a very strong need to suck, you can give her a pacifier or a security blanket.

Mistake No. 2: Failing to Recognize Fatigue Signals

The baby has drunk well, has everything she needs, and is in a good mood and ready to play some. The mother does some

243

Rubbing the eyes is a clear statement: I am tired. When your baby sends this signal, the only thing to do is put her to bed!

finger games, tickles the baby all over—and the baby squeals with delight. When the phone rings, the baby sits calmly and happily on the mother's lap. But soon thereafter the mood changes quickly: The baby fusses, rubs her eyes, throws herself rearward. "She wants to play," thinks the parent, who resumes the previous activity. The baby responds with loud crying.

➤ Problem: The baby was tired and wanted to go to sleep. She first expressed this need with fussing, and then escalated into crying. The parent interpreted the crying as boredom.

➤ Recommendation: Don't neglect pauses for rest. Take the trouble to recognize the signs of fatigue. As soon as your baby fusses, put her to bed—provided, of course, that she has already had a meal and been changed.

Sleeping Through the Night

Most parents would like to know when their child will finally sleep through the night for the first time. The answer: In the first three months, a baby is not able to distinguish day from night. It sometimes can take four to six months until the inner clock is adjusted. When this is ticking properly, the baby's nighttime temperature drops, and the child's body switches over to sleep.

The first undisturbed nights come when your baby is around six months old. Only then are babies in a position to make it through ten to twelve hours without food. Until that time they are awake two to three times every night and want milk, which they are entitled to until their gastric capacity is big enough to tolerate a longer time period.

How to Keep Your Baby in Slumber Land All Night Long

Here is a list of the most important points that will make it easier for your baby (six months and older) to sleep through the night.

1. Don't Turn the Night into Day

Always keep in mind how many hours of sleep your child needs at the present age (see page 235). Most of the sleep time should be at night, so a two- to four-month old child shouldn't need more than two naps of around two hours each during the day. A child who sleeps eight to ten hours during the day has had enough sleep before night and is ready to go. Starting at around six months, you should limit the daytime naps to an hour or two.

2. Babies Sleep Best When Full

Sometimes it is recommended to give babies six months and older one last meal in the late evening—that is, when the mother goes to bed. The baby is taken out of bed asleep and offered the breast or bottle. Normally babies begin to suck as soon as you touch their lower lip. Make sure your baby doesn't wake up entirely. In other words, you don't need a lot of light for this meal, and you shouldn't speak to the baby. Usually you don't even have to burp the baby, for babies are calm and relaxed when they drink during sleep, so they don't swallow much air. As long as the diaper is not full or excessively wet, you also should not change the baby. Once the baby is done, simply put her back to bed asleep. Children who get another meal in the late evening generally have enough calories in their stomach to sleep well through the coming hours.

3. Don't Jump Up Right Away

If your baby wakes up at night and fusses, you shouldn't rush to the crib. Give your child a chance to fall back asleep. You should comfort the child only when the crying becomes really loud.

If It Doesn't Work, What Did We Do Wrong?

When it comes to getting the baby to sleep through the night, many parents make mistakes that turn night into day. Here are the most common mistakes.

Mistake: Winding Up Rather Than Winding Down

Here's what happens: An older baby keeps

> ### TIP | SLEEP RECORD
>
> Sometimes it makes good sense to write down a type of sleep record. In the morning note when the baby wakes up and what her mood is like. And how long does she sleep during the day? When does the baby go to bed at night? How long does it take to go to sleep? When does the baby wake up at night? It's worthwhile to write these things down. After just four or five days you can form a picture of your child's individual sleep pattern.

waking up. The baby should have settled into a four-hour rhythm long ago. Instead, he sleeps an hour to an hour and a half, and then wakes up again and cries. What's going on? The baby can't be hungry, since it's barely been an hour since the last meal. The mother doesn't know what to do. "Just don't pick the baby up," the mother and mother-in-law have urged, "otherwise you'll get the child used to it and then you're stuck." When the baby cries, the mother gets up, pushes the bassinet back and forth. It doesn't do any good; on the contrary, the baby cries even louder. So she takes the baby out and carries him around on her shoulder through the house, moves the mobile above the chest of drawers, sits on the sofa and turns on the television—anything to calm the baby. She also pats the baby on his back and rocks him back and forth. But nothing works; the baby continues squealing. At last the mother offers the breast.

245

TIP | A ROOM CHANGE

We often hear that changing from the parents' bedroom to a sibling's room is good for many babies. Whether this is due to the (snoring) noises of the parents or the positive vibes of the sibling, there is no explanation for it. However, amazingly, it often works.

Thankfully, the baby sucks the breast and calms down. When the mother tries to put the baby back down, the bellowing starts again. Now the agitated father gets into the act, for he can't sleep a wink with all the yelling. The mother shoves the baby into his arms and says, "I've done all I can; your turn." The father tries a similar program to the mother's (looking out the window, flying like a plane, and so on), and it doesn't work this time either. The child screams and screams.

➤ Problem: The baby couldn't fall back asleep by himself and was looking for comfort; instead, he is overloaded with stimuli. The baby woke up and became curious, but couldn't get to sleep. The parents are also in a volatile mood. Both are suffering from a sleep deficit and are clearly agitated—and the baby picks up on it.

➤ Recommendation: Pick up your baby and hold him tight and lovingly to your body. Speak to him and comfort him. Once again, it's important to keep a separation between eating and sleeping. Don't let the baby fall asleep at your breast; keep him awake a few minutes longer after drinking before your put him back to bed.

Sleep Disorders in Babies

It's possible that babies who have difficulties falling asleep and sleeping through the night in the first six months simply have not yet settled into a regular rhythm of wakefulness and sleep. This is not yet a true sleep disorder. Experts speak of sleep disorders when a child around six months or older meets the following criteria:

➤ The baby wakes up more than three times.

➤ On the average the child is awake for more than twenty minutes.

➤ The child always needs Mom or Dad in order to fall asleep again.

➤ The problems have been going on for several weeks.

➤ There are physical causes (e.g., constricted air passages or enlarged tonsils).

"Sleep Thieves"

It's fortunate for all parents when babies learn to go to sleep by themselves and sleep through till daybreak. Experts speak of "sleeping through the night" when the baby sleeps from midnight to five o'clock. It is entirely possible that your baby will sleep wonderfully for a few nights—and then suddenly things aren't working any more. There may be several reasons for this that you should clear up.

1. Is Your Child Going Through a Growth Spurt?

Scientists have determined that in the first fourteen months babies go through eight growth spurts (see front cover flap).

Personal Experience

Bonnie (34), mother of Leah (5) and John (7 months)

The Nights Have to Get Better!

Johnnie came into the world in just an hour and a half. Because of this quick delivery, his head was very distorted. When he at first refused to drink from the breast, we consulted a lactation specialist about his not being able to latch on. He could drink out of a bottle, for it was easier for him. So I pumped my breasts. During the day that was no problem, but at night it was stressful: getting up, taking the pumped milk out of the refrigerator and warming it up, giving it to the crying baby, pumping more milk, and so on, night after night. During this time I got about one good hour of sleep at a time. This lasted seven full weeks—until I was at the end of my strength. Around this time, Johnnie got better at latching. It worked so well that in the following months I breastfed him exclusively. But suddenly things took another turn for the worse: Johnnie got out of the four-hour rhythm and into a two- or three-hour one. Once he was asleep, I had to keep putting the pacifier back into his mouth because he would lose it in his sleep and wake up.

I did this for three months, until I was physically and mentally exhausted. It was time to change something. When I heard about writing down the baby's sleep habits, I did it for two weeks. I wanted to know how much sleep Johnnie got all together, and especially when. In fact, Johnnie was getting enough sleep, but split up differently. At night he would drink frequently and copiously, so often in the morning he wasn't hungry. He simply was still full from the night and during the day he wanted to catch up on the sleep he'd lost during the nighttime meals. I realized I had to change this routine. The child couldn't drink himself full in short intervals at night and then rest up and forego meals during the day.

From that day on I made sure that he got no more than two and a half hours of sleep during the day and was breastfed five or six times before bedtime. And you know, ever since, things have been going much better.

During these times, the baby's accustomed world goes topsy-turvy, and they only want to get back to the most trusted place in the world—Mom. So don't be surprised if your child whines, still wants the breast, and clings to you. Once the spurt is over, the sleep will be back in order. And your baby will have taken a big step in development.

2. Is Your Baby Especially Hungry Because of a Growth Spurt?

During a growth spurt, many babies need so much energy that they simply are hungrier. So in the first night, offer your baby an additional meal (but thereafter no other nighttime meals), and get used to the fact that your baby also needs more during the day in a growth spurt.

3. Is Your Baby Teething?

We adults can't remember, but children keep showing us that growing teeth can hurt a lot and rob you and your baby of

TIP | HELP FROM THE PROS

If you believe that your child suffers from sleep problems, you should not hesitate to get professional help. Consult your pediatrician, who can direct you to other resources. This is especially important if you have a sense that your baby may have a sleep disorder caused by a physical problem, or if you, your partner, or a sibling can't take any more because of the baby's sleep disorder.

nighttime sleep. Let the baby chew on a chilled teething ring or pacifier before going to bed. You can also try using homeopathic teething gels or capsules which contain camellia, available at a store that sells natural remedies.

4. Does Your Baby Have Gas?

Gas can occur as soon as a baby's digestive system changes over to solid food. Sometimes it can be so bad that it wakes babies up. If you are not sure which foods cause gas, ask your pediatrician.

5. Is the Baby's Diaper Full?

Some babies don't care about this, but others are extremely sensitive; your child may wake up when her diaper is full or wet. Then you should change the diaper—preferably without much light and lots of hubbub. Then pack her off to bed again.

6. Has the Baby Lost Her Pacifier?

Has your baby gotten used to the pacifier as an aid in falling asleep? Then in the future you have to live with being awakened until your child can find the pacifier in the dark and put it into her mouth by herself. This will happen around age one. Tip: If your baby can find the pacifier by herself, put several pacifiers into the bed with her. Until that time, though, unfortunately you will have to get up—or else break the pacifier habit. After a few (difficult) days, your baby will forget the pacifier.

Pacifier or Thumb?

With young babies, the inborn sucking reflex helps them find the food source and ensure their survival. But the breast or bottle is not always available, so many children have to content themselves with their fingers when they want to suck on something. The alternative to the fingers, or later on the thumb, is a pacifier. Both satisfy the baby's sucking reflex with both advantages and disadvantages.

What Does a Pacifier Provide?

Scientists have in fact determined that babies sleep better at night when they suck on a pacifier. Just the same, the pacifier pleasure also has its side effects:

➤ In the first few months, little babies are not able to keep a pacifier in their mouth for a long time. As soon as it falls out, many babies wake up and cry. They can't get back to sleep unless the pacifier is put back into their mouth. This amounts to a sleep disturbance.

➤ With larger babies, weaning from the pacifier is usually accompanied by lots of drama. It's important to be done with the pacifier as soon as possible, for the longer and more frequently the pacifier is used, the greater is the risk of damage to the jaw. Ideally, the pacifier should be history by the first birthday.

➤ A string for the pacifier can help the baby find the favorite item quickly. But this must never be used in the baby's bed because it could strangle the child.

➤ See if it's enough for your baby to use the pacifier only occasionally and in exceptional circumstances. Keep the pacifier phase short, and carefully take the pacifier out of the baby's mouth once he falls asleep.

What's the Right Type of Pacifier?

In any case, you should choose a type that is shaped properly for the jaw, that is, flat on the underside. In the long term, pacifiers shaped like a cherry can produce an open bite. Regarding the materials, there are the following options:

➤ Latex pacifiers are made from the high-quality natural-material latex, which is very supple and durable; however, it ages quickly. They should thus be replaced every four to six weeks.

➤ Silicone pacifiers are made from high-quality, very durable plastic; they last for a long time and can withstand frequent boiling. However, silicone pacifiers are more easily bitten through when the first teeth come in. So they are available only in sizes one and two, which are not appropriate for older children (over eighteen months).

TIP | **SPARING THE BREAST**

Nursing mothers should avoid offering their breast as a substitute for the pacifier, especially because in the first days and weeks after giving birth, a breast performs heavy duty. Regular recovery breaks are urgently needed.

When Does a Baby Need the Next Larger Pacifier?

Consider a larger pacifier when your baby is six or eighteen months old. Pacifiers come in three different sizes that match the size of the child's jaw. Be aware that as soon as your child can put the whole pacifier in his mouth (including the shield), it's time for the next size.

What Care Does My Baby's Pacifier Require?

It is very important to boil the pacifier before it is used for the first time. Put all pacifiers and nipples into a pot of water at a rolling boil and leave them in for at least five minutes. Sterilization is required, especially for newborns if the pacifier has fallen onto the floor, another child has had it in his mouth, or it otherwise appears dirty. It's better to boil a pacifier once too often than once too seldom. At first this may happen every day. Never put your baby's pacifier into your mouth to lick it clean because you will load it up with countless germs. Your baby will be much better off if you always keep a replacement pacifier in a container.

Whether babies use a thumb or a pacifier, sucking helps them fall asleep.

Is It Better to Suck the Thumb?

No. Sucking the thumb does have the advantage that the fingers are always available; however, a child who once uses his thumb for comfort can find it hard to do without it later on.

Sudden Infant Death Syndrome

This is the worst thing that parents can imagine: going to the crib in the morning and discovering a dead child. Unfortunately, this happens in 1 per 10,000 infants. SIDS (Sudden Infant Death Syndrome) though rare, is a tragedy whenever it occurs. Why babies—usually between the second and fourth months of life—die is still not clear. But usually there are several factors that contribute to the fatal result.

What You Can Do

Even though the exact cause is still obscure, the following preventive measures are recommended:

➤ In the first nine months, babies must sleep only on their backs.

➤ Babies should fall asleep in such a way that they cannot pull the blanket over their head. Larger babies should sleep in a sleep sack.

➤ Avoid pillows. Your baby doesn't need a pillow and could suffocate if it covers the head.

➤ Don't use a fleece blanket in the crib. It could encourage heat buildup.

➤ In the first few months the child should sleep in his own bed, cradle, or bassinet next to your bed. That way you can check on his sleep.

➤ The ideal sleeping temperature for babies is 64–68°F (18–20°C) during the day, and 63–65°F (17–18°C) at night. Don't place the child's bed right next to a heater or in the direct sun.

High-risk Babies

Babies who meet the following criteria are considered to be at particularly high risk:

➤ Babies who sleep on their stomachs or in an unstable position on their sides;

➤ Babies who had a sibling who died of SIDS;

➤ Babies who experience breathing interruptions;

➤ Preemies or babies with birth defects;

➤ Babies whose parents are heavy smokers or drinkers, or who take drugs;

➤ Babies whose mother smoked during pregnancy;

➤ Babies whose parents are low on the social ladder;

➤ Babies of very young mothers;

➤ Babies who sleep on soft surfaces such as blankets or waterbeds, or under blankets in the parents' bed.

INFO | SIDS STUDIES

There are approximately 2,500 SIDS-related deaths every year in the United States alone. However, since 1983, the rate of SIDS has fallen by over 50%. For more information on SIDS, go to http://sids.org.

Questions and Answers

1 *Why do people wake up briefly after each REM (dream) phase?*

Experts consider this brief awakening a type of warning system and explain it this way: In ancient times people were exposed to dangerous situations day and night. People had no fixed dwellings, but generally spent the night under the stars and were thus always exposed to enemies. If nature had equipped humans with only deep sleep, they would not have been able to respond to threats so quickly. So today when we wake up briefly after every dream phase, we can react quickly to suspicious factors such as the smell of fire, or to unaccustomed noises. It's the same with children: When they wake up at night, they check out the surroundings: Is my pacifier within reach? Am I in the right position? Is Mom there?

2 *Should I let my baby sleep in bed with us?*

Let's put it this way: The worry of crushing your baby to death is unfounded. A mother's light sleep and instinct protects against that. And yet this is still a problem: Often parents mean well and cover up the baby with their blankets. The danger is that the baby will become overheated or slip under the covers and suffocate. There is only one compromise: Your baby can get into bed with you if he has his own means for conserving body heat, such as a sleep sack.

Do not cover your baby also with your blankets! There are at least two other points that you need to consider if the baby is to sleep with you:

First, this must not place a strain on your partnership; that is, both partners must agree to the baby's visit. Second, the baby must not be emboldened by Mom's closeness to continue suckling or to wish for a bottle. Since this is generally not so easy to get across to a newborn, you should look to the future and select a dedicated sleeping location for the baby. This can be in the parents' bedroom. A cradle or a bassinet that you can set up next to your bed is fine. Both variants can move, so the baby can even enjoy rocking.

3 *How can I help my baby get used to the day-night rhythm more quickly?*

Set an example showing that the day is the active half. This is when we speak, sing, laugh, eat, and work—the baby can play, be read to, get massage, take baths, and so on. Important: show your child the daylight. If possible, take a walk every day and put a bassinet near the window (but avoid direct sunlight). Let your baby experience the night as the quiet part of the day. Now there are no major activities. Nighttime feeding takes place in a darkened room. If you have to change a diaper, do so without a bright light. You should also avoid loud talk at night.

4 *It's so difficult for me to let my baby cry. Am I bad parent if I don't go to the child when she cries?*

Don't cause yourself any unnecessary grief over this. From the looks of things, your heart is in the right place. That's great! However, when a baby cries, this doesn't necessarily mean that she feels miserable. Babies also use crying as a type of communication—they can't yet speak, after all. By crying they communicate, "I am hungry," "I am tired," "That's enough," "I'm cold," or "My tummy hurts." Crying doesn't mean, "I am angry with you," "I am sad," "I am lonesome," or "I want a different mother or father!" Crying is healthy, totally normal with babies, and even important. But check with a doctor if a normally happy baby cries longer than two hours or violent crying is accompanied by fever, vomiting, diarrhea, rash, or similar conditions. It should also get your attention if your baby never cries and then suddenly whimpers pitifully.

5 *I am afraid that my baby could die from Sudden Infant Death Syndrome. How can I tell if she is at risk?*

Unfortunately, there is never any way to tell for sure. Still, there are a couple of points that suggest an elevated risk. Today we know from studies that children who sleep on their stomachs or in a stable position on their sides are affected. Also babies who lie in excessively soft beds (e.g., on blankets) are more frequently affected. If your baby sleeps on her back on a hard mattress, she is in the right position. Babies who had siblings who died from SIDS or who experience breathing interruptions also have a greater risk. Mothers who smoked during and after pregnancy, drink lots of alcohol, or take drugs heighten the risk even further. Then there are the premature babies and others who are too small and light for their age.

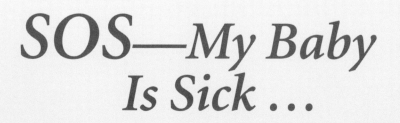

SOS—My Baby Is Sick …

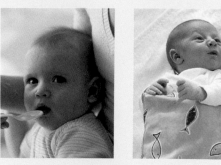

*First the good news: Pediatricians say
that the first year of life is basically a
healthy, stable phase in a human's life.
But if your child doesn't feel well, or is
really sick, you will find a number of
tips and information on how you can
help him regain health.*

Major and Minor Complaints

Alas, when things hurt, it's always tough for parents to watch their children suffer. Still, getting sick is quite normal for children, for there are many minor and major maladies that the young body has to deal with. Generally, this is not too severe because infectious diseases usually are quite mild in the first year of life, especially since serious disabling conditions (measles, mumps, polio haemophilus, pneumococcal meningitis) are preventable with immunization and carry children one step farther in their development of immunity. To keep you better prepared, here is a list of the most common illnesses and complaints and the best ways of dealing with them.

Diaper Rash—When Baby's Bottom Hurts

Sometimes this is what happens: You open up the diaper and see that the baby's bottom is red. Even if the baby gets conscientious care, nearly every baby experiences this at one time or another.

Sore Bottom (Diaper Dermatitis)

Diaper rash refers to a skin irritation in the diaper area with a wide range of symptoms that require special treatment.

Symptoms
The entire bottom is red. The skin infection often spreads to the genitals and the insides of the thighs, too. The redness is the first step; the second is that the bottom develops open areas that bleed. Of course, these are very painful, especially when the baby does his bowel movements in the diaper.

Causes
Breastfed babies are susceptible if the mother eats fruits high in citric acid (berries, pineapple, and citrus fruits). But acidic, strong urine (if the diaper is changed too infrequently) and frequent bowel movements, with the attendant cleanings, attack the sensitive skin.

See a Doctor
Seek help from the child's doctor as soon as the diaper area becomes very red, certainly by the time bloody sores appear on the skin.

Treatment
Now the theme is change, change, and keep changing the diaper in the first couple of days on an hourly basis. Drugstores sell a good zinc-based ointment for soreness. A soothing, soft zinc paste that limits inflammation is recommended; you need to spread it on thin so that it covers the afflicted skin with a protective film. Ointments with the effective ingredient Dexpanthenol also produce good results. Do not use moist or oily cloths. All you need for cleaning is clean water. Let the baby romp around as often as possible without a diaper on. This should be no problem in summer temperatures; in the winter, you can do this near a heat source. The doctor will prescribe appropriate medications for weeping, open areas on the skin. By the way, disposable diapers keep a baby drier than cloth diapers.

INFO | ZINC OINTMENT

Pastes and salves that contain zinc are available without prescription in drugstores. Don't use these preparations over the long term to prevent diaper rash because other germs or infrequent changing could be contributing to the sore bottom.

257

Diaper Thrush

Thrush is a fungal infection that occurs primarily in the diaper area, but it can also appear in the mouth. It can be transferred from one body area to another. If a fungal infection and diaper rash are found on an infant, this is an indication that the entire stomach and intestinal area is infected with the *candida* fungus.

Symptoms

The baby suddenly doesn't drink well and generally doesn't feel well. She whines more and is not as happy when placed at the breast. Thrush can hurt while sucking. With an extensive infestation, the entire mouth can be inflamed and sore. Inside the mouth, white coatings with red borders form on the tongue or on the mucous membranes of the lips or cheeks.

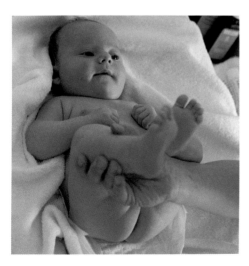

If the baby's bottom is sore, the only solution is lots of care (frequent changes), air, and lots of love.

INFO | A DIFFICULT DIAGNOSIS

At first mothers frequently mistake the whitish thrush coating inside the baby's mouth for milk. But if the baby's tongue and the mucous membranes in the mouth display white coatings that are fairly difficult to wipe off, this is probably thrush.

In the diaper area, thrush is visible as clearly defined spots with a scaly border than may blend with one another. They often build so-called satellites on the upper thighs and stomach. The inflamed areas on the skin may display moist, open areas.

Causes

The germs are encouraged by a warm, moist diaper environment and transmitted through unwashed hands, pacifier, knives and forks used by several people, kisses on the baby's mouth, an infected toy in a play group, and many other means. In other words, thrush is the result of faulty hygiene, in combination with the child's underdeveloped immune defenses.

Consulting a Doctor/Treatment

If thrush is suspected, consult a pediatrician, who can treat the condition with a prescription anti-fungal diaper creme. With a particularly stubborn infection, especially with breastfed children, the pediatrician should ascertain if the baby has a zinc deficiency.

Fever—When the Body Is Fighting Pathogens

Fever is not an illness, but rather a natural defensive reaction by the body. As soon as bacteria or viruses get into the body and weaken it, metabolism goes into high gear: an elaborate process causes the body temperature to shoot up from the average of 98.6°F (36.7°C). The goal of the higher temperature is to kill the invaders and eliminate them, which happens around 102°F (39°C).

Symptoms

With a fever, the child appears sick and weak and is noticeably hot. Her forehead feels significantly warmer than normal, but the hands and feet can be uncommonly hot or cold. There are various types of fever: many babies experience a dry, hot fever; others, a cold (hands and feet) and damp one (sweat). In the center, however, that is, on the body and the head, both types of fever are equally hot. Many children with a fever have no appetite and no desire to drink, while others thirst for something cold.

Causes

Triggers for fever include bacteria, viruses, fungi, and/or parasites. They can cause countless illnesses, such as a cold, a stomach and intestinal infection, or an infection in the tonsils, throat, or ears. A shot can also cause a fever, as so can many classic childhood diseases such as whooping cough, chickenpox, and others.

See a Doctor

There are feverish conditions that don't require a visit to the doctor—such as when the child seems to feel all right despite an elevated temperature and is drinking enough. However, a very high fever (over 102°F /39°C) that appears with no apparent cause and doesn't go down, plus any deterioration in general condition (breathlessness or rapid breathing, pale or bluish skin tone, crying, poor drinking in newborns up to the age of four weeks), requires a prompt visit to the doctor or emergency room.

Treatment

The child needs bed rest. The little body is working at high speed; every effort means additional energy consumption and hinders recovery. Basically it makes sense to help a low-grade fever through sensible measures, for it's the means to rid the child's body of bacteria and viruses. If you strangle the fever too quickly with medications, you interrupt the natural healing

---

INFO | **INTERPRETING THE TEMPERATURE**

Here's what your baby's body temperature (taken rectally) means:

Low temperature	below 97°F (36°C)
Normal temperature	97–99.5°F (36–37.5°C)
Elevated temperature	99.6–100.5°F (37.6–38°C)
Fever	over 100.5°F (38°C)

If you want an accurate reading you can't get around taking the temperature in baby's bottom.

of the sixth month of life, the ingredient ibuprofen is also acceptable. There are two different ways to administer them:

➤ Syrup: Soothing or fever-reducing ingredients are usually given in the form of syrups. It is easy to administer and measure; however, to make it palatable and keep it from going bad, it contains sweeteners and preservatives that have nothing to do with the therapy (reducing the fever).

➤ Wiping down: Rubbing the feverish body with a damp washcloth can hasten recovery. Don't dry off the baby, but dress him immediately and put him to bed.

Good to Know

A child with a fever may refuse to eat. That's not necessarily bad, for eating and digesting are tiring. It is, however, important that the child take in adequate fluids because the body loses water with a fever. Per centigrade degree of fever, a baby loses 0.07–0.15 ounces of water per pound (5–10 milliliters of water per kilo) of body weight per day, and that's a lot! So keep offering your baby water or formula, if necessary in a teaspoon. Put breastfed

process. However, any fever in an infant younger than six months old or a fever above 102.6°F (39°C) in an infant older than six months old deserves prompt medical attention and treatment.

You should use fever-reducing medications only if the temperature rises above 102.2°F (39°C) in an infant 6 months of age or older. Only then is the following an option: With pain and fever medications, the traditional effective ingredient for infants is acetaminophen. After the end

INFO | **LIGHT CLOTHING**

Often children with a fever are dressed too warmly. Light cotton clothing (like a long-sleeved body suit or long-sleeved T-shirt) and a light blanket are adequate at room temperatures between 64 and 68°F (18 and 20°C).

babies to the breast frequently so they can quench their thirst.

➤ Modern glass thermometers contain no mercury; they are instead filled with an alloy of gallium, indium, and tin. They are very precise and produce the most accurate readings when used rectally (see page 261). They have one disadvantage: With a three to four minute delay, you have to wait quite a long time for the results. They cost around $5.00.

➤ Digital thermometers have the advantage of taking only a minute to produce a reading. Normally you can get 2000 to 3000 measurements from a single battery. They are priced around $6.

➤ Aural thermometers provide a reading in a matter of seconds, but it is not always precise. For a precise measurement, you must pull the outer ear rearward and upward to straighten the ear canal, and that doesn't always work. For that reason, and because earwax or secretions in the auditory canal can interfere with the measurement, the result can vary a degree from one ear to the other. Important: don't use with infants younger than six months because their ear canals are too narrow. These are a good choice for a quick reading with children older than six months. Prices range from about $25 to $60.

➤ Forehead thermometers produce results quickly and are very simple to use because it's relatively easy to measure the temperature on the forehead. Variations can result due to factors such as sweat. Prices start around $37.

➤ Pacifier thermometer: The idea is brilliant, but there are some dangers in the

> **TIP | MEASURING THE PRECISE TEMPERATURE**
>
> If you want a precise measurement, you should take the temperature in the bottom, and for at least a minute. Digital thermometers are the easiest to handle. Dab a little Vaseline or cream onto the tip. Place the child on his back, lift the legs, and carefully insert the thermometer a little less than an inch (2 cm) into the anus. Wait patiently until a signal indicates that the measurement is complete.

execution. For one thing, pacifier thermometers measure the temperature inside the front of the mouth, where it can be a fraction of a degree cooler than at the baby's bottom. In addition, it takes up to five minutes to get a reading, and not every infant accepts this pacifier. Prices start around $10.

Febrile Seizures

Febrile seizures are generalized tonic clonic minor epileptic seizures that can occur at the age of six months through five years. They do not just accompany a high fever, as the broadly accepted opinion holds, but have even been associated with a body temperature of 101°F (38.5°C). A quick rise in temperature and a family predisposition are usually responsible for these seizures. Parents should seek medical attention once the seizure has stopped. (And any seizure that lasts five

261

> ### INFO | STRESS-FREE TEMPERATURE TAKING
>
> Some parents take the baby's temperature every half hour. For precision, they use the rectal method (in the bottom), which the little patient doesn't really like (and will like even less as he grows older). The question arises why parents really need an exact temperature reading. What's the difference if the child has a fever of 100.2°F or 101.3°F (37.9° or 38.5°C)? The important thing is that the child has a fever. It is an essential defense for the body to keep disease-causing pathogens in check. So a fever shouldn't be brought down rashly. (An exception is children who are prone to fever convulsions; see page 261.) As long as your child has a "good" fever, that is, a painless one and feels as good as can be expected under the circumstances, the precise temperature is a secondary consideration. Soon you will also be able to determine by placing your hand on your child's neck if he has a high temperature, and by checking if something is "brewing." The important thing is for you to keep a close eye on your child and how the illness is progressing. If you visit the pediatrician, you merely need to mention that your baby has had a fever. Oftentimes the precise temperature is unimportant. Using an ear or a forehead thermometer can also be useful. They generally cause no stress, for they display the temperature in a matter of seconds, although they are not always 100 percent accurate; however, as a general indication, the results are entirely adequate.

minutes or more requires immediate emergency help—dial 911.)

Symptoms

The child doesn't react when spoken to or stimulated, and is unconscious. There is also a rhythmic twitching in the extremities—arms and legs contract and jerk straight out again, as if flailing about. Ninety percent of fever convulsions affect the entire body. Usually the children stiffen their heads on their necks and roll their eyes upward. Saliva flows more copiously, and the child may lose control of bowels and bladder. But other children simply are unresponsive when spoken to, and instead of twitching, they display increased muscle tension. The child may have noisy breathing and often has a brief pause in breathing at the end. Because a seizure with a fever is not necessarily a fever convulsion, you should contact your pediatrician right away.

Cause

The cause of fever convulsions is not entirely clear from a scientific viewpoint. It is suspected that it's not the fever itself that produces a sudden interruption in the functioning of the brain but rather the rapid increase in temperature. This is why a febrile seizure does not mean your child has epilepsy, or even that the seizure will ever happen again.

Treatment

It is important to stay calm, make your child comfortable after the seizure is over but make sure to call the doctor or go to an emergency room! Protect your child from injury (don't place the child on the changing table) by placing them on the floor and on their sides. That way the baby cannot choke on vomit. Place a cool cloth on the forehead and loosen the clothes. When your child is lying down securely, call 911. Generally the seizure stops after one to five minutes.

Good to Know

If your child has had several febrile fever convulsions, you may get a prescription for the appropriate medications for emergency use. You always have to have these handy for use, even while traveling. With children who are prone to fever convulsions, the fever should be lowered as soon as it reaches 101°F (38.5°C). Consult with your pediatrician about this.

Roseola (Exanthema Subitum)

Symptoms

For three to five days, sometimes even two to eight days, but rarely over ten days, the child has a significantly elevated temperature (up to 104°F/40°C), usually without further signs of illness. When the fever disappears, small, pink, blurry spots appear on the back, chest, and stomach and sometimes also on the arms. Side effects of exanthema subitum can include diarrhea, swollen lower eyelids, spots on the roof of the mouth, coughing, swollen lymph nodes, and an arched

fontanel. Eight percent of all children with *exanthema subita* also suffer a fever convulsion.

Cause

A virus from the herpes family is responsible for *exanthema subita*; it is transmitted by airborne infection, and this means that your baby is contagious, but only as long as the outbreak lasts. The treatment for *exanthema subita* depends on the fever (see information starting on page 259). By the end of the second year of life, nearly 100 percent of all babies have experienced this three-day fever. Thereafter they have a lifelong immunity to the virus.

INFO | STATISTICS

Generally fever convulsions last only a minute or two—and are inconsequential. About 5 percent of all children between six months and five years are affected. They often come from families with a relevant predisposition. Eighty-five percent of all convulsions occur before the fourth year of life; 70 percent disappear spontaneously after less than five minutes, and 25 percent of all children experience another uncomplicated febrile seizure. Almost all children outgrow them before school starts.

Fever with No Recognizable Cause

If your child has a fever with no ascertainable cause—she neither coughs nor vomits, doesn't have diarrhea or a stuffy nose, and doesn't even look sick, but simply has an elevated temperature—the cause may be viruses or bacteria. Consult a doctor,

who may find the source of infection by process of elimination. Generally a urine sample is analyzed. Possible causes include an infection of the urinary ducts or harmless viral infections that require no further treatment. Severe infections such as meningitis have become rare if the child is generally in good health, has not traveled abroad, and is immunized.

264

When the Stomach Causes Problems . . .

Constipation

Symptoms
Pediatricians speak of constipation when the baby's stool is very hard. This often leads to tears in the mucous membranes of the anus, which begins a vicious circle: Because of the pain, the stool is held back, thereby becoming even harder and making the squeezing more painful.

Causes
Insufficient intestinal movement and the food itself may be responsible. Babies who are given commercially manufactured formulas frequently experience constipation. Parents of these children must precisely observe the feeding instructions, for an overdose of the milk powder can lead to intestinal problems (see page 209). Breast-fed babies suffer from constipation less frequently.

Treatment
➤ Milk sugar has a laxative effect. One to three times a day give your baby two to four teaspoons of milk sugar dissolved in water. Prune or vegetable juice are other liquids with a laxative effect.
➤ Glycerin suppositories soften hardened stool, thus reducing the effort required.

Alternative Medicine
➤ Sulfur C12 helps with constipation and anal itching.
➤ Alumina D6 is used for small, dry stool and very little intestinal movement.

Diarrhea and Vomiting

Diarrhea and vomiting are two symptoms that are side effects of many illnesses. Both serve to cleanse the body. The important thing is to make sure your baby is not losing too much fluid. A fluid deficiency is generally evident through dry, cracked lips, a lusterless tongue, insufficient tearing, concentrated (dark yellow) urine, and/or a sunken fontanel.

Diarrhea

Symptoms and Causes
Diarrhea means very watery stool, often in combination with vomiting. In serious cases (an infant loses 10 percent of her weight), babies must be treated in a hospital. Diarrhea often accompanies other illnesses, but it can also be caused by a viral infection.

TIP | DEHYDRATION

Carefully press your fingernail onto your child's fingernail. If the child's nail remains white from the pressure longer than three seconds, she has a fluid deficiency that is interfering with circulation.

See a Doctor

If a baby experiences diarrhea for longer than two days, the pediatrician should verify the extent of the fluid loss. The doctor will then advise on how to feed the baby in the future.

Treatment

Diarrhea shouldn't be stopped at first, for the cause (usually a virus) and its toxic excreta should be driven from the baby's body. However, there are some home remedies that get the bowels back to normal more quickly.

➤ Nutrition up to the sixth month of life: Research has shown that breastfed children should continue to get mother's milk. Bottle babies should also continue to get their formula—or, in consultation with a doctor, a special formula. But in both cases,

1. The fluid loss must be quickly replaced. Small amounts (in some circumstances 5 ml every two minutes) of an electrolyte solution (like Pedialyte®) are helpful, with a total amount of intake of 100 cc/kg per day, are required. That is, a baby weighing 11 pounds (5 kg) needs approximately 16 ounces (500 ml) of solution. Normally an improvement is seen in half a day. If not, the lost fluid must be replaced as described (this can take four to five days). In the meantime the child must be under a pediatrician's regular care.

2. Bottle babies should be switched back from the special formula to the usual one quickly. This means that at first they get 3.4 ounces (100 ml) of infant formula per kilogram of body weight (16.9 ounces/500 ml per day for an 11-pound baby).

➤ Nutrition starting in the sixth month of life: Babies accustomed to supplementary foods can be given various foods that help to reduce diarrhea: rice cereal, carrot mash, grated raw apples, pressed bananas, fruit with zwieback softened in water, and cooked potatoes are most commonly used. It is important to consult your pediatrician.

TIP | BREASTFED BABIES

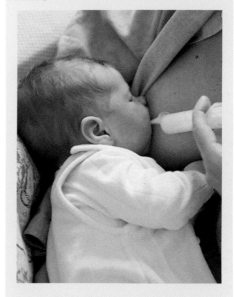

Breastfed babies should continue to get mother's milk. If necessary, they must be returned to the breast to be sure that they are taking in adequate fluids. In extreme cases, breastfed babies also get an electrolyte solution to counteract the fluid loss. This works quite well when the solution is administered with a syringe while nursing.

Vomiting/Spitting Up

If a baby occasionally vomits, this is no cause for concern. But if the child keeps vomiting and the condition is clearly connected to food intake, when there is a fever, and/or when the general condition deteriorates rapidly because of the vomiting, you must consult a pediatrician.

Effusive Spitting Up/Reflux

If babies spit up in great quantities, this is a special case. The cause for this pronounced vomiting is usually a lax lower esophageal sphincter, which allows stomach contents to reflux back up the esophagus and into the mouth. However, sometimes the cause is a pyloric stenosis, which is a tightening of the passage from the stomach to the intestines. Both of these conditions need to be evaluated by a pediatrician. Reflux is a chronic problem that is usually treated with medicines and altering your feeding technique. Pyloric stenosis, on the other hand, is an acute problem and is treated by surgery.

Go to the Doctor

Go to the doctor if your baby vomits copiously several times a day. The doctor must determine if there are any organic causes.

Treatment

As long as the child continues to gain weight and develop normally, no treatment is required. Raising the upper body can reduce the symptoms. Studies have shown that lying on the stomach is preferable for children who spit up, but this is

TIP | PEDIALYTE®

Use Pedialyte® and then enhance the diet with toast, applesauce, rice, and bananas.

controversial because of the risk of sudden infant death.

Thickening the food seems to reduce vomiting. In exceptional cases various medications can reduce reflux, but there may be side effects. If your baby doesn't

INFO | VOMITING

Some popular wisdom says that children who spit up are healthy children. The intention is good, but you have to make a distinction. When babies drink too much or too quickly, they may spit up the small excess. The cause is reduced muscle tension in the lower esophagus. Since there is equal pressure in the stomach and esophagus, the food doesn't stay in the stomach, but blows back into the mouth. Spitting up is encouraged by an open entrance to the stomach, which is normal in infancy. This condition improves by itself in the following weeks and months. In the meantime, you have to be patient. The common wisdom mentioned above is right, because nearly all children who spit up develop just fine.

267

gain weight, or even loses weight, because of vomiting, further investigation such as ultrasound and X-rays of the upper thorax are necessary to rule out other organic causes (such as pyloric thickening).

Other Causes for Spitting Up

It is also possible that the baby is suffering from a viral stomach-intestinal grippe, an allergy (to the protein in cow's milk, for example), a metabolic disorder, or a pyloric thickening. This is the case in one of a thousand children who experience vomiting.

See the Doctor/Treatment

If the baby continues to spit up, you need to consult a doctor, who will check out all these possibilities. For continued copious vomiting can lead to serious fluid loss, electrolyte disturbances, and even inflammation of the esophagus. If your baby suffers from a stomach and intestinal infection, the pediatrician will suggest the right treatment. In this case the information on diarrhea and vomiting starting on page 265 applies.

Colic

Young parents sometimes have to deal with a child with colic. With this, babies have such severe digestive problems that after every meal they have persistent crying, sometimes for hours at a time. Boys are affected more frequently than girls; preemies and babies who are too small and underweight for their age are most commonly afflicted. The difficulty for the parents is in determining if the baby is really crying because of colic or because of a gastrointestinal condition.

Symptoms

The baby cries from pain after a meal. His stomach is hard and swollen, the hands are clenched into fists, and the head is bright red. The infant draws up his legs to his body or becomes stiff as a board and arches his head rearward. With colic you can hear a rumbling in the stomach. And yet other children with severe stomachache are very quiet but breathe very quickly and suddenly look sick.

Causes

There may be many types of causes. It is possible that the baby's digestive system is not yet fully mature. Or the baby drinks too hastily and swallows too much air, or there is an intolerance to certain types of protein. Sometimes even medications that were given to the mother (e.g., painkillers for birthing) are responsible for the gas. Regardless of where it comes from, it always occurs without regard to time of day. Affected babies have problems especially in the late afternoon and evening, but experience no pain during the night.

See a Doctor

If your home treatment doesn't produce results, you should consult a doctor. If the gas comes on quickly and severely, with serious stomach pains or blood in the stool, get to a doctor right away so you can rule out gastrointestinal disorder or a similar condition.

Treatment

The pediatrician can make sure that the baby does not have a serious illness. Here are some things you can do yourself:
➤ Make sure that your baby drinks calmly to avoid swallowing a lot of air that can't escape from the stomach.
➤ Nursing mothers can avoid gassy foods, but this is often overrated. Find out what gives you gas and avoid it (also see page 199). It generally is helpful for nursing mothers to drink anise-fennel-caraway tea (found in herbal stores), for these herbs have a calming effect on their baby's intestine.
➤ If you suspect allergy to cow's milk protein, ask your pediatrician for advice, but don't deny yourself milk.
➤ Gentle caresses with baby massage oil frequently work wonders. Use it to "paint" an increasingly large spiral with your fingertips on the baby's tummy, starting at the navel and working in a clockwise direction. You can also lay the baby naked on the changing table. Use your left hand to hold up the baby's legs and stroke gently with your right hand from the navel to the loins. This is one way to let gas out.

➤ In flying position, the baby lies on Mom's or Dad's forearm, with his head face-down and toward the elbow. The adult's hand exerts gentle pressure on the baby's stomach; this often helps.

➤ Massage in succession the point on both feet between the heel and the middle of the foot; this relaxes the stomach and intestinal tract.

Good to Know

When a baby has pain, he needs you! Pick up your baby; show him your love and that you are not leaving him alone with his problems.

INFO | THE INFAMOUS THREE-MONTHS COLIC

It is a normal evening, and the baby is freshly diapered and full. And yet she is crying; she cries a lot, nearly always in the evening hours and for no apparent reason. Often the parents are at the end of their nerves and stumped. The fact is that one of every ten babies has these screaming attacks, boys more commonly than girls, and the high point is in the second month. This much is clear: No baby cries for fun; a baby cries when something is wrong. As for the causes, the experts are divided. One group believes that babies cry because they have gas, and the other believes that the baby has gas because he has swallowed so much air while crying. As is often the case, the truth probably lies midway between the two. Possible reasons for the screaming attacks are an immature digestive system, lots of swallowed air, and an immature central nervous regulatory system. The same measures as for gas help in this situation. Afflicted babies need a calm, well-structured daily routine without a lot of (loud) stimuli. Make sure the baby gets regular sleep and is dealt with as quietly as possible—ideally at home, without much hubbub.

If additional help is needed, a useful service is the Fussy Baby Team at the Erikson Institute (http://www.fussybabynetwork.org/). After three months, the colic-like attacks generally disappear without obvious reason.

Support for Young Mothers

Nearly every pregnant woman and mother knows the importance of information and support. Listed below are several books and web sites that health professionals and families have found helpful. It's also a good idea to ask your doctor and see what he/she recommends based on your and your child's needs.

General Baby Guides

Robert Needlman, MD. *Dr. Spock's Baby Basics: Take Charge Parenting Guides.* Pocket Books, 2003. New York, NY.

Burton L. White. *Raising a Happy, Unspoiled Child.* Fireside, 1995. New York, NY.

Craig T. Ramey, PhD and Sharon L. Ramey PhD. *Right From Birth: Building Your Child's Foundation for Life—Birth to 18 Months.* Goddard Press. 1999. New York, NY.

Marilyn Segal, PhD. *Your Child at Play— One to Two Years: Exploring, Daily Living, Learning and Making Friends.* Newmarket Press, 1998. New York, NY.

Burton L. White. *New First Three Years of Life: Completely Revised and Updated.* Fireside, 1995. New York, NY.

Jackie Silberg. *Games to Play with Toddlers.* Gryphon House, 1993. Beltsville, MD.

Jackie Silberg. *Games to Play with Two Year Olds.* Gryphon House, 1993. Beltsville, MD.

Sleep Guide

Judy A. Owens, MD and Jodi A. Mindell, PhD. *Take Charge of Your Child's Sleep.* Da Capo Press, 2005. New York, NY.

Richard Ferber, MD. *Solve Your Child's Sleep Problems: New, Revised, and Expanded Edition.* Fireside, 2006. New York, NY.

Guides for Children with Disability

Betsy Santelli, Florence Stewart Poyadue, and Jane Leora Young. *The Parent to Parent Handbook: Connecting Families of Children with Special Needs.* Paul H. Brookes Publishing Co., 2001. Baltimore, MD.

Mark L. Batshaw, MD. When Your Child Has a Disability: The Complete Sourcebook of Daily and Medical Care, Revised Edition. Paul H. Brookes Publishing Co., 2001. Baltimore, MD.

Mark L. Batshaw, MD, Louis Pellegrino, MD, and Nancy J. Roizen, MD. *Children with Disabilities.* Paul H. Brookes Publishing Co., 2007. Baltimore, MD.

Guide for Behavioral Management

Lynn Clark and John Robb. *SOS: Help for Parents.* Parents Press, 2005. Bowling Green, KY.

Helpful Web Sites

La Leche League International (http://www.llli.org/): Provides information on breastfeeding.

American Association of Poison Control Centers (http://www.aapcc.org/)

Fussy Baby Network (http://www.fussybabynetwork.org/): Support and guidance for families with babies who colic.

American Academy of Pediatrics (http://www.aap.org/): Guidance and information on health, immunization, and safety.

Other Things That Afflict Babies . . .

Coughing/Bronchitis

Fortunately, infants rarely develop a cough. A cough is extremely unpleasant for little babies.

Symptoms

At first the children have a dry, clipped, chesty cough that wakes them up at night and makes them tired. Later the cough becomes moist and looser and can produce mucus. In many cases the nose is also congested, so the babies can't drink properly and sometimes even lose weight.

Causes

Bacteria or viruses infect the airways in various degrees, and airborne infection usually is caused by family members.

See a Doctor

When an infant has a cough, visit a doctor! An untreated cough can develop into bronchitis or even pneumonia.

Treatment

The pediatrician will use a stethoscope to listen to your baby's lungs and bronchi.

➤ Normal cough: The baby coughs, the nose is clear, the baby is drinking well and doesn't feel too bad overall: Moist air, warm water, warm cloths, and a warm chest wrap will help—along with lots of parental patience.

➤ Upper respiratory infection: The baby coughs and has a congested nose. Since the nose is plugged, secretions flow rearward into the throat, producing a reflexive cough, especially at night. Don't use any cough suppressant medication. It is important to first free up the nose, for example with saline nose drops. Various products containing thyme (anti-inflammatory), primrose (anti-inflammatory), and/or marshmallow (protects mucous membranes) may decrease symptoms.

➤ Infection of the middle airways (throat and larynx area): The infection causes pain on swallowing, so the little patients generally refuse to drink. Warm milk is just what's needed. An appropriate medicinal plant is sage tea. If the throat and larynx are infected and the baby is already coughing up phlegm, everything that cuts mucus will help including a moist atmosphere.

➤ Lower respiratory infection (bronchi): If there is mucus in the large bronchi or the airways, you can feel the "rattling" with your hand. Expectorant medications, damp heat (atmospheric humidity), inhalants, and a warm drink can help. But if the little bronchi are infected, with no mucus present, we are dealing with bronchiopneumonia. Since this can very easily lead to shortness of breath and respiratory failure in infants, a pediatric evaluation and hospital stay are usually required.

➤ This too can help: Drinking a lot—preferably lukewarm water liquefies and cuts mucus.

➤ Humidifier: Be sure to provide high humidity, especially at night, by using a humidifier.

TIP | **NOSE DROPS**

To administer nose drops, lay the child on her back and put one drop into one nostril. Turn the child onto this side for a minute so the drop can get into the throat to opening of the tube. Then treat the second nostril in a similar way.

Middle Ear Infection

A middle ear infection frequently occurs in winter and spring as the result of a cold and can be extremely painful.

Symptoms

Infants roll their head back and forth, are very restless, and cry shrilly from pain (it sounds quite different from crying from hunger or boredom!), and their face is distorted with pain. Sometimes they refuse to eat. The child may have a fever and/or a stuffy nose. It is important that you take your baby's behavior seriously and do not simply attribute it to teething.

Causes

Middle ear infections are caused by viruses, or most commonly, bacteria, which get into the middle ear from the throat or the nose by way of the eustachean tubes, or from the inside through the nasal passages.

See a Doctor

As soon as you suspect that your baby is experiencing ear pain, take her to the doctor.

Treatment

➤ If the cause is a virus, symptomatic treatment with pain medication is helpful. The badly congested nose must be treated. The pediatrician will often suggest saline nose drops and, when necessary, appropriate decongestants. In addition, the child should drink a lot to dissolve the mucus. The infection will heal by itself, but the doctor should monitor that the middle ear cavity recovers.

If bacteria are the cause, most doctors prescribe an antibiotic, for without antibiotic treatment a number of complications can set in, including perforated eardrum (ear infection) and mastoiditis (inflammation or infection of the mastoid bone).

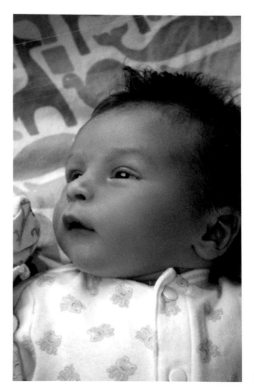

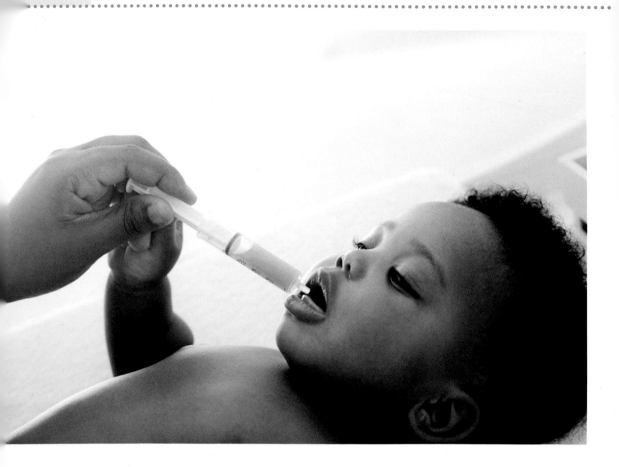

INFO | KEY WORD *CROUP*

Croup refers to an infection of the upper airways caused by viruses. It produces a swelling in the mucous membranes at the narrowest place in the airways, the transition from the larynx to the trachea. In the evening and early night hours, the child develops a characteristic, barking cough. It is hoarse and wheezy, and every time the child breathes in, you can hear a loud, strange grumbling. Croup occurs primarily in the first through third years of life, especially in the fall and late winter. Boys are affected more frequently than girls. In acute cases, call the emergency room. Fresh, moist, cool air provides quick relief because it shrinks the swelling in the breathing passages. Bundle your child up well and sit in front of an open window or take the child outdoors. You can also turn on the shower with hot water, open the window, and let the child breathe in the moist steam on the fresh air.

Shots

At the time of birth a baby is free of pathogens, but as soon as the baby is touched he comes into contact with many germs.

The Body Helps Itself

Once a germ gets into the human body, the white blood corpuscles become active and fend off the intruder; it is killed and digested. Concurrently the white blood vessels note which pathogen it is and form special defensive compounds (antibodies) and so-called helper cells to combat this pathogen. This reaction by the body is called an immune response. If the pathogen gets back into the body, the immune system can immediately release the appropriate defense to neutralize the recognized intruder.

Naturally or with a Shot

Today people prefer that the body immunize itself actively in advance, in other words, that it form antibodies to a pathogen through direct contact, whether through natural invasion by the pathogen or through a shot. With a shot, weakened or dead pathogens, or parts of pathogens, are injected into the body. Once they are inside the body, the immunization program kicks in: The body's own defensive cells (antibodies) are formed, and they attack the invader and get rid of it. At the same time, the characteristics of the pathogen are stored in the "memory." After the first shot, there is an immune response. If the same pathogen crops up again through a booster shot, the antibodies formed after the first contact become

INFO | NO COMPLICATIONS

Shots can imitate natural infections, but without triggering the dreaded complications of illness. The immune system is similarly conditioned by shots instead of by infections involving the natural germ (the "wild type").

active and mature further in their functioning, until they become fully effective after the completion of the basic immunization. With many shots the protection decreases after a certain time, so a booster is needed at regular intervals. This is especially true for tetanus and diphtheria.

Vaccines Through the Years

In the last century, vaccines have been improved tremendously. Today's vaccines contain just a fraction of the antigens that were used fifteen years ago (fifty today, previously three thousand antigens!). This works, for the new vaccines are so effective in promoting the formation of antibodies that a tiny amount of antigen is sufficient to form an effective immunity to diseases.

How Is the Shot Given?

Before the inoculation, your child is checked over thoroughly to make sure he is truly healthy. Then the doctor inserts a thin, inch-long (2.5 cm) hollow needle into the fatty tissue in the thigh muscle and administers the vaccine. This generally takes a few seconds and causes very little pain.

275

INFO | **THE NEONATAL IMMUNE SYSTEM**

A baby can fall back on passively acquired immunity in the first months of life. This involves an antibody from the mother (immunoglobulin), which is transferred to the child at the end of the pregnancy. It gives the baby all the defensive cells that the mother has formed in her body. The child is initially protected against all the diseases for which the mother has antibodies. After three to six months (up to twelve months for measles) the child's body breaks down the mother's antibodies, and now the child needs his own immune defense, which must be built up independently.

What Gets Injected?

So-called combination vaccines are common; they are used to immunize against several diseases at the same time.

➤ Combination vaccines: With these vaccines, several shots are combined in a 0.5% solution. They contain water, vaccine antigens, and stabilizers. Most frequently a five-part shot (diphtheria, tetanus, polio, hepatitis B, and pertussis) is given. The advantage of combination vaccines is that they decrease the number of shots.

What Do the Shot Critics Say?

There are always critics who hold that the multiple vaccines contribute to the appearance of chronic diseases. Currently there is no proof of this. This also applies to the mumps-measles-rubella vaccine, which is frequently accused of being connected to an increased incidence of autism. Nor is there any verification that an increase in allergies is attributable to multiple vaccines. Talk to your pediatrician about this. Get some information about the advantages of the planned immunizations and the possible consequences of not having the shots.

The Immunization Schedule

The American Academy of Pediatrics recommends starting certain immunizations right after the end of the second month of life. That way the declining passively received infant antibodies meld seamlessly into the independent immunity of the child's body. This is especially necessary for pathogens that can cause complications in infants, such as whooping cough or the hemophilus influenza bacteria that cause purulent meningitis. Go to the American Academy of Pediatrics web site for tables showing the recommended childhood immunization schedule for ages 0 to 6 years as of January 2, 2008, and a corresponding catch-up schedule for children aged 4 months to 18 years who have delayed immunizations.

An Overview of Standard Shots

➤ Diphtheria is an infection caused by bacteria that produce a toxin that damages the heart and other organs; in spite of antibiotics, it can lead to death. Lifelong booster shots at regular intervals (every ten years) are necessary.

➤ Tetanus is a bacterial infection. The bacteria get inside the body through wounds and form a toxin that damages the nervous system and can lead to death through persistent muscle cramps—even with antibiotic treatment. The inoculation is reliable but must be renewed regularly throughout life.

➤ Pertussis (whooping cough) is a bacterial infectious disease that can be transmitted through airborne infection. Here too the bacteria produce toxins that damage mucous membranes and produce coughing bouts with vomiting. Infants are at mortal risk of respiratory failure, and antibiotic treatment usually comes too late. The first shots provide good protection against complications.

➤ Poliomyelitis is a viral infection that is transmitted via unwashed hands or objects. Usually it takes the form of harmless diarrhea, but some patients experience paralysis, which is permanent in 10 percent of them. There is no known treatment. Basic immunization is highly recommended. A series of three injections during infancy followed in six to twelve months by a booster shot is recommended.

➤ Haemophilus influenzae Type b (Hib): The responsible bacteria can cause life-threatening diseases through airborne infections. Usually they turn out to be harmless, but in one out of every 500 cases it produces purulent meningitis, acute epiglottitis with danger of suffocation, bone and periorbital infections, and blood poisoning. In spite of treatment with antibiotics, up to 20 percent of the consequences (such as deafness) remain. Shots during babyhood provide lifelong protection against these effects of the disease.

INFO | DANGER OF EPIDEMIC

Since children have been immunized with highly effective vaccines in the last few decades, many diseases are essentially extinct and are disappearing from our bodies. A logical question is, "Why should I get my child immunized against diseases that hardly ever crop up?" Here's the answer: Many diseases that seem to be conquered suddenly make a resurgence. They infect patients who have not had the appropriate shots. The larger this group is, the greater is the danger of epidemics, since the susceptibility of the entire population to a disease is higher.

➤ Liver inflammation (hepatitis B) is caused by a virus. The younger the child is at the time of infection, the more common it is to experience chronic effects. Treatment of the severe, often chronic infection with medications produces only inadequate success. There are thousands and thousands of new infections every year.

➤ Measles-mumps-rubella is a reliable three-part inoculation for these viral diseases (airborne infections).

Measles, contrary to common opinion, should be classified as a dangerous viral infection. In addition to fever, coughing, and the typical skin rash, consequences can include pneumonia with respiratory failure and death, encephalitis (inflammation of the brain) with epilepsy, deafness, and intellectual disability. Very rarely a late side effect is a progressive brain infection, that leads to paralysis, seizures, and death. The older the patient is, the higher is the risk of experiencing complications.

Mumps entails fever, headache, and painful inflammation of the parotid glands on both sides. Possible late consequences include meningitis, diabetes mellitus, hearing impairment, and sterility in boys.

Varicella vaccine (twelve months)

Pneumococcal vaccine (two, four, and six months)

Rotavirus (two, four, and six months)

Hepatitis A (twelve months)

Rubella generally runs its course without problems, but infections in pregnant women with no immunity can cause congenital rubella syndrome. This is characterized by cataracts, deafness, microcephaly (small head circumference), and congenital heart disease in infants. Developmental consequences include deafness, blindness, autism, intellectual disability, epilepsy, and cerebral palsy.

Varicella (chicken pox) is a highly contagious illness that can sometimes cause pneumonia. Scratching the itchy rash can lead to skin infections. Varicella can be especially severe in individuals with poor immune systems. If a pregnant woman develops varicella during the first two trimesters, it could cause birth defects in the fetus. Varicella immunization is given at twelve months and again between four and six years.

Influenza is a viral illness that occurs mainly during the winter. Influenza is spread between people by coughing or sneezing. Influenza can result in fever, sore throat, headache, chills, and muscle ache. It can even cause complications such as ear and sinus infections and pneumonia. The rates of infection are particularly high among children. Influenza vaccine is recommended yearly because the virus that causes it changes from year to year. Infants can be vaccinated against influenza as early as six months.

Pneumococcus is a bacterium, which can cause pneumonia; blood, ear, and sinus infections; and even meningitis. African Americans, Native Americans, Alaska natives, and children with sickle cell anemia have a particularly difficult time fending off pneumococcal disease. The vaccine is given at two, four, and six months with a fourth dose between twelve and eighteen months.

Hepatitis A is a viral disease that affects the liver. A severe case can lead to liver failure and death. It is recommended that the vaccine be started at twelve months. Two doses need to be given six months apart.

Rotavirus is a common cause of severe diarrhea in infancy. It can cause dehydration especially in young children. A child with a rotavirus infection may even be hospitalized for treatment. Rotavirus vaccine can eliminate or decrease the severity of infections with this agent. It is given at two, four, and six months of age.

INFO | **CRITICAL CONSIDERATIONS**

Inoculations are generally required for school/day care. A non-inoculated child is at higher risk for several diseases that can result in disabilities or death.

For Further Reference

What to Expect at the Doctor's Office in the First Year of Life

As a new parent, you must be feeling excited, happy, nervous, and overwhelmed at the same time. Many questions and concerns are racing through your mind. At the same time, you might be afraid you'll forget to ask important questions during your next doctor's visit. Here are some guidelines (based on Bright Future's Encounter Forms for Families; http://www.brightfutures.org/) on what to expect and things you can keep in mind during your visit to your baby's pediatrician.

Newborn Visit

➤ **What to Expect:** Your baby will go through a routine physical examination. The pediatrician will also check your baby's hearing and ask for blood tests to be done. Your baby will receive immunization for hepatitis at this time.

➤ **Possible Things to Discuss:** Talk about your family members' reaction to the new baby, including you and your partner. If this is not your first child, talk to your pediatrician about the impact the arrival of the baby has had on your other child(ren). Be prepared to discuss your physical and emotional well-being. If you have concerns regarding breastfeeding or bottle feeding your baby, don't forget to bring it up. And lastly, do you have questions on safety regarding your environment (car seats, cribs, baths, nail trims)?

➤ **Prepare for Your Next Visit:** Keep track of your baby's illnesses and injuries. Continue to observe your baby's sleeping and eating behaviors as well as your family members' feelings and level of adjustment to the new baby.

One Week Visit

➤ **What to Expect:** Your baby will go through a routine physical examination. The pediatrician will also check your baby's hearing and ask for blood tests to be done. Your baby will receive immunization for hepatitis at this time.

➤ **Possible Things to Discuss:** You may see your baby's personality developing during the first week of life. This will be a good time to discuss your baby's personality with your pediatrician. Talk about your baby's fussy period, and what you have been doing to soothe her. Discuss your physical and emotional well-being and the progress you are making with breastfeeding/bottle-feeding.

➤ **Prepare for Your Next Visit:** Keep track of your baby's illnesses and injuries. Continue to observe your baby's sleeping and eating behaviors. Complete any questionnaires or forms given to you by your pediatrician and prepare to bring them in to your next visit.

➤ **And Don't Forget!:** If you don't have a postpartum checkup scheduled with your OBGYN already, be sure to do so!

One Month Visit

➤ **What to Expect:** Your baby will go through a routine physical examination as well as a hearing checkup. Your doctor will talk to you about your baby's growth and development. The pediatrician will also ask about your baby's possible exposure to lead. Your baby may receive an immunization for hepatitis at this time.

➤ **Possible Things to Discuss:** Bring up your baby's personality and the effect it's having on you and your family. Talk about your baby's fussy period, and what you have been doing to soothe him. Discuss your physical and emotional well-being and the progress you are making with breastfeeding/bottle-feeding. If you have plans to return to work or school, this will be a good time to talk to your pediatrician about it. Also, don't forget to inform the doctor the results of your postpartum checkup.

➤ **Prepare for Your Next Visit:** Keep track of your baby's illnesses and injuries. Continue to observe your baby's sleeping and eating behaviors. Complete any questionnaires or forms given to you by your pediatrician and prepare to bring them in to your next visit.

Two Month Visit

➤ **What to Expect:** Your baby will go through a routine physical examination. Your doctor will talk to you about your baby's growth and development. You baby will receive one or more immunizations for hepatitis, diptheria, Haemophilus influenzae type b (Hib), tetanus, pertussis, and polio.

➤ **Possible Things to Discuss:** Inform your pediatrician about your baby's sleeping habits and schedule. Any observations you've made regarding your baby's vision and hearing, concerns regarding breastfeeding/bottle-feeding, and your family's level of adjustment to your new baby should be discussed at this time. If you and your partner were thinking about family planning, it'll be a good idea to inform your pediatrician about it. If you thought about spending time with other parents and babies (such as play dates), seek feedback or advice from your pediatrician.

➤ **Prepare for Your Next Visit:** Keep track of your baby's illnesses and injuries. Continue to observe your baby's sleeping and eating behaviors. Note any changes. Be prepared to bring in the Individualized Family Service Plan for early intervention if your baby has special needs. Also, be prepared to talk about your baby's possible exposure to lead, asbestos, violence, or hazards.

Four Month Visit

➤ **What to Expect:** Your baby will go through a routine physical examination. Your doctor will talk to you about your baby's growth and development. You baby will receive one or more immunizations for hepatitis, diptheria, Haemophilus influenzae type b (Hib), or polio.

➤ **Possible Things to Discuss:** Inform your pediatrician about your baby's sleeping and eating habits. Talk about how your family is getting along with the baby. If you're having a difficult time getting the help you need with the baby, bring it up. You might also want to discuss with your pediatrician your plans to return to work or school and subsequent child care arrangements.

➤ **Prepare for Your Next Visit:** Keep track of your baby's illnesses and injuries. Continue to observe your baby's sleeping and eating behaviors. Note any changes. Be prepared to give information about your baby's possible allergies to food or medication. Consider how many children you want to have and be prepared to discuss future pregnancies or prevention of pregnancies.

Six Month Visit

➤ **What to Expect:** Your baby will go through a routine physical examination. Your doctor will talk to you about your baby's growth and development. You baby may receive one or more immunizations for hepatitis, diptheria, Haemophilus influenzae type b (Hib), or polio. You will be asked about your baby's possible exposure to lead. Your baby may be assessed for anemia (low level of iron in blood).

➤ **Possible Things to Discuss:** Update your doctor on your baby's health status, as well as feeding and sleeping patterns. In addition to questions about breastfeeding or bottle-feeding, inform your doctor concerning your baby's diet and any reactions to foods. If you have concerns about your baby's hearing or vision, don't forget to bring that up too. You may also want to discuss with the pediatrician the stress (if you have any) of balancing the roles of partner and parent, as well as child care arrangements. Questions regarding child-proofing your home can also be addressed at this time.

➤ **Prepare for Your Next Visit:** Keep track of your baby's illnesses and injuries. Continue to observe your baby's sleeping and eating behaviors, and note any changes. Be prepared to provide information about changes in your family (births, deaths, divorces, marriages, losses of income, moves, etc.).

Nine Month Visit

➤ **What to Expect:** Your baby will go through a routine physical examination. Your doctor will talk to you about your baby's growth and development. You will be asked about your baby's possible exposure to lead, and your baby may be tested for lead. Your baby may also have a test for tuberculosis, in addition to a blood test, and may receive one or more immunizations for hepatitis or polio.

➤ **Possible Things to Discuss:** Discuss your baby's eating and sleeping habits. Child-proofing your home and checking for hazards should also be discussed at this time. Talk to your pediatrician about your baby's increasing independence and the stress of keeping up with your baby. Changes in your family since the last visit should also be discussed. Ask about infant fluoride supplements for your baby and see what your doctor's advice is on brushing your baby's teeth.

➤ **Prepare for Your Next Visit:** Keep track of your baby's illnesses and injuries. Continue to observe your baby's sleeping and eating behaviors. Prepare and bring in questions about your baby's development (eating, temperament, activity level, thumb sucking, or use of pacifier). Keep note of any reactions or side effects your baby has experienced as a result of immunizations.

One Year Visit

➤ **What to Expect:** You and your doctor will discuss your toddler's growth and development. Your toddler will have a routine physical examination, and she will be tested for tuberculosis, screened for lead, and receive a blood test. Your toddler may receive one or more immunizations for hepatitis, Haemophilus influenzae type b (Hib), polio, MMR, or chicken pox.

➤ **Possible Things to Discuss:** In addition to your child's sleeping, eating, and playing patterns, you may want to discuss with your pediatrician what you and your partner think about discipline. Child-proofing your home and checking for possible hazards should also be brought up.

➤ **Prepare for Your Next Visit:** In addition to keeping track of your child's illnesses and injuries, note changes in her eating, sleeping, and social behaviors. Be prepared to speak to your doctor about some of the games and activities you enjoy doing with your baby. Start talking to your toddler about the visit to the pediatrician and try to explain and prepare her for the physical exam, immunizations, and other procedures.

Helpful Addresses

➤ **La Leche League International.**
Web site: http://www.llli.org
La Leche League focuses on breastfeeding.

➤ **Poison Control.** Since different cities and localities have different poison control centers, it is recommended that expectant mothers should find the contact information of the local poison control center before their due date and keep that information handy (save it to speed dial, tape it to the refrigerator, etc.). For more information, parents should visit the web site of the American Association for Poison Control Centers (http://www.aapcc.org).

Index

Copyright

English translation © Copyright 2009 by Barron's Educational Series, Inc.

Published originally under the title *Das Grosse GU Baby Buch* © 2005 by Gräfe and Unzer Verlag GmbH, Munchen

GU

German edition by Birgit Gebauer-Sesterhenn, Dr. Manfred Praun

Consulting editor: Dr. Michael Msall, M.D.

Photography: Antje Anders

Photo Editor: Henrike Schechter

Photo credits: Angelika Salomon: pp. 47, 271; Corbis: C4 left, pp. 32, 203; Fotosearch: C3 left, pp. 15, 194, 203, 210, 274; Getty: C4 right; GU archive: pp. 70 (B. Büchner), 101, and 218 (K. Dingel), 187 and 266 (A. Peisl), 195 (A. Hoernisch), 221, (J. Rynio); Marina Raith: C1, p. 1; Mauritius: pp. 9, 197, 232, 233; Mother & Baby Picture Library: pp.17, 35, 209, 217, 236, 249, 260; Picture Press: pp. 6, 94/95, 240; Shutterstock: C3 right, pp. 4, 41, 51, 57, 58, 73, 75, 76, 111, 115, 120, 126, 129, 189, 191, 200, 211, 223, 227, 231, 264, 268, 270, 273, 282, 287; Superbild: pp. 205, 210, 225, 254, 255; Vario-Press: pp. 36; Zefa: pp. 6, 10, 11, 12, 177, 207

Illustrations
Association for Dental Health: p. 145; GU Archive: p. 80 (Nike Schenkl), p.193 (H. Vignati)

English translation by Eric A. Bye, M.A.

All inquiries should be addressed to:
Barron's Educational Series, Inc.
250 Wireless Boulevard
Hauppauge, NY 11788
www.barronseduc.com

Library of Congress Control No.: 2008928364

ISBN-13: 978-0-7641-3796-9
ISBN-10: 0-7641-3796-4

PRINTED IN CHINA
9 8 7 6 5 4 3 2 1

Disclaimer
All medical advice contained herein should not be taken as a substitute for medical care, and all practices or suggestions should be reviewed with an actual healthcare practitioner before initiating care of a child.